SHIA
POWER
COMES
OF AGE

A CENTURY FOUNDATION BOOK

SHIA POWER COMES OF AGE

THE TRANSFORMATION OF ISLAMIST POLITICS IN IRAQ, 2003-2023

Thanassis Cambanis
Sajad Jiyad
Editors

About The Century Foundation

The Century Foundation is a progressive, independent think tank that conducts research, develops solutions, and drives policy change to make people's lives better. We pursue economic, racial, gender, and disability equity in education, health care, and work, and promote U.S. foreign policy that fosters international cooperation, peace, and security.

Library of Congress Cataloguing-in-Publication Data Available from the publisher upon request.

Manufactured in the United States of America

Cover design by Jamal Saleh
Text design by Cynthia Stock

Shia Power Comes of Age: The Transformation of Islamist Politics in Iraq, 2003–2023
Thanassis Cambanis and Sajad Jiyad, Editors

ISBN 978-0-87078-570-2 (paperback)
ISBN 978-0-87078-571-9 (e-book)

Contents

Introduction

Thanassis Cambanis and Sajad Jiyad
Understanding Shia Politics When Everyone's
a Shia Islamist   3

Defining Shia Politics

1 *Fanar Haddad*
Shia Rule Is a Reality in Iraq. "Shia Politics"
Needs a New Definition.   13

2 *Ali Al-Mawlawi*
Iraqi Shia Factions Are Supposedly "Anti-state."
But State Power Is What They Want.   37

Clerics

3 *Marsin Alshamary*
Shia Clerics in Iraq Haven't Lost Their Authority   61

4 *Sajad Jiyad*
Guide and Critic: Sistani from 2014 to 2023   81

Politicians

5 *Ben Robin-D'Cruz*
The Sadrist Electoral Machine in Basra   105

6 *Maria Luisa Fantappie*
Men of Dawa: How the Personalities of
One Party Shaped Iraq's New Politics   129

Protest

7 *Taif AlKhudary*
Young Revolutionary Parties Are Still Iraq's
Best Hope for Democracy   157

Systemic Constraints

8 *Renad Mansour*
The Logic of Intra-Shia Violence in Iraq   183

9 *Thanassis Cambanis*
Sectarian Relapse: Lessons of "the Shia House"   197

Notes   221

About the Editors

Thanassis Cambanis is an author and journalist, and the director of Century International. His work focuses on U.S. foreign policy, Arab politics, and social movements in the Middle East. He is currently working on a book about the impact of the 2003 invasion of Iraq. He is the author of *Once upon a Revolution: An Egyptian Story* (Simon and Schuster: 2015); *A Privilege to Die: Inside Hezbollah's Legions* (Free Press: 2010); and editor of five volumes about politics, conflict, and citizenship in the Middle East. He regularly contributes to *Foreign Affairs*, *The New York Times*, *World Policy Review*, and other publications. He is an adjunct professor at Columbia University's School of International and Public Affairs.

Sajad Jiyad is a fellow at Century International and director of the Shia Politics Working Group. An Iraqi political analyst based in Baghdad, he is the managing director of Bridge, an Iraqi nongovernmental organization and consultancy focused on development projects for young people. Sajad's main focus is on public policy and governance in Iraq. He is frequently published and cited as an expert commentator on Iraqi affairs. Sajad's educational background is in economics, politics, and Islamic studies.

About the Authors

Fanar Haddad is assistant professor at the Department of Cross-Cultural and Regional Studies, University of Copenhagen. He previously served as senior advisor on international affairs to the prime minister of Iraq. His most recent book is *Understanding "Sectarianism": Sunni-Shi'a Relations in the Modern Arab World* (Oxford: Hurst/Oxford University Press, 2020).

Marsin Alshamary is assistant professor of political science at Boston College. She is currently working on a book that examines the role of Shia clerics in anti-government protests in Iraq from 1920 to 2020.

Ali Al-Mawlawi is an analyst and consultant with a specialist interest in Iraqi politics, political economy and governance.

Renad Mansour is an academy fellow at the Middle East and North Africa Programme at Chatham House, where his research focuses on Iraq, Iran, and Kurdish affairs and a lecturer at the London School of Economics (LSE), where he teaches a MSc course on the International Relations of the Middle East. He is also a fellow at the Cambridge Security Initiative based at the University of Cambridge, where he previously held positions as lecturer and supervisor at the faculty of politics. Renad has also held research posts at the Carnegie Middle East Center and the Iraq Institute for Strategic Studies. He received his PhD from Pembroke College, Cambridge.

Ben Robin-D'Cruz is a postdoctoral fellow in Aarhus University's Political Science Department, where he works on the Bringing in the Other Islamists project. His academic research focuses on the Sadrist Movement, Shia Islamist politics, and Iraq's protest movements.

Taif Alkhudary is a research officer at the London School of Economics Middle East Centre. She previously worked for various nongovernmental organizations, where she conducted research on women's and girls' rights and strategic litigation on violations of civil and political rights in the Gulf and Iraq.

Maria Luisa Fantappie holds a Phd from King's College London, Department of War Studies. She has served as senior adviser at the Centre for Humanitarian Dialogue and International Crisis Group conducting fieldwork across Iraq and the Middle East for more than a decade. In 2018, she was seconded by the Italian Ministry of Foreign Affairs as a strategic adviser for security sector reform to the European Union Mission in Baghdad. She is currently an associate fellow at the Istituto Affari Internazionali.

Acknowledgments

T he project would not have been possible without the generous support of the Henry Luce Foundation, which has enabled a multiyear research effort, and of the Carnegie Corporation of New York and the Open Society Foundations, which made it possible to see this stage of the work to its conclusion.

We are grateful to the board of trustees and our colleagues at The Century Foundation (TCF), led by Chairman Bradley Abelow and President Mark Zuckerman, who have created the space for Century International to extend its commitment to innovative policy research. Century International's Advisory Board provided critical guidance and support: thanks to Lina Attalah, Melani Cammett, Mona Fawaz, Michael Wahid Hanna, and Marc Lynch. Former Luce program director Toby Volkman helped conceive the Shia politics project.

Members of the Shia Politics Working Group whose research is collected in this volume generated years of fruitful and challenging discussion: Taif Alkhudary, Ali Al-Mawlawi, Marsin Alshamary, Ben Robin-D'Cruz, Maria Luisa Fantappie, and Renad Mansour. Along the way, many other researchers and reviewers offered important insights and feedback, including Lahib Higel, Abbas Kadhim, Haley Bobseine, and Abbas Anbori.

Eamon Kircher-Allen, editor-in-chief at Century International, labored from the ground up to shape the reports in this collection, greatly enhancing their clarity and accessibility.

As always, we hold our contributors and supporters responsible for any insights in this volume, and ourselves for any mistakes.

—*The Editors*

Introduction

Understanding Shia Politics When Everyone's a Shia Islamist

Thanassis Cambanis and Sajad Jiyad

Iraq's unique trajectory in the region since 2003 has made it both a test lab and a model of new approaches to religion, politics, and power. Sect and religion alone cannot explain politics and the pursuit of power. Additional factors include the importance of personalities in shaping politics; the historic networks and ties that underpin Shia parties; the ongoing importance of clerical authority; and, most clearly, the subservience of sect and ideology to the pursuit of power, by any means necessary.

Shia Islamist politics have dominated Iraq since 2005, when Iraqis chose their first representative government under U.S. military occupation. Clerics and political leaders have built networks of power and amassed followings, often under the banner of sect. Religion and sect hardly explain everything about Iraq's competitive and pluralistic political scene—but they must be part of any attempt at a complete explanation.

Iraq's new politics exploded into being in the violent shadow of the U.S. invasion and occupation. Twenty years ago, many politicians and scholars in the Middle East and abroad believed the region's future lay in "Islamism" or "political Islam." Perhaps intentionally vague, the terms were nonetheless in common use among many clerics, politicians, activists, and faithful.

In Iraq, leaders in a new state were able to quickly test the tangible meaning of the terms. When everyone at the center of a new government defines themselves as a Shia Islamist, even as they compete for resources, weapons, and religious legitimacy, how then should we understand Shia politics?

Messy, Malleable Labels

Century International convened a group of Iraq researchers in early 2021 to explore the transformation of Shia politics in Iraq since the U.S. invasion, in order to better understand the role of religion in politics, and the nature of religious politics. The researchers worked in concert to chart the development of Shia Islamist politics through the cycles of power-sharing and armed conflict that have marked Iraq over the last two decades. They studied the leaders who espoused the label of Shia Islamist—and how we might more usefully describe and understand Iraqi politics today.

Iraq has always been an important driver of Middle East regional politics, and a bellwether of new thinking and trends. Under Saddam Hussein, Iraq was a minority-ruled authoritarian republic, a critical oil producer, and an engine of regional conflict. Two decades later, Iraq remains a republic, though its flawed but pluralistic democratic power-sharing system is now dominated by factions representing the Shia majority.

In practice, Shia Islamist power has shattered any consensus about the meaning of either the term Shia or Islamist in politics— and not just in Iraq. The evolution of Shia Islamist power in Iraq has significance for the entire surrounding region, where complex political struggles are often misleadingly framed—often by the participants themselves—as Islamist versus secular, or Shia versus Sunni.

In contemporary Iraq, Shia politics are only partly about religion or identity. A clear understanding of Iraqi Shia agendas and power struggles reveals politics that are messy and malleable. The concepts of Islamism and Shia politics hardly explain any of Iraq's political motives and divides, even as pious Shia figures play a leading role on all sides of the country's many political struggles. This volume, *Shia Power Comes of Age: The Transformation of Islamist Politics in Iraq, 2003–2023*, maps the radical transformation of Shia Islamist politics in Iraq during a tumultuous historical period.

Explaining Everything and Nothing

Careful study suggests that in some way all the important decisions in Iraq trace back to Shia politics—and at the same time, none of them do. Two processes have unfolded in parallel: Shia preeminence, and the natural limits of a pluralistic political system.

Under majority rule, Shia politics have become the most important politics in Iraq, but by no means the only important ones. The "Shia house," as Iraqi politicians call the squabbling and heterogenous spectrum of Shia political factions, gets to select the prime minister and fill the most important and lucrative government posts. Shia factions are supposed to defend Shia interests, but actually spend much if not most of their time struggling with one another for a larger share of power or resources. They often try to summon independent clerics as referees or change agents, and Grand Ayatollah Ali al-Sistani, the most senior Shia cleric, has regularly intervened to nudge Iraq away from catastrophic escalations in conflict. None of Iraq's disputes or their resolutions make sense solely as avatars of Shia Islamism. Yet at the same time, religion and identity play an important role.

And the Shia house operates not in a vacuum, but in constant negotiation with other forces, some denoted by identity (Kurdish, Sunni Arab, and other communities) and some by institutional affiliation or interest (the security services, the business elite). Iraqis have carefully orchestrated a political system that prevents any single faction or identity group from dominating the others—not only at the national level but even within any one community. Iraq's post-American power-sharing arrangement grants winners and losers alike shares of government power; this consociational system promotes corruption and bad governance, but it also makes it difficult for a single authoritarian to ever take full control of state resources. This built-in balance that so frustrates reformers and long-suffering Iraqi citizens has also yielded a system characterized by hybrid actors, overlapping and layered identities, and political compromises.

Century International's Shia Politics Working Group brought together experts on Shia Islam and the socio-politics of the Middle East to produce unique research that might inform debate and provide insights into the current affairs not only of Iraq but of other countries with significant Shia populations, including Iran, Lebanon, and Bahrain. The group began with workshops and field research, and continues to recruit new researchers and widen the scope of its research. In the future, we expect the project that yielded *Shia Power Comes of Age* to extend the study of Shia politics in other directions, in Iraq and beyond, from the interaction of religion with politics to the rule of the transnational Shia diaspora, the influence of alms, and government efforts to harness religious authority for state ends.

The research collected in this volume can enrich the current policy debates focused on Iraq—and prompt new, wider discussions about the Middle East, Shia politics, and the intersection of religious communities, political power, and armed conflict.

Neither researchers nor the Iraqi politicians who use the term to describe themselves have a clear definition of Shia politics, though the state of play in Iraq unambiguously suggests that Shia politics means, at a minimum, Shia *Islamist* politics.

Each of the studies in this book is based on original fieldwork conducted in Iraq in the past five years, giving a detailed and nuanced view of a particular aspect of politics in Iraq. The 2021 elections and the sometimes violent competition to decide the shape of the new government altered the course of several of the research projects collected here, underscoring the dynamic nature of the topic.

The working group members pursued complementary questions, but this work is by no means comprehensive. A great many areas require future research. Several themes come through consistently: the importance of personalities in shaping politics, the historic networks and ties that underpin Shia parties, the ongoing importance of clerical authority, the continued relevance of sectarian identity politics, and, most clearly, the subservience of sect and ideology to the pursuit of power, by any means necessary.

Beyond Islamism and Identity

Shia Power Comes of Age opens with a pair of essays that challenge established thinking about sectarian politics and consider alternate frameworks and definitions of terms. Subsequent chapters explore various sections of the architecture of power: clerics, politicians, and protest movements. The final pair of essays return to framing ideas and examine changes over the last decades to structural factors, including violence and sectarian political identity.

In the first section, "Defining Shia Politics," Fanar Haddad questions the very terms Shia politics and Shia Islamism, and builds on his extensive earlier work to put the sectarian dimension of contemporary Iraqi politics in its proper context: as just one of the factors that helps explain Iraq's shifting political alliances and rivalries. If we cannot explain crucial forces through concepts like Shia politics or Shia Islamism, then how *should* we understand those forces—especially as intra-Shia cleavages are increasingly the most important points of conflict in Iraq and Iran?

Ali Al-Mawlawi's study of Shia political rhetoric about the state helps anchor intra-Shia political competition in a shared desire to harness the resources of the state. Even among rival Shia factions, a debate still flares over who is loyal to the state and who is not. Al-Mawlawi's analysis suggests Iraq's Shia factions might accuse one another of undermining the state, but all of them ultimately want more of its resources and power—so on that level, at least, they are all invested in the state.

In the second section, "Clerics," Marsin Alshamary draws on extensive field research in the Shia seminaries of Najaf, and interviews with clerics who have actively participated in electoral politics, to assess clerical authority in Iraq. Alshamary charts how Iraq's repeated crises and governance failures have affected the standing of clerics with their followers—and their authority relative to the Shia political class.

Sajad Jiyad's assessment of Grand Ayatollah Sistani's role during the Islamic State war and its aftermath suggests the direct and indirect power of the Shia clergy, especially during periods of crisis.

In the third section, "Politicians," Ben Robin-D'Cruz's deep study of the Sadrist electoral machine casts new light on Muqtada al-Sadr's ability to command enduring support, while pointing to some of its limits. Robin-D'Cruz's detailed depiction of the Sadrist movement's mobilization mechanics provides a corrective to analysis that has attributed Sadr's electoral prowess to religious pedigree, or to political ideology, rather than to the construction and maintenance of a network.

Maria Luisa Fantappie's historical study of the three Iraqi prime ministers who hail from the Shia Islamist Dawa Party makes a compelling case that personalities and leadership styles have played a determining role at key historical junctures.

In the fourth section, "Protest," Taif Alkhudary has produced a deep study of the ideology and goals of the Tishreen movement beyond protest, and suggests paths it might take as its followers gain power and their political movements mature.

In the fifth section, "Systemic Constraints," Renad Mansour researches the ways in which violence has usurped other mechanisms of negotiating competitions for power in Iraq. The centrality of violence has specific historical roots in each of the major ethnic and sectarian communities. For Shia factions, that history includes a power struggle between armed groups that returned from exile in 2003 and rivals who never left Iraq.

Thanassis Cambanis focuses on moments of "sectarian relapse," such as the tense and violent confrontation over government formation in 2022. Despite growing public aversion to sectarianism, sectarian and ethnic identity continue to dominate Iraqi politics.

Test Lab and Model

Iraq's unique trajectory in the region since 2003 has made it both a test lab and a model of new approaches to religion, politics, and power. As a pluralistic republic with majority rule and a system that has effectively prevented the emergence of a single dominant ruler or faction, the lessons of Iraq's experience are valuable for a region that witnesses little political experimentation or evolution. Iraq is surrounded by countries ruled by authoritarians and despots, who are often desperate to instrumentalize religion, either to legitimize their regimes or else to serve as a bogeyman, the terrifying alternative to whatever the existing ruler offers.

But in Iraq, religion has saturated and suffused politics, and those politics have evolved—not transcending religion but absorbing it. "Shia" and "Islamist" were apt terms for a segment of Iraq's politics in the immediate aftermath of the U.S.-led invasion in 2003; many Iraqis themselves embraced the labels. In a relatively short historical period of time, identity and political practice have shifted. The terms Shia and Islamist no longer contain the same specificity and explanatory power in Iraq. And more widely across the Middle East, the implications of sectarian and religious labels have dramatically changed, or even lost meaning, in one generation. "Shia" and "Islamist" might have the same limited utility in Iraq as "Catholic" or "Protestant" and "Christianist" do for politics in North America and Europe. Religion and religious histories are relevant but not necessarily a dispositive factor in explaining motives and events.

We intend the research, analysis and argument in *Shia Power Comes of Age: The Transformation of Islamist Politics in Iraq, 2003–2023* to help advance the understanding of Shia politics, Islamism, and more widely, religious politics in the Middle East among policymakers, researchers, and even political actors themselves.

Defining Shia Politics

1

Shia Rule Is a Reality in Iraq. "Shia Politics" Needs a New Definition.

Fanar Haddad

In Iraq, the conventional definition of Shia politics refers to sect-centric actors and Islamists. Today, that definition excludes too many politically active Shia Iraqis. A new analytical framework is necessary for today's Iraq. Iraqi politics are today driven not by a competition of Islamists versus non-Islamists, but by other divides, including intra-elite competition; status quo actors versus revisionist actors (from within the system and beyond); and core versus periphery. "Shia politics" could still accurately describe a subset of broader Iraqi politics; more accurately still, the term could be retired altogether.

Like any term associated with such a vast socio-religious group, "Shia politics" is inherently difficult to define. Does it refer to the sectarian identity of its protagonists? Is it a synonym for Shia Islamism? Must a movement speak in the name of "the Shia" to be considered Shia politics? Or does the term Shia politics refer to a particular set of discursive practices—a style of political rhetoric?

However it is defined, the term "Shia politics" is in need of reconceptualization, at least in the context of today's Iraq, because of several developments in the country's recent history. For one, the vague
notion of Shia rule is no longer an aspiration, but a reality: the dominant political actors in Iraq are Shia and, more so, Shia-centric politicians. (The terms Shia-centric and sect-centric denote a self-defining
focus on sect—this helps us better differentiate, for example, a politician who just happens to be Shia from a Shia-centric politician.)
Further, since Shia rule is a reality, it no longer has to contend with
sect-coded existential threats, as it once did after the U.S.-led invasion of 2003. The lack of such threats naturally blunts the salience of
the politics of sect, and more generally calls into question the purpose
of political sect-centricity in Iraq—a phenomenon that has traditionally been closely associated with conceptions of Shia politics.

Additionally, the empowerment of Shia elites has not translated
into any material benefit for the average Iraqi—Shia or otherwise—
save for those with elite connections. The lack of such gains has further dented the relevance of sect-centricity in Iraqi politics. In other
words, the protagonists of so-called Shia politics have failed their
supposed constituents.

As a result, the primary challenge to the dominance of today's
Shia political elite comes from Shia quarters in the form of intensi-
fying intra-Shia (and intra-Shia Islamist) elite fragmentation on the
one hand, and popular mass mobilization (mainly Shia) against the
status quo on the other. Where identity politics once animated a
critical mass of Iraqis, today the more resonant themes of political
mobilization employ the language of change and reform, in line with
popular demands for good governance, social justice, and the promise of a better life.

All of these developments call into question what is meant by
Shia politics: whom does the concept include, and whom does it
exclude? As this report shows, the complexity of contemporary Iraqi
politics means that the answer to these questions is far from obvious.

Divides between core and periphery, competing elite factions, and status quo actors and reformist challengers all better explain Iraqi politics than the obsolete frameworks of Islamism and Shia politics. At the very least, retaining the term Shia politics requires us to broaden what it refers to beyond conventional assumptions that approximate it to Shia Islamists and Shia political sect-centricity.

Profound and protracted political change and upheaval of the kind that Iraq has witnessed often necessitate a reassessment of conventional wisdom. The Arab uprisings of 2011, for example, have inspired a growing literature that interrogates how terms such as Islamism are understood in the wake of the uprisings.[1] Similar retrospection is all the more urgent in the case of Shia politics in Iraq, given the structural transformations that have unfolded since 2003.

What Are Shia Politics?

In the literature, Shia politics have traditionally been taken to mean a combination of Shia Islamism (sect-centric or otherwise) and Shia-centric political actors—while also occasionally including clerical networks.[2] At first glance, this seems like a reasonable premise, as it may be misleading to include, in conceptions of Shia politics, political actors who simply happen to be Shia—say a member of the Iraqi Communist Party from a Shia background. Including coincidentally Shia politicians in the definition insists on the political relevance of sectarian identity where it does not necessarily exist. This type of thinking created the problems of the Iraqi Governing Council (the provisional government of Iraq in 2003–4). The body was formed on the basis of communal proportional representation. As such, the general secretary of the Iraqi Communist Party, Hamid Majid Musa, was often described as a Shia who was a communist, rather than a communist who happened to be Shia.[3]

Equally reasonable, at first glance, is the assumption that Shia politics are a spectrum of politics that are sect-centric to varying degrees: political actors who, to one extent or another, claim to speak in the name of "the Shia," champion Shia causes, lobby on the basis of Shia victimhood or entitlement (or both), or otherwise exhibit and instrumentalize their Shia identity in politics. In the context of Iraq, analysts often view Shia political sect-centricity and Shia Islamism (itself a notoriously difficult term to define) as synonymous, because it is Shia Islamist actors who have most forcefully taken up the causes of Shia empowerment and Shia representation, especially since the latter decades of the twentieth century.[4] Hence, for example, the cast of characters in Faleh Abdul Jabar's seminal 2003 history *The Shi'ite Movement in Iraq* are almost entirely Shia Islamists: the Dawa Party, Munadhamat al-Amal al-Islami, the Supreme Council of the Islamic Revolution in Iraq (SCIRI), the Sadrs, the Hakims, and broader clerical networks.[5]

But, as this report argues, these assumptions are not entirely problem-free: sect-centricity is not the preserve of Islamists, nor have Islamists always adopted sect-centricity. This report therefore discusses the question of whether or not the concept of Shia politics should encompass more than Shia Islamists or sect-centricity, or both. This concern is particularly relevant today, given the transformation of Shia political sect-centricity: At one time, Shia-centric politics constituted an oppositional current that sought to remedy what adherents regarded as historical wrongs relating to Shia marginalization and underrepresentation. But today, Shia political sect-centricity is a status quo force that seeks to maintain the established hierarchies of power within an identity-based political system that is increasingly out of touch with ordinary Iraqis, Shia or otherwise.

Sect-Centricity, Shia Islamism, and Shia Politics

Abdul Jabar notes that Shia Islamism in the Arab world has a higher propensity than its Sunni counterpart toward sect-centricity (or, as he labeled it, to exhibit "communal militancy").[6] Whereas

Sunni Islamism, in his view, is a populist movement and ideology that emerged in defiance of postcolonial, authoritarian nationalist regimes and their socioeconomic policies and international alignments, Shia Islamism was often marked by communal militancy (or sect-centricity), which is a "responsive, segmentary movement caused by political, economic or cultural group-discrimination... in multi-communal societies."[7] Such communal militancy is a function of the relations of power underpinning sectarian relations, and the way that these sectarian relations have been shaped by state formation, nation-building processes, and more recent history—the Iranian revolution of 1979 being a particularly relevant milestone. This pattern emerged in Saudi Arabia and Bahrain, as well, where political sect-centricity in the twentieth century (especially the latter half) emerged as a more pronounced feature of Shia Islamism and activism than was the case with Sunni Islamists. The features of Shia Islamism in these countries were a response to feelings of sectarian victimhood, marginalization, and discrimination—real or perceived.[8]

However, as is widely noted, Shia Islamism in Iraq (and elsewhere) was not always sect-centric.[9] Iraqi Shia Islamist movements emerged in the mid-twentieth century in response to concerns about the rise of the secular Left; Shia identity or Shia victimhood were not the initial motivations for Iraqi Shia Islamism. In that sense, Iraqi Shia Islamism's foundational impulse was, much like its Sunni counterparts, a conservative modernism rather than sect-centricity. There is no singular moment that heralded a "sectarian turn" in Iraqi Shia Islamism. Rather, it was a gradual process that built on preexisting, though latent, feelings of Shia victimhood, and that was shaped by Iraqi and regional currents.

The policies of Abd al-Salam Arif (president 1963–66) and Abd al-Rahman Arif (president 1966–68) at times fostered feelings of sectarian discrimination in some Shia quarters. These policies included the expropriation of some Shia religious endowments, the adverse impact of nationalization and regulation policies in 1964, which negatively affected the Shia merchant classes, and discriminatory hiring practices.[10] The increasing authoritarianism of the state—particularly after the Ba'ath coup of 1968—was accompanied by an intensification of Shia activism, much of it driven by feelings of sectarian victimhood that in turn were driven by state policy.[11] This cycle resulted in the sharpening of the state's suspicions of Shia political activism and of the mobilization of Shia identity, which in turn raised the political salience of Shia sect-centricity.

Shia Islamists clashed with the state on several occasions in the 1970s, which further accelerated these dynamics. Most notable among these disturbances was the government's violent clampdown on Shia processions in 1977, and on the protests that followed the arrest, in 1979, of Shia activist cleric Mohammad Baqir al-Sadr.[12] This escalation was partly shaped by the regional environment and Iraq's deteriorating relations with Iran—naturally this downward spiral only accelerated after the Iranian revolution of 1979. The demise of Arab nationalism and communism as popular mobilizers and the emergence of the Islamic Republic of Iran (and the rise of other Islamist movements in the region) further explain the growing political relevance of Shia sect-centricity in Iraq. The 1980–88 Iran–Iraq War, the uprisings of 1991, international sanctions against Iraq, mass exile, and the growing international discourse of human rights and communal rights meant that by the 1990s, Iraqi Shia Islamism was firmly wedded to sect-centricity, based on feelings of Shia victimhood and political entitlement.

This culture of political sect-centricity (and ethnocentricity in the case of Kurdish nationalists in the Iraqi opposition) converged with official U.S. policy views toward Iraq. After 2003, sect- and ethnocentricity became the foundational principles of the new political order—an enormous change from the relative irrelevance of sect-centricity among Shia Islamists less than four decades earlier.

While sect-centricity did not always characterize Shia Islamism, it is also important to recall that, contrary to conventional assumptions, sect-centricity was never the exclusive preserve of Shia Islamists. A variety of Shia figures intermittently voiced Shia-specific grievances such as political underrepresentation throughout the twentieth century. For example, in the 1920s, Amin al-Charchafchi's Hizb al-Nahda adopted an openly sect-centric platform that stressed Shia political grievance.[13] A variety of prominent non-Islamist figures raised the issues of Shia underrepresentation and perceived anti-Shia discrimination throughout the twentieth century. These include nationalist politician Muhammad Ridha al-Shabibi, historian and Arab nationalist Abd al-Razzaq al-Hassani, nationalist politician Muhsin Abu-Tabikh, former foreign minister and minister of reconstruction Abd al-Karim al-Uzri, political activist and intellectual Hassan al-Alawi, and many others.[14] All of these non-Islamist examples revolved around the twin pillars of Shia political sect-centricity: victimhood and entitlement.[15] This fact further problematizes any assumption that treats Shia politics and Shia Islamism as synonymous.

The synonymity that arose—both for analysts and political actors—between Shia politics and Shia Islamism was a result of contingent factors, some of which no longer hold. Toward the end of the twentieth century, Shia Islamism was increasingly intertwined with sect-centricity, to the point where they became indistinguishable to observers. However, the overlap between the two was never complete: as this report has already shown, Islamism does not necessarily have to be sect-centric, and Islamists are not the only actors who adopt sect-centricity. Nevertheless, the tendency to conflate Shia Islamism and Shia political sect-centricity persisted and was reinforced by the political changes of 2003 and the entrenchment of a political system based on ethno-sectarian identities—and dominated by Shia Islamists.

Yet it is those very changes that call for a reconceptualization of the term Shia politics away from a narrow focus on Islamism and sect-centricity. Simply put, both Shia Islamism and sect-centricity—and hence Shia politics—have been fundamentally transformed by Shia elite empowerment since 2003.

Regime Change and the Politics of Sect

The sect-centricity and ethnocentricity of the Iraqi opposition in exile neatly converged with how the U.S. administration viewed Iraq in the run-up to 2003: as a country fundamentally defined by communal identity, with oppressive Sunnis on the one hand and oppressed Shias and Kurds on the other, alongside an assortment of lesser minorities. The political system that was created by the U.S.-led occupation and its Iraqi partners after 2003 followed this communal logic.

Soon after regime change, the Shia-centric actors (Islamist and otherwise) of the pre-2003 Iraqi opposition rose to the top of the political pyramid. The sect-centricity that marked their oppositional politics in exile was superimposed onto post-2003 governance and political practice. A key enabling factor in that regard was that, despite the fact of Shia (elite) empowerment, the main themes of Shia political sect-centricity retained much of their salience in the years after 2003. For one thing, newly empowered Shia-centric actors played on themes of Shia victimhood and entitlement that resonated with parts of an Iraqi generation that was formed under the shadow of late Ba'athist Iraq.[16] In that sense, sect-centric opponents of the Ba'ath appealed to the regime's sect-coded victims, and played up the mythology of unique Shia victimization.[17] Another thing that sustained sect-centricity in the early post-invasion years was the precariousness of Shia empowerment, and the sect-coded hopes and fears that regime change and its ensuing chaos engendered. These conditions meant that the pre-2003 pillars of Shia political sect-centricity—victimhood and entitlement—persisted after the invasion, albeit for new or modified reasons: fears of a Ba'athist return; sectarian violence by Sunni militants; the regional backlash against the new Iraq, and against the empowerment of Shia-centric actors; and what the general atmosphere of violence and sectarian polarization portended for the future. Shia political actors now dominated Iraqi politics, but this ostensible Shia empowerment had to be defended against both internal and external sect-coded threats. In such a context, it made some sense for the concept of Shia politics to refer to a mélange of Shia Islamism and sect-centricity: the two were intertwined.

Finally, and as a result of all of this, ethno-sectarian categories profoundly shaped the politics of the early years following the U.S.-led invasion. In the elections of 2005, the political classes, despite their internal divisions, coalesced into three major identity-based blocs—Shia, Sunni, and Kurdish—thereby validating the cartoonish conception of a tripartite Iraq that was so in vogue amongst American officials and their Iraqi interlocutors. The division of Iraqi politics into these categories, and the dominance of sect-centric Shia Islamists, further reinforced the association of Shia politics with sect-centricity and Shia Islamism.

An Altered Landscape

However, today's Iraq is vastly different from what it was during "the long 2003"—a term that refers to the five or so years after the 2003 invasion, when the basic outline of the new political order was being contested.[18] The political classes, and perhaps Shia elites more than any others, have undergone a deep and continuous process of fragmentation. This is most obviously evident in electoral politics. In the elections of January 2005, the three ethno-sectarian blocs secured 87 percent of the vote, with the Shia-dominated United Iraqi Alliance, the top vote-getter, receiving 47 percent of the vote.[19] In 2010, the top performer's share of the vote dropped to a mere 24 percent, which went to Ayad Allawi's al-Iraqiya coalition.[20] This trend continued in the elections of 2014 with Nouri al-Maliki's State of Law

Coalition securing only 24 percent of the vote and no other entity receiving more than 7.5 percent of the vote. Further, in 2014, the Shia vote was split among three major electoral lists, while the Sunni vote was split among four main lists.[21] The process of fragmentation accelerated in the elections of 2018: the top nine lists shared 80 percent of the vote, with the largest share—a modest 14 percent—going to the Sadrist Sa'iroun list.[22] Finally, the elections of October 2021 yielded the most fragmented result yet: The top performer in 2021, the Sadrists, received a mere 10 percent of the vote.[23]

This fragmentation reflects the increased complexity of Iraqi politics, governance, and political competition. During the long 2003, basic questions relating to the nature of the new governing order were being contested: the survival of the post-2003 order; the question of identity politics and whether ethno-sectarian identities would form the basis of the new state; the question of so-called Shia rule; the nature of the emergent hierarchies of power; and the territorial integrity of Iraq. The polarization surrounding these issues was very much (though never entirely) mapped onto ethno-sectarian categories. This was a period of intense inter-sectarian competition in which sect- and ethnicity-coded political and militant camps struggled over the definition of the new Iraq and the relations of power within it.

With time, these broad-brush foundational issues were settled (though not necessarily resolved), and an order of sorts emerged out of the embers of civil war. As the relations of power and the vested interests that underpinned them crystallized, and as the roots of the post-2003 state deepened, political uncertainty and sect-coded existential fears receded. With them, the political salience of sectarian identity in contentious politics also diminished, as did the drivers of sectarian polarization. Today, and for some years now, the primary lines of political contestation have been intra-sectarian, with rival, amorphous, cross-sectarian alignments competing over the political and economic spoils of the state. In particular, in recent years, the primary challenge to Iraq's political stability and to the empowerment of the Shia political elite has been intra-Shia elite competition on the one hand, and public discontent and mobilization (largely Shia) on the other.

Political Discourse Evolves

The transformations of political discourse over the years illustrate the shifts described above. The changes in the discourse, in turn, reflect the shifting parameters of political contestation, political correctness, and populism.[24] To take one of countless examples, in 2003 Fa'iq al-Shaikh Ali was a noted non-Islamist figure in the Iraqi opposition in exile. While perhaps not a Shia-centric actor, he was not oblivious or insensitive to the issue of Shia victimhood under the Ba'ath regime; for example, he signed the intensely sect-centric Declaration of the Shia of Iraq in 2002.[25] He engaged directly with Iraqi politics after 2003, and became a member of parliament in 2014. A populist media figure and critic of the system, his evolution with regard to Shia sect-centricity is relevant here.

Immediately after regime change, al-Shaikh Ali was among many who cautioned against the possibility of Shia fragmentation. In an interview just months after the invasion, he expressed dismay at the rise of Shia religious and political leader Muqtada al-Sadr. Even more so, he criticized the United States' seeming willingness to turn a blind eye to Sadr and his militant brand, and claimed that the Central Intelligence Agency was seeking to instigate a Shia–Shia clash by pitting the Sadrists against SCIRI (an important player in the Iraqi opposition) and their armed wing, the Badr Brigade.[26] The idea of external powers seeking to ignite intra-Shia rivalries is a ubiquitous trope of Shia-centric political discourse today (as I discuss in the following section).

Today, however, al-Shaikh Ali positions himself against that very discourse, challenging the status quo and the rhetoric of sect-centricity. In late October 2021, he described that month's elections as signaling the defeat of "the Iranian project," which he defined as being composed of a blunt element (militias, suppression of protests, and the like) and a soft element, in the form of Shia, Sunni, and Kurdish political factions that do Iran's bidding. Among the Shia actors in this project, he explicitly called out the Islamic Supreme Council of Iraq (ISCI—the rebranded version of the aforementioned SCIRI), Hikma, and Badr.[27] Far from seeking to avoid Shia fragmentation, al-Shaikh Ali—and countless others besides him, not least the Sadrists—are today agents of that fragmentation, as they challenge the ossified hierarchies of power underpinning the status quo.

Al-Shaikh Ali's contradictory statements should not be taken as signs of hypocrisy or political fickleness. Rather, they reflect the transformations that Shia political sect-centricity have undergone after nearly two decades of supposed "Shia rule" characterized by abject governance failure and increasing distance between Shia-centric elites and a growing segment of the Shia public. Where once even some secular Shia perceived a historic opportunity requiring the maintenance of a united Shia front, today such discourse is primarily the preserve of Shia-centric status quo actors.[28]

Shia Sect-Centricity as the Establishment

Shia politics, as a concept, once referred to a populist sect-centricity, which emphasized Shia victimhood and Shia political entitlement combined with varying shades of Shia Islamism. But today the term may need to encompass a lot more. Shia political sect-centricity today is primarily a tool and a discourse for maintaining the status quo and the empowerment of increasingly unpopular Shia-centric political elites. Previously, Shia political sect-centricity appealed to a constituency that viewed it as a vehicle for empowerment and for the righting of historical wrongs, as they perceived them. In recent years however, it is viewed as part of the problem by a growing number of Shia who have known no reality other than that of a Shia (elite) empowerment that has failed the vast majority of Iraqis, Shia or otherwise. Put differently, politicians today deploy sect-centricity to defend Shia rule primarily from *Shia* challengers to the status quo. These challengers include Islamists from within the system—the Sadrists—a fact that further complicates the dated analytical conflation of Islamists, sect-centricity, and Shia politics.

At the time of writing, Iraq's primary political contest was related to the fallout of the October 2021 elections and the ongoing attempts at government formation. The contest was primarily split between the Shia-centric and pro status-quo Coordination Framework and its allies, on the one hand, and the Sadrists and their allies on the other. Despite being a pillar of the political system, Sadr has positioned himself as an outsider, railing against the establishment (of which he is very much a part) and promising radical change. Crucially, he vowed to do away with the post-2003 practice of "consensus governments" whereby all major political actors are included in government. Instead, he has promised to form a "majority government," where a parliamentary majority forms a government and those excluded go on to form a parliamentary opposition. Sadr gathered a cross-sectarian, cross-ethnic, but Sadr-dominated, alliance that could have theoretically formed a government without the Coordination Framework. Having fared poorly in the elections, and alarmed at the unprecedented prospect of being excluded from government, the Coordination Framework resorted to a combination of coercive, political, and legal measures that successfully blocked Sadr from forming a government. Sadr, in turn, used his street power and coercive capital to prevent the formation of a government led by the Coordination Framework. The political stalemate lasted for just over a year: in mid-October 2022, the Coordination Framework's nominee for prime minister, Mohammed Shia al-Sudani, was officially tasked with forming a government.

The details of the crisis need not detain us. What is relevant is the framing strategy adopted by the Coordination Framework in its rivalry with Sadr. Rather predictably, it stressed the need to maintain the post-2003 system of consensual governments, and in doing so have employed the language of Shia-centric politics: emphasizing the necessity of maintaining a united Shia front and, by extension, Shia rule. The alternative, according to proponents of this view, is chaos and possibly reversion to a state of Shia oppression. In June 2022, the head of Badr, Hadi al-Amiri, invoked the clerical leadership in Najaf (the marja'iyya) when he argued in a television appearance that it was essential to uphold the status quo and the political process: "The marja'iyya knows more than us that any eventuality that threatens the political process means placing an entire history of sacrifices and victories and martyrs' blood on the edge of a precipice."[29] A variety of spokespeople affiliated with the Coordination Framework repeated, ad nauseum, the key elements of this discourse—victimhood (historic and potentially reemerging), political entitlement, and warnings of the dangers of Shia fragmentation and a Shia–Shia clash. Interlaced throughout this discourse is the vague notion of Shia rule (or, more accurately, Shia-centric rule) and the need to maintain it.

For example, in a tediously repetitive sermon in November 2021, a month after the elections, Sadr al-Din al-Qubanchi, who is affiliated with ISCI—which itself is part of the Coordination Framework—commended the efforts of the political elites to find a "national solution" to the country's political crisis. The implication of this phrase suggests a solution that transcends the boundaries of sect and ethnicity. However, his comments leave no doubt as to the nonnegotiable necessity of Shia dominance in any "national solution":

> We say: all initiatives are accepted on the condition that the Shia House is not dismantled. This initiative, that initiative, a third, a fourth, on the condition of what? That the Shia House is not dismantled. The initiatives are acceptable on the condition that the Shia House is not dismantled because

the dismantling of the Shia House means the end of Iraq. The end of the new Iraq and the return of dictatorship and authoritarianism. There will be no more elections or freedom, everything will go if we [the Shia House] are dismantled, God forbid. If we are dismantled it would mean that our experiment is finished. It would mean that Saddam and those like Saddam will come back.

Qubanchi went on to call on Iraqis to accept the election results once they were released and ratified, and to allow the "political majority" to steer the country. However, like "national solution," the phrase "political majority" is also contingent on Shia dominance:

God willing, [the political elites] will give us glad tidings this week: they will announce a solution that they agree upon. The Shia House must not be dismantled. All of you [Shia politicians] sit down and unify the position and form a majority. And that is that: the political majority has the right to steer the country—with the unity of the Shia House.[30]

Here, "political majority" is being used in much the same way that the franker "majority rule" (hukm al-aghlabiyya) was used in the early post-2003 years. The political majority, in this conception, has to be a Shia-dominated majority; more than that, it must include all Shia (and particularly Shia-centric) actors. A cross-sectarian political majority, even if it is Shia-dominated—as would have been the case with Sadr's proposed coalition—is rejected in Qubanchi's framework if it excludes some Shia factions, and particularly if it excludes Qubanchi's Shia factions. In this formula, elections, parliamentary politics, and government formation are a charade for maintaining the demography-equals-democracy basis of the post-2003 identity-based system, and the power that it has delivered to the sect-centric and ethnocentric political elites. The new phrasing is a clumsy attempt at softening the blunt rhetoric of "vote for the mathhab [Shiism]" that was used by Shia-centric actors in earlier elections—particularly in 2005 and 2014. The new language reflects the shifting parameters of populism over the course of the last nineteen years and the fact that openly sect-centric political strategies are now less effective.

The Sadrists, having emerged from the 2021 elections with a stronger hand, insisted on the necessity of a majority government with political losers— the Coordination Framework—going into opposition. The Sadrists framed this position as a necessary course correction in the quest for political reform. Needless to say, one should take such assertions with a large grain of salt: while a break with the practice of consensus governments would be a major step forward, there is little reason to suppose that a Sadrist-led majority government will fundamentally alter the political economy of Iraq. The Sadrists claimed the competition that followed the elections of 2021 was between the forces of reform and the corrupt political classes. The Sadrist stance, however, is better understood as a power play against their rivals in the political system, within which the Sadrists are as complicit as anyone else. Nevertheless, the divide between the Sadrists and the Coordination Framework illustrates the need to reconceptualize the concept of Shia politics. If Shia politics are (at least partially) about sect-centricity, then the term would have to exclude today's Sadrists because of their stance—an implausible exclusion given their importance. The discourse of sect-centricity and Shia entitlement has become divisive among Shia and Shia political actors themselves, and hence cannot be used as a marker for *their* politics.

Defining the Borders of Shia Politics

As already mentioned above, besides sect-centricity, Islamism is the other characteristic that many scholars and analysts assume is a defining feature of Shia politics. Rightly or wrongly, Islamism was often regarded as the most important vehicle for Shia political activism. If this may have been somewhat inaccurate in the past it is patently counterfactual today. Whatever electoral advantage Shia Islamists commanded in the early post-2003 years has considerably dissipated. It can be argued that this again reflects the diminished populist currency of sect-centric politics. In their early years, Islamist actors such as the Dawa Party or ISCI articulated an ideological vision rooted in varying notions of an Islamic order. Yet by 2003, they had abandoned such visions as unworkable in the context of Iraq, even if they were desirable in the abstract.[31] All that remained in terms of political vision was sect-centricity: validating Shia victimhood and realizing Shia-centric notions of political entitlement by attaining and securing Shia rule. Given how undefined the concept is, this equated to ideational bankruptcy. This bankruptcy of ideas explains the remarkable fact that, after two decades in which Shia Islamist parties and political actors have been the dominant partners in six governments, they have not managed to articulate, let alone implement, any discernible Islamist program. Even matters of public morality—commonly an object of special focus for social conservatives such as Islamists—have not been a high priority on these parties' legislative agenda. Indeed, given the similar legislative outlooks, the lack of distinguishable political programs, and the collusion and mutual interests that often tie them together, one may fairly ask what actually differentiates a self-described Islamist from a non-Islamist in elite Iraqi politics.[32]

As this report has shown, the past two decades have illustrated the relatively precarious shelf life of sect-centricity as a populist political trope. In some regards, Shia-centric political actors have been victims of their own success: the more they succeeded in turning Shia-centric state-building into a reality, the less cause there was for the sectarian entrenchment upon which populist sect-centricity depends.[33] Yet Shia Islamists proved unable to offer much beyond a sect-centric outlook, and have struggled to keep up with the shift in popular sentiment toward issue politics that analysts have observed since at least 2018.[34] This gulf separating Shia Islamists from a widening swath of Iraqi Shias, and the ideological hollowness of contemporary Shia Islamists in Iraq, again raises questions as to the validity of reducing Shia politics to Shia Islamism (however defined).

Today, the public often distills its anger at the political system into anger against Shia Islamists, because of their role as architects, beneficiaries, and guardians of the system. In a paper published in April, political scientist Marsin Alshamary clearly describes this distillation in an analysis of the protest movement and its usage of concepts such as "civic state" and "secularism" as shorthand for a rejection of the Shia Islamist parties that have dominated post-2003 Iraq.[35] It therefore makes just as little sense to exclusively associate Shia politics with Islamism as it does to associate it entirely with sect-centricity. The relative unpopularity of Shia Islamists means that any formulation of Shia politics that is centered on Islamism would detach a critical mass of Iraqi Shias from the concept. Whether or not such a formulation is helpful is open to debate.

The Protest Movements

If sect-centricity and Islamism are not the defining features of Shia politics, where should we situate the protest movement in the discussion? On the one hand, including the protest movement in understandings of Shia politics risks sect-coding an avowedly non-sect-centric phenomenon just because its protagonists are Shia. On the other hand, can we exclude such an important political current from Shia politics? The protests of 2019–20 have left a lasting imprint on Iraqi political culture and, at the very least, have had a discursive effect on formal Iraqi politics. The protests turned vast segments of the Shia public into a key political force in 2019 and 2020. They forced the resignation of a government and the drafting of a new electoral law, which in turn enabled new entrants affiliated or claiming affiliation with the protest movement into parliamentary politics. A case can be made that, given its demographic weight and political significance, protest activism in Shia areas is as much a part of "Shia politics" as any Islamist party.

The protests of 2019 were a primarily Shia challenge against the dominant Shia-centric political parties. The latter, quite predictably, employed the pillars of Shia political sect-centricity (victimhood and entitlement) to counter the threat. But while this strategy might have been effective in tarnishing activism emanating from Sunni quarters, it was much less powerful when deployed against Shia, since there was no sect-coded threat to counter. For example, in a sermon shortly after the start of the protests in 2019, Hasan al-Zamili, another cleric affiliated with ISCI, articulated how Shia-centric actors viewed the protests:

> We have two choices: either we leave the government to battle on its own, with the prime minister bare-backed, fighting on his own in the field with the arrows pointing at him, even from participants in the government. This would mean that we have destroyed and lost our entitlement as Shia [istihqaquna nahnu ka Shia]. Let some people call this a sectarian message, [but] this is reality: we are the majority of the Iraqi people, and this is our entitlement [istihqaquna] after having been marginalized for tens of years and even hundreds of years [during which] we were enslaved, attacked, killed, and dispersed. Today, power [hukm] is in our hands. If we do not preserve this power, O parties of Iraq, where are we heading? After you took the spoils, benefits, gains, and privileges, you left the prime minister to fight on his own.[36]

Of course, the irony here is that the threat Zamili referred to is the threat of a Shia public furious at what the political parties have done with the Shia power that he is so keen to maintain. It may be tempting to conclude that Shia politics is what Zamili is defending, and is a part of, while the protests are not. Yet this would again bring us back to a definition of Shia politics based on sect-centricity which, as seen above, does not stand up to critical scrutiny—not least because it would exclude the Sadrists. It seems problematic to restrict Shia politics to the likes of Zamili: a status quo actor resented by a significant section of Shia Iraqis.

The decision of whether or not to include the protest movements in the concept of Shia politics is a difficult one for the analyst. Including them risks artificially sect-coding them (and thereby possibly misrepresenting them); yet excluding them and restricting Shia politics to the unrepresentative and unpopular Shia political elite risks detaching the concept of Shia politics from an increasing number of Iraqi Shia.

The protests of 2019 were primarily in Shia areas and were primarily composed of young Shia. On the one hand, this was a function of geography and demographics rather than sectarian dynamics; on the other, the protestors employed Shia symbolism (among other frames) to express their outrage at the political classes. As commented upon at the time, the very same symbols that were used by the political classes in pursuit of Shia-centric state-building were now being used against them by young protesters.[37] In that sense, an argument can be made for including non-sect-centric Shia challengers to the status quo in understandings of Shia politics, if the concept were taken to mean the discursive, political, and ideational space in which Shia Iraqis engage with politics—particularly if they are employing Shia symbolism when doing so. It is another debatable question whether or not it is wise to include such a diverse range of actors under any single term—ranging from Iran-leaning paramilitaries, such as Kata'eb Hezbollah, to the protest-inspired Imtidad.

Political scientist Harith Hasan has made an insightful sociological observation that is relevant here. In his analysis, the

Iran-leaning paramilitaries and political parties (the so-called resistance factions) should not only be understood through the prism of ideology or Iranian sympathies but should also be seen as part of a sociological process of challengers rising from the periphery against the center. Hasan makes the point that this applies to a succession of movements: Shia Islamist challengers to the pre-2003 Ba'ath; the post-2003 Sadrist challenge to both the political center in Baghdad and to the religious center in Najaf after 2003; and the challenge of Sadrist splinter groups and resistance factions to the Sadrists more recently. Hasan argues that the latest iteration of this cycle is the challenge posed by impoverished Shia youth rising against the Islamist-dominated center.[38] Employing Hasan's framework, it can be argued that all of the actors mentioned by him, including the impoverished youth who made up the bulk of the 2019–20 protests, are protagonists in Shia politics. Such a formulation—while not entirely free of analytical problems—may be more consistent with the realities of contemporary Iraq. Other concepts of Shia politics that this report has referred to are rooted in pre-2003 and early post-2003 history.

New Definitions

The term "Shia politics" is hardly unique in its definitional issues. Liberalism, sectarianism, Islamism and any number of other concepts are similarly open to multiple definitions and are the subject of vast literatures grappling with what they mean and how they should be understood. What may set the concept of Shia politics apart (at least in Iraq) is the profound transformation that has been imposed on the term's ingredients: Shia identity, sect-centricity, the political economy of Iraq, Iraqi sectarian relations, Shia Islamism—all of these have been radically transformed over the last two decades in ways that render somewhat obsolete many of our assumptions as to what Shia politics mean.

Several questions arise from the preceding discussion. Key among them is what and whom the term "Shia politics" refers to. Unfortunately, there are no easy answers: Do all Shia political actors collectively constitute "Shia politics"? If not, who is to be excluded?

As this report has argued, standard assumptions regarding Shia politics as a combination of sect-centricity and Islamism simply do not work. Anchoring the term in Shia sect-centricity would mean restricting it to a narrowing section of the Shia political elite while excluding—unconvincingly—other Shia political actors, most egregiously the Sadrists. The term "Shia politics" may have been less complicated when it referred to an oppositional trend that focused on communal rights, but such a framing has been made obsolete by Shia elite empowerment and the intensification of intra-Shia political competition. Previously, and particularly since the closing decades of the twentieth century, Shia-centric movements were juxtaposed against "Sunni regimes," with Shia victimhood forming a key part of such movements' political outlook. Today, the dominant political actors are Shia and Shia-centric ones, and their primary opponents are each other and much of the Shia public.

Shia-centric political actors are finding it increasingly difficult to convince a critical mass of Shia Iraqis of the benefits of so-called Shia rule and, more importantly, they are having a difficult time convincing Iraqis that such rule is in a precarious position. The idea that, for example, Shia rituals and processions or the expression of Shia identity can be suppressed by anyone is simply too implausible in 2022. Nor can they plausibly claim to be defenders of Shia rights, given their failure to deliver basic economic and political goods to ordinary Iraqis, Shia or otherwise. As the protests of 2019–20 and the aftermath of the 2021 elections showed, Shia-centric actors will self-defensively try to revive the discourse of Shia political sect-centricity, but the efficacy of this discourse is severely curtailed by the intra-Shia nature of the political challenges they face and the absence of a sect-coded threat. The discourse struggles to gain currency beyond the (rather limited) choir.

Like sect-centricity, Shia Islamism is often assumed to be the substance of Shia politics. Yet, this, again, is no longer tenable. Two decades of Shia Islamist empowerment have altered Shia Islamists' politics, and the way that they are viewed by the Shia public. A critical mass of Shia Iraqis arguably saw these Islamists as champions of Shia causes in 2003, but now an increasing number of these Islamists' supposed constituents view them as part of the problem. Therefore, restricting the concept of Shia politics to Shia Islamists would exclude far too large a segment of Iraqi Shias and Iraqi Shia political actors. Furthermore, Shia Islamist empowerment and the relative success of Shia-centric state-building (at least in turning it into a reality, as opposed to success in the sense of a positive contribution) has fostered a profound ideational and ideological bankruptcy in so-called Shia Islamism in Iraq. After nearly twenty years in power, it is difficult to identify anything discernibly "Islamist" in Iraq's Shia Islamists—be it in their political behavior, their political programs, their legislative agenda or what, if anything, supposedly sets them apart from non-Islamists.

Rather than Islamists versus non-Islamists, Iraqi politics are today driven by other divides. These divides include intra-elite competition (which obliterates the Islamist–non-Islamist binary), and status quo actors versus revisionist actors (from within the system and beyond). These are some of the factors that should compel us to reevaluate the concept of Shia politics—what it refers to and whom it includes.

Two suggestions come to mind, neither of which is satisfactory. There undoubtedly exists a Shia political field that interacts and partially overlaps with broader Iraqi politics. Perhaps it is this that should be labeled Shia politics irrespective of the ideological convictions or sect-centricity of individual actors. After all, the Shia political field today is too complex for the assumptions that have traditionally underpinned understandings of Shia politics.

But as this report has shown, using the term "Shia politics" in this way risks artificially and incorrectly sect-coding actors who do not merit such labels. Alternatively, perhaps the changes of the past two decades and the complexity of Iraqi politics have simply rendered the term obsolete. Retiring the term might make sense, particularly given the fact that it is a Western term that is not derived from an Iraqi or Middle Eastern equivalent. The problem here, of course, is the notorious difficulty in retiring commonly used terms, such as Shia politics, and what to replace them with.

Ultimately, this report does not claim to provide an answer to these questions. But it does highlight the need to ask these questions, reevaluate the meaning of the concept of Shia politics, and whether or not the term is still useful. Its current usage is based on out-of-date assumptions, and our understanding of what the term entails has not kept up with the fundamental transformations of the past two decades.

2

Iraqi Shia Factions Are Supposedly "Anti-state." But State Power Is What They Want.

Ali Al-Mawlawi

In Iraqi politics and analysis, and even among activists, it has become popular to describe the country's Shia Islamist groups as being "anti-state"—inherently against the Iraqi state. But this narrative is problematic. In reality, the dominant Shia political factions all believe in the Iraqi state; what distinguishes them are their different aspirations for the state's identity. Worse, the anti-state narrative risks smearing Shia Iraqis in general, and further exacerbating political polarization, leading to more instability. The anti-state label is a politically expedient accusation that plays a role in the narratives employed by competing Iraqi factions—Shia or otherwise—to assert greater influence and control over Iraq.

Shia Islamist parties have dominated politics in Iraq since the first post-Saddam Hussein elections in 2005. The political narrative for much of this period has revolved around two often misleading debates: about the role of Shia Islamism in politics, and whether Iraq's leading movements are loyal to the Iraqi state or are subordinate to foreign interests.

This narrative has continued to shape even more recent developments. During the Tishreen protest movement that erupted in Iraq in October 2019, a fierce public discourse emerged over who could lay claim to being the defender of the Iraqi state, and who was bent on undermining its authority. In particular, the debate focused on whether Shia Islamist movements helped fortify the Iraqi state or eroded it. Detractors of Shia Islamist groups portrayed them as inherently antagonistic to the state—and this view took hold among protesters.

In the context of the Tishreen movement, there was a clear appeal to this narrative: The marchers were decrying the chronic dysfunction and corruption of the government, and Shia Islamist groups have been central to Iraqi politics for many years. Although most of the protesters were themselves Shia, it is easy to see how the dysfunctional government and Shia Islamist parties could be lumped together in the fervor of a street movement.

But the narrative that Shia Islamist groups are inherently *against* the Iraqi state is also facile, and problematic. This report seeks to explore political rhetoric and public debates as an indicator of how Shia Islamists conceive of their relationship with the Iraqi state, and how their adversaries perceive that relationship. This study, based on interviews with members of a prominent Shia Islamist group and a study of Iraqi political rhetoric, suggests that rootedness in the state is a misleading metric that fails to shed light on the goals of leading Shia Islamist political factions or the differences between them. To the contrary, a careful reading of Iraq's political discourse shows that the dominant Shia political factions all believe in the Iraqi state; what distinguishes them are their different aspirations for state identity. These differing aspirations vary according to how they see the role of religion in politics, which regional alliances should be prioritized, and how the state's power structures should be configured.

Brushing off Shia Islamists as being "anti-state" is plainly erroneous, and the ideological offspring of anti-Shia prejudices that date back to at least the beginning of modern Iraq. Throughout Iraq's recent past, the country's ruling elites deployed similar frames to smear the entirety of Shia Iraqis as fifth columnists for Iran or other outside actors. Previous regimes used these accusations to silence political dissent and justify the persecution of Shia Iraqis.

In reality, Shia Islamists in Iraq see themselves as earnest patriots with political ambitions within the existing Iraqi state. This report reveals a far more nuanced picture of how Shia Islamists conceive of their relationship with the Iraqi state, and how they reconcile their sect-based identity with a national identity. The extent to which they rely on an ethno-sectarian framework to assert their political voice is largely a reaction to the ethno-sectarian framework that had long kept them silent. There is little evidence that their identity as Shia Islamists reduces their sense of belonging or allegiance to the multi-confessional Iraqi state.

There may be truth to the idea that Shia Islamist factions have, at times, eroded the state's authority and its institutions. But a more constructive discourse should focus on identifying these factions' specific practices and understanding the motivations behind them. A crude labeling of these factions as being inherently "against the state" does little to advance the analysis.

The salience of the corrective offered in this report has broader implications, as well. It also sheds light on how Iraqis think of their own politics more generally, and the narratives that are employed by competing factions—Shia or otherwise—to assert greater influence and control over the country.

And at the heart of this discursive contest over the political narrative lies a struggle over the identity of the Iraqi state. As this report shows, this contest should not be conceived of as a struggle between those who believe in the state and those who do not. Rather, it is a contest between antagonistic visions of what Iraq's state should look like—competing visions of state identity. In this contest, allegations that Shia Islamist groups stand against the state are merely a politically expedient accusation—one that risks smearing Shia people in Iraq in general, and further exacerbating societal divisions and political polarization that will inevitably lead to more instability and political turmoil.

The State and the Anti-state

In late September 2019, jobless graduates gathered outside the office of the prime minister, Adil Abdul-Mahdi, to protest their lack of prospects and the dysfunctionality of the Iraqi state. Security forces turned water cannons against the protesters, sparking a wave of public outrage that gave rise to the biggest protest movement in Iraq in the post-2003 era.[1]

On October 1, 2019, protesters gathered in Baghdad's Tahrir Square, and the Tishreen movement began. As the protest movement gained momentum, demonstrators viewed their stance as a defense of the state against the corrupt ruling elite and the armed actors—some of whom were fighters affiliated with Shia Islamist factions—who were attacking them. The protesters' relationship with the state was articulated through the popularized protest movement slogan, "We want a homeland" (*nureedu watan*).

Over the first three days of October, some twenty protesters in Baghdad and the southern governorates were killed by live fire and tear gas canisters.[2] In the early hours of October 4, Abdul-Mahdi went on television to warn that the deterioration of the country's security situation could lead to "the destruction of the state." He ominously declared that Iraq was faced with a choice between the state (*dawla*) and the anti-state, using the Arabic term *la-dawla*. (The anti-state is an imperfect translation of la-dawla, since it is essentially a unique term in Arabic; la-dawla more pointedly refers to the absence of the state.) Abdul-Mahdi added that building the state was the ultimate goal that would guarantee freedom and a dignified life for all Iraqis.[3] In his view, those who posed a threat to state-building were violent saboteurs within the protest movement who had stormed government buildings and party headquarters and had attacked security forces with Molotov cocktails.[4]

Abdul-Mahdi's October 4 remarks introduced into the public discourse the dichotomous tension between the state and the anti-state. The remarks sparked a fierce debate among competing political and civil actors over who should be considered a defender of the state and who was seeking to sabotage it. The debate quickly became central to the country's discursive politics, and it ultimately shaped the principal themes around the run-up to the October 2021 parliamentary elections.

Abdul-Mahdi juxtaposed the security forces as defenders of the state against the violent elements of the protest movement, whom he viewed as challenging and undercutting the authority of the state. But leading voices within the protest movement took an entirely different view. From their perspective, it was the government's repressive actions that were undermining the state's legitimacy—and their demonstrations were an attempt at salvaging the state.

But it was ironic when, facing a popular revolt over his own governance failures, Abdul-Mahdi invoked the specter of a dissolving state. Abdul-Mahdi himself exemplified a trend toward state weakness. Formerly a member of the Shia Islamist party the Supreme Council for the Islamic Revolution in Iraq (SCIRI), he ended up in the 2010s as an independent politician who claimed technocratic prowess. He was nominated prime minister by the harder-line Shia Islamist factions, including the Sadrist movement and groups that identified most closely with Iran and with autonomous, nonstate militias.

Of course, the presence of armed actors in Iraq committed to subverting the state's authority long predates the October 2019 protests. After 2003, a variety of Sunni insurgent groups emerged, all dedicated to inflicting bloodshed and civil strife as a means to undermine the legitimacy of the Shia-led order. There was also the rise of Muqtada al-Sadr's Mahdi Army, which at its height represented a major repudiation of the authority of state security forces across large swathes of Baghdad and the southern provinces. But there is a marked difference between these earlier armed actors and those whom the protesters of Abdul-Mahdi referred to as *qiwa al-la-dawla,* or forces of the anti-state. These latter groups were supposed to be deeply embedded within the state apparatus, sustaining themselves through access to formal state resources. In recent years, the concept of "hybridity" has emerged to describe armed actors that "sometimes operate with the government and sometimes compete against it," as analyst Renad Mansour has written.[5] Over time, "forces of the anti-state" took on broader connotations, referring not just to the paramilitary groups that were targeting protesters, but also to the political parties that both sustained those groups and benefited from their existence.

Understanding how discursive frames emerge and evolve in Iraq's body politic is important because it sheds light on how political competition is framed among rival actors that seek to utilize these frames to shape the narrative to their advantage. While many of the early proponents of the state-versus-anti-state construct were Iraqi writers and social media influencers, Arab media platforms and Western think tanks were often instrumental in disseminating the analytical construct more broadly. This has important implications for how we interpret discursive shifts and their appropriation at the local level.[6]

What is most relevant to the discussion on Shia politics is that, even though forces of the anti-state should, by definition, denote a broad spectrum of political and paramilitary actors, a close look at the use of the term shows that, when it was first popularized in 2019–20, it referred exclusively to Shia groups that critics regarded as closely aligned with Iran. This history suggests that the term emerged more as a political attack than an analytical tool. It is important to deepen the inquiry into the term's emergence in the public discourse to determine what intellectual utility it has—if it is indeed useful at all.

La-dawla Goes Mainstream

It is difficult to pin down the origin and rise in popularity of the term la-dawla. One possible source is a book by the renowned sociologist Faleh Abdul Jabar, published in 2019, about a year and half after his death.[7] The volume, which was a follow-up to a famous 2017 work, had little to do with the political narrative advanced during the Tishreen movement, and did not even contain the term la-dawla in the text. But the book's title—Kitab al-la-dawla, or Book of the Anti-State—did contain the unique term, and may have popularized it, especially among intellectuals in the Tishreen movement.

But Jabar did not coin the term, and its use in reference to Iraq predates this period. During the outbreak of the Basra protests in the summer of 2018, a Swiss media outlet published a collection of opinions by Iraqis living in Switzerland about the ongoing events back home. One person, named Sabah, declared that "Iraq is a country of the anti-state," before adding that there was no real government, but rather a quasi-government whose role was to legitimize the corruption of the ruling elite.[8]

Within the first month of the Tishreen protests, the anti-state concept gained notoriety among Iraqi writers and social media influencers. But it is noteworthy that many of the most prominent writers chose to publish their thoughts not in Iraqi outlets, but in other Arabic-language media outlets. Writing for the website of Al Jazeera (which is owned by the state of Qatar) on October 8, 2019, Iraqi commentator Muhammad al-Najjar asserted that Iraq was an anti-state because of what he described as the chaos and proliferation of arms in urban areas.[9] Omar al-Jaffal made a similar case in his October 22 piece for the Lebanese outlet *As-Safir*.[10] Meanwhile, another renowned Iraqi commentator, Ayad al-Anbar, sought to set the anti-state discourse in Western frames around failed and fragile states in a January 2020 article for the website of the state-funded American outlet Alhurra. He referenced global indices from Transparency International and the World Bank to reinforce his thesis.[11]

While these writers focused on the anti-state to describe the situation in Iraq, others chose to concentrate on identifying the political and armed actors that could be described as forces of the anti-state—in other words, forces that were seen as perpetuating the anti-state. One Iraqi writer published a piece for a Jordanian outlet in March 2020, in which he discussed the need for the U.S.-led international coalition to counter the Iran-backed militias of the anti-state, despite the fact that the coalition's stated mission was to fight the Islamic State (which some of those Iranian-backed militias had helped defeat).[12] In the same month, another Iraqi writer, Ayad al-Dulaymi, used anti-state in the context of ongoing attacks by Shia paramilitary groups against American targets in Iraq. For him, these attacks were an affront to Iraq's sovereignty.[13] Dulaymi then wrote a column for Al Jazeera in July 2020, in which he described the "project" of the anti-state that the newly elected government of Prime Minister Mustafa al-Kadhimi would, as he put it, inevitably have to confront.[14] By the summer of 2020, "forces of the anti-state" had become synonymous not only with Shia paramilitary groups but also with political parties that critics saw as being aligned with Iran. A case in point is the Sadrist movement, which has been vocally critical of Iran. Despite the fact that the Sadrists had turned on the protest movement by the end of 2019 and engaged in a violent confrontation with them in several protest squares, including in Nasiriyah, the protesters did not use the anti-state label to refer to the Sadrists.

Selectively labeling Shia Islamist groups with ties to Iran as the forces of the anti-state explicitly suggests that their allegiance is not to the Iraqi state. This was illustrated in an August 2020 piece published by the London-based Arabic-language newspaper *Al-Arab*. The editorial, "Iraq: The State of the Anti-state," describes how Iraqis have employed the anti-state discourse on social media to point to "the absence of a state and the rule of the jungle, which has transformed Iraq into a 'country of the anti-state.'" According to *Al-Arab*'s definition, "the concept of the anti-state [la-dawla] means the confiscation of Iraq's sovereignty for the benefit of armed groups backed by political parties and clerics subject to the orders of Iran."[15] The article cites prominent Iraqi social media commentator Steven Nabil, who wrote in an August 2020 tweet that if the forces of the anti-state emerged victorious against the state, Iraq would be "almost entirely beholden to the eastern neighbor."[16] The editorial also cites a tweet by former speaker of parliament Osama Al-Nujayfi, a man known for his close ties to Turkey, in which he urges "the forces that believe in the state to unite their efforts in challenging the forces of the anti-state," warning that failure to do so would result in chaos and a state of "subordination" (*taba'iya*).[17]

La-dawla in the 2021 Elections

Commensurate with the violent crackdown on the protest movement and the chaos that ensued was a growing popular sentiment that Iraq had lost what is often described as *haybat al-dawla,* meaning the state's ability to project or assert authority. The first two months of the Tishreen protests were particularly damaging to public perceptions of such state capacities. There was recurrent torching of government and party offices across the southern governorates. Impromptu roadblocks, often orchestrated by teenage protesters, became daily occurrences in urban centers because security forces were seemingly unable or unwilling to intervene for fear of recriminations. Protesters also began to establish pickets outside of government buildings to call on public employees not to go to work. Blockades were set up outside schools and universities, forcing most educational institutions to shut down.

It was these acts that Abdul-Mahdi had in mind when he first used the la-dawla expression in his October 4, 2019 speech. Following the resignation of his government, all these events fomented greater public discourse about the need for a new government that could reassert the authority of the state. In fact, support for Kadhimi's premiership by some of the leading political parties was conditioned on his commitment to prioritizing the reassertion of haybat al-dawla. In one of his earliest public addresses, Kadhimi seemed to mimic Abdul-Mahdi's rhetoric by talking about the imperative of confronting ongoing acts of vandalism against government targets by elements purporting to be protesters. Kadhimi also used an almost identical turn of phrase to Abdul-Mahdi, declaring that the country was faced with a choice between the state and the anti-state.[18]

By the run up to the October 10, 2021 elections, the public and political discourse was fixated on the imperative of salvaging the state. All of the leading Shia Islamist parties focused their electoral campaigns on showcasing their credentials as defenders of the state and pledging to bring a semblance of order back to the country.[19] This focus was in stark contrast to the 2018 election campaigns, when the victory over the Islamic State had ushered in—albeit momentarily—a sort of post-sectarian moment, with competing parties seeking to emphasize cross-sectarian, nationalist credentials. A national opinion poll in April 2021 found that only 41 percent of respondents believed that the state had greater control over politics than nonstate armed groups.[20]

During the 2021 elections, cross-sectarian cooperation was far less prominent within the public discourse than debates over haybat al-dawla and the state-versus-anti-state construct. The electoral coalition between Ammar al-Hakim and Haider al-Abadi, for example, was named the State Forces Coalition (*Tahaluf Qiwa al-Dawla*). The coalition's campaign slogan was "We want a state" (*nureedu dawla*). During the coalition's launch event, Abadi played on the dichotomy between the state and the anti-state in an attempt to illustrate his credentials as someone who could offer voters the choice of a strong and confident state. Meanwhile, Nouri al-Maliki's State of Law coalition adopted similar campaign messaging with the slogan "We will revive the state."

An incident just before the election showed the extent to which support of the state had become a key messaging point for political parties. In an October 2, 2021 televised interview, the Fatah Alliance's Qais al-Khazali spoke about the importance of Shia consensus in selecting the next prime minister. When he said that all the main Shia Islamist parties—including the Sadrists—had been meeting over the past several months in order to build consensus, the interviewer quipped that the forces of the state had sat down with the forces of the anti-state. Khazali responded that *all* were "forces of the state" and that he had reservations about using the "forces of the anti-state" expression.[21]

The Problems with the Anti-state Discourse

In April 2021, Alaa al-Hattab, a presenter on Iraqiya, the state television channel, published a column in the state-owned *Al-Sabah* newspaper calling into question the utility of the state-versus-anti-state construct.[22] Hattab posited that the term anti-state was not constructive, because no political party claims to be opposed to the state, and that political parties, by definition, implicitly acknowledge the legitimacy of the Iraqi state, since parties compete for power within the confines of that state. Hattab also questioned whether those parties that claim to be on the side of the state were actually free of problems, like corruption, that undermine the state.

Indeed, the state-versus-anti-state construct is problematic on several levels. First, it is far too nebulous to be used in an intellectually consistent manner. Had its intended use been to identify *practices* that undermine the authority of the state, there would have been greater scope for advocating for its utility. These practices would then invariably apply to every political actor that engages in siphoning of state funds for private gain; the blatant transgressions against constitutional provisions; and the widespread practice of drawing on resources from foreign patrons. But as this analysis has demonstrated, the anti-state label is used exclusively as a put-down against Shia Islamist actors to suggest that they are *inherently* against the Iraqi state. It is merely a political slur masquerading as analysis.

There is a historical precedent for this sort of discursive politics whereby Shia religious actors are dismissed as fifth columnists in Iraq. Two essential points form the basis of this accusation. The first is the notion that religious Shia are not loyal to the Iraqi state, because of the erroneous notion that their sect has Persian roots. The second point is the idea that Shia identity is inherently antithetical to national identity. The claim is that a religious identity conflicts with loyalty to the country. Indeed, there are several instances where derogatory terms that were historically deployed by the ruling elite against Shia Iraqis have reemerged in recent years. One notable example is the concept of taba'iya, a term used to suggest subordination of individuals or a communal group to a foreign entity. The concept of taba'iya was instrumentalized by the ruling Ba'ath regime as a means to crush dissent. The term was used to justify the deportation of tens of thousands of Shia Iraqis to Iran (1969–80), and its use today in relation to Shia Islamists with ties to Iran could lead to a broader smearing of Shia Iraqis in the public discourse.

The anti-state discourse also overlaps with aspects of how sect-based identity is problematized in relation to national identity, which emerges most clearly in the way public opinion polls frame questions. A 2021 national poll commissioned by the Center for Strategic and International Studies (CSIS), a U.S. think tank, measured the strength of national identity by asking respondents, "Which of the following do you consider most important for giving you a sense of who you are?" Respondents could choose from a list of options that included sect, ethnicity, tribe, locality, gender, and "being a citizen of Iraq." The report of the poll's findings separated the answers according to whether respondents mainly identified as Shia, Sunni, Kurd, or "I am Iraqi above all."[23] The construction of the poll appears to have imposed a hierarchical conception of identity that makes it hard for respondents to express both a strong national identity and a separate ethnic or religious identity. Being asked to choose between the two suggests that they cannot exist in harmony as a set of co-identities.

In a similar vein, a 2018 CSIS-commissioned poll deduced that the country was shifting from what it described as "sub-identities to a national identity" based on polling data that found that the popularity of "Islamic parties" was declining.[24] This conclusion assumes that there is something antagonistic about how political parties that are based on religious identity relate to the state. In contrast, no such tension is generally assumed in Western countries that have Christianity-inspired political parties. Furthermore, the pollsters came to this conclusion despite the fact that the data showed an even greater decline in the popularity of what it called "secular movements."

Anti-Shia Analytical Bias

The misrepresentation of Shia Islamist groups as anti-state is especially dangerous because of the potential of discrediting Iraq's Shia more broadly. The efforts of ruling elites to wholesale smear the country's Shia as a Persian fifth column date back to Iraq's modern founding. The British shared this view, and propagated it, during the early mandate period in the 1920s. Shia were viewed as seditious and pro-Iranian, leading British officials to install to power King

Faisal, a Sunni Arab from Mecca, and other, largely Sunni notables.[25] Gertrude Bell, then the British Oriental secretary in Iraq, expressed a typical sentiment in an October 1920 letter to her father: "I don't for a moment doubt that the final authority must be in the hands of the Sunnis, in spite of their numerical inferiority; otherwise you will have a mujtahid-run, theocratic state, which is the very devil."[26]

The British had no interest in ensuring that Iraq's institutions reflected the country's demographic makeup—which at the time was more than 50 percent Shia and included many other religious minorities. The first British-installed government was made up of twenty-three ministers, only two of whom were Shia. Writing in November 1920, Bell dismissed Shia demands for greater representation on the grounds that "nearly all their leading men are Persian subjects."[27]

Elites not only portrayed Iraq's Shia as seditious pro-Iranians, but even questioned their Arab roots. The scholar Yitzhak Nakash points out that in 1933, a Sunni Iraqi called Abd al-Razzaq al-Hasan published a book, *Al-uruba fi al-mizan* (*Arabism on the Scales*), that claimed that Shia Iraqis, by virtue of their alleged Persian inclinations, were unable to reconcile their sectarian identity with Arab nationalism.[28] When the Ba'ath Party came to power in Iraq in 1963 and took on the mantle of Arab nationalism, they ostensibly avoided sect-based identity politics. But as prominent academic Juan Cole explains, "the Baath rhetoric of universalism was subverted for the purposes of enriching and enhancing the power and prestige of the Sunni minority."[29] The Ba'ath Party tried to counter Shia opposition to the regime through a concerted campaign to portray members of the Dawa Party (the first Shia Islamist movement in the country) as Iranian agitators. During the 1970s and 1980s, this culminated in mass arrests and executions of party members, and the deportation of thousands of Shia Iraqis who were deemed to be of Iranian origin. In response to the 1991 Shia uprising, the regime revived this approach to justify the violent suppression of the rebellion.

Aside from the erroneous claims about their lineage, the idea that the Shia are not committed to the Iraqi state is based on two key assertions. First, its proponents point to a consistent pattern of rejection of state authority by the Shia religious leadership and their followers, from the mandate period through to the Ba'ath era. Secondly, they claim that the centrality of the Shia sect-based identity, including the distinctive Shia religious beliefs and practices, make them inherently antagonistic toward the notion of coexistence with their Sunni coreligionists.

Debunked Theories

These assertions have been adequately refuted in Western academic literature. On the first charge, Nakash asserts that Shia contestation was never with the state per se; rather, Shia contestation was over their political role within the state. The Shia sought greater influence within the state as a means to preserving their identity and how they were being perceived as citizens of the state. During the monarchy, contestation included issues around the education curriculum and versions of Islamic history that were being taught that the Shia did not subscribe to. Other issues include opposition to conscription because it was regarded as a means of Sunni domination since the Shia were denied the right to occupy senior ranks within the armed forces.[30]

Furthermore, as Iraq scholars Reidar Visser and Gareth Stansfield point out, there have been almost no recorded instances of Shia figures calling for a separate Shia entity or the merging of a Shia Iraqi state with their counterparts in Iran.[31] Fanar Haddad and Sajjad Rizvi also reinforce the point that Shia opposition groups and figures have never, throughout the country's modern history, supported a Shia secessionist state or the redrawing of Iraq's borders. Rather, these figures' political opposition pertains to their role within the unitary state, and demands for greater power sharing that is commensurate with their demographic weight.[32] During the post-2003 period, despite the onslaught of civil war and the Islamic State's takeover, the Shia parties never seriously considered challenging Iraq's territorial integrity. Even when SCIRI, one of the leading Shia Islamist parties, led by Abdul Aziz al-Hakim, pushed for a southern super-region in 2005, it had more to do with intra-Shia politics rather than ideological conviction. SCIRI thought it could assert itself as the preeminent Shia party by establishing control over a southern region, but the idea received little popular support and ultimately went nowhere.[33]

The second charge, that a Shia-centric identity is incompatible with multiconfessional coexistence, misses a key point: Shia Iraqis have actually found the iterations of Arab nationalism that emerged in the region in the late 1960s to be problematic, not because they do not see themselves as Arabs, but because that strain of Arab nationalism was always framed through an exclusionary Sunni lens. As the renowned American historian Phebe Marr puts it, "In some senses [Sunnis] may be compared to WASPs [White Anglo-Saxon Protestants] in the American experience. Since Iraq's founding, Sunnis have been the dominant political and social elite. . . . They perpetuated their status and their hold over the political system, not through sectarian identity, but rather through nationalist ideologies."[34] Shia identity arguably poses no *inherent* obstacle to multiconfessional coexistence, and as Haddad and Rizvi contend, sect-based identity can be "a vehicle for national identity rather than its substitute."[35]

Another way to understand Shia identity and its relationship with the state is to look at the ideological roots of Shia Islamist movements in Iraq. Here, it is incumbent to focus on the Dawa Party, since it was the first Shia Islamist movement in the country. Founded in Najaf in 1957, the Dawa Party began as an underground movement, formed by a group of Shia religious scholars and intellectuals, primarily as a response to the growing appeal of communism and anti-religious fervor in Iraq. It sought to offer a coherent and holistic

Islamic alternative to the intellectual thought of Marxism and Arab nationalism. But with the rise to power of the Ba'ath Party in 1963 and its growing authoritarianism, Dawa's rank and file organized as an opposition movement to the regime. It subsequently paid the price, suffering mass arrests and executions of its party leadership and activists.

All the subsequent Shia Islamist trends have, either directly or indirectly, emerged from the intellectual thought of Dawa's founding ideologue, Muhammad Baqir al-Sadr. For instance, although SCIRI was established in Iran, its leadership, including Muhammad Baqir al-Hakim, were among the original members of Dawa. Even the Sadrist movement (named for Muqtada al-Sadr), which is arguably distinct in its origins as a movement, regards Muhammad Baqir al-Sadr (that late father of Muqtada al-Sadr's wife) as a founding father.

Although the Dawa Party of today is commonly regarded in Western circles as a Shia sectarian party, a number of contemporary academics including Nakash, Abdul Jabar, and Joyce Wiley have pointed out that Dawa's initial message throughout the 1960s and 1970s went beyond sectarian interests. In his renowned 1991 study on Shia Islamic movements in Iraq, Wiley asserts that "in the hundreds of books and papers on the [Shia] Islamic movement . . . I encountered no derogation of Sunnism."[36]

Muhammad Baqir al-Sadr's message was never about pitting Shia against Sunnis. In fact, religious Sunnis were seen as natural allies against what was viewed as the common threat of communism, and the defense of the Global South against the Global North. Nor did Sadr view Shia opposition to the Ba'ath regime through an anti-Sunni lens. In his final message, shortly before his arrest and murder by Saddam Hussein's regime in 1980, he distinguishes between Sunnis and Ba'ath rule: "The actual [Iraqi] rule today is not a Sunni rule, although the ruling gang deceitfully claims to belong to the Sunni branch of Islam. Sunni rule does not mean the rule of a person who

descended from Sunni parents. . . . The tyrant rulers of Iraq today
. . . violate Islam, and they abuse Ali and Omar together every day in
every step they take."[37]

Muhammad Baqir al-Sadr wrote about what he saw as the illegit-
imacy of the government rather than the state.[38] It was not the state
that was inherently flawed, but rather the practices of those who
wielded the power of the state.

Dawa Party Members React

Muhammad Baqir Sadr's intellectual legacy continues to shape the
identity and ideological convictions of the Dawa Party today. His
publications and teachings remain central to the education of the
younger generation of cadres. A nuanced understanding of how the
Dawa Party conceptualizes its relationship with the Iraqi state provides a useful illustrative case because of Dawa's rich intellectual heritage in comparison with other Shia Islamist groups, and the party's
continued relevance in Iraqi politics. My interviews with party members focused on younger members, because their formative experiences were primarily shaped by post-2003 Iraq rather than a bygone
era, and their views offer important insights into the party's political
and ideological trajectory over the long term.[39]

In my interviews with these younger party members, our discussions ranged from their views on the state-versus-anti-state construct, whether national and sect-based identities were irreconcilably
antagonistic, and how their conceptions of the state had evolved
since 2003.

From the outset, interviewees asserted the salience of discursive
politics in relation to the Iraqi context. One party member explained
how language is constructed and instrumentalized for political gain,
and described the state-versus-anti-state construct as "problematic,"
because he viewed it as an oversimplification of the divide among
political actors. Others expressed concern about the binary framing

of the construct, describing it as a reductionist approach that was unhelpful in addressing societal polarization in the country.

A key objection that some interviewees expressed concerned the very definition of the state. They cautioned against the forced adoption of Western conceptions of the state. As one respondent asserted, Iraqis should not confine themselves to Western frames of thinking about the role and functions of the Iraqi state. Although there may be much in common between Weberian views on the state as a polity and how Iraqis conceive of the state, interviewees emphasized the need to account for the Iraqi context before determining what governing arrangements would be most suitable for the country.

Many interviewees tied perceptions about the legitimacy of the state's governing arrangements to preserving the country's Islamic roots. In other words, while they viewed state identity pluralistically—as an expression of the country's diverse inhabitants—they placed great importance on preserving the Islamic facets of state identity. In this regard, they saw political opposition to a ruling power or to foreign influence as incumbent in response to any attempts to uproot the Islamic aspects of the country's identity. Pressed on the key facets of this identity, respondents agreed on the centrality of preserving an Islamic ethical code within society.

Throughout the discussions, Dawa members often expressed a sense of pragmatism about the type of state identity that they should aspire for. "We must deal with reality," said one respondent, noting that the current configuration of the state may not meet all the aspirations of Dawa Party members, but it does achieve a bare minimum in terms of guaranteeing the rights of all citizens to express themselves without fear of persecution.[40] In a similar vein, while interviewees viewed the constitution as being deeply flawed, all respondents believed that it should nevertheless be upheld as the basis for the state's polity. Members agreed that the state should safeguard the interests of all citizens rather than just those in power. As one interviewee put it, state legitimacy is inextricably linked with this function.[41] Another referred to a concept, which was developed by earlier Dawa ideologues, known as *wilayat al-ummah*, meaning "the authority of the people." He asserted that legitimate governance should be based on entrusting the people to freely express their will and determine the trajectory that the country takes.[42]

Interviewees also linked state identity to structural aspects of power. One respondent described how the nature of the state itself had evolved since its modern founding. He believed that Iraq under the monarchy (1921–58) was qualitatively different to that under Abdul Karim Qasim (prime minister from the end of the monarchy in 1958 until 1963). Similarly, the interviewee felt that Iraq had fundamentally changed under the Ba'ath regime. He cited Saddam Hussein's notorious Republican Guard to illustrate how the type of state security apparatus can have a major impact on the nature of the political system.[43]

Addressing the issue of whether national and subnational identities could be reconciled, one interviewee pointed to problems with how sect-based identity is often defined, noting that there was a major distinction between sectarian practices—defined as discriminatory acts based on sect—and engaging in sect-based identity politics. One member described how the ethno-sectarian nature of Iraqi political movements was a natural consequence of the environment in which they emerged. He noted that many existing Shia parties began as movements rather than political parties seeking power. He pointed to how Western frames about the relationship between political movements and the state do not account for religious institutions like the hawza (the Shia seminaries, collectively), which has an important transnational dimension. Since the hawza in Najaf is a primary center of Shia religious learning, its authority extends far beyond Iraq's borders. He also pointed out that Dawa was not established exclusively for Iraqis and that it later had to refocus itself on domestic matters. According to this party member, this need to make itself domestic does not mean that Dawa's loyalties lie outside of Iraq. Rather, Dawa's origins as a party with an international focus simply reflected the environment in which it emerged, and the fact that it was forced into exile for a large portion of its history.[44]

Similar interviews with Sadrists, and groups that are more closely aligned with Iran, could explore in detail the views of those Shia movement supporters about the state. But even a cursory analysis of the political discourse of those movements makes clear that, no matter what their differing views on Iran, militia regulation, or anti-corruption, all of them invoke the goal of effective government and a strong state, and seek to control, rather than erode, state institutions.[45]

A More Nuanced Analysis

While it is often said that Iraq's ethno-religious diversity is a source of strength for the country rather than a weakness, it is hard to deny that identity-based contests have driven much of the violence and political instability of the post-2003 period. Shia Islamist parties and movements, by virtue of their central role in governing Iraq, have borne the brunt of widespread public blame and anger about the chaotic state of the country. In recent years, discursive politics in Iraq have turned to the "state versus anti-state" construct as a way to frame criticism of Iraq's ruling elite. This construct has focused almost exclusively on Shia Islamist parties and movements that enjoy political ties to Iran, brandishing them as inherently antithetical to the state.

There is a strong need for a more nuanced and measured discussion about how Iraq's broad spectrum of Shia Islamist groups conceive of the Iraqi state and view themselves within it. This discussion should first begin by differentiating the views of Iraq's Shia Islamist groups along ideological and political lines in order to understand who they are, what they stand for, and how they conceive of their relationship with the state. While understanding the convictions of Dawa Party members is a useful entry point for this endeavor, further inquiry is needed to understand the views of other Shia Islamist groups.

Shia Islamists are an integral part of Iraq's body politic and will continue to be so by virtue of their reach within Iraqi society. If political stability and conflict resolution are to be truly prioritized, policymakers, academics, and pundits should be cautious about using discursive frames that have the potential to exacerbate societal schisms and ultimately undermine Iraq's fragile social fabric. Iraq's modern history is replete with instances in which Shia have suffered wholesale smearing as fifth columnists that are antagonistic towards the state. Thus, whenever Shia Iraqis engage in politics—particularly when they are religious Shia—there is a danger that they will automatically be portrayed in erroneous and harmful ways.

Further, discursive politics that seek to frame sect-based identity as invariably incompatible with nationalism should also be avoided. Such discursive politics imply that there is something *inherently* antithetical about identity politics and nationalism. There are many examples around the world where subnational identities have been embraced as the bedrock of pluralistic coexistence. The cases of both Sri Lanka and Bosnia and Herzegovina illustrate the persistent salience of ethno-religious identities in postwar contexts and how the idea of negating these identities is not a realistic prospect. Instances where identity politics do lead to civil strife should be identified and countered, but the wholesale rejection of ethno-sectarian frames of thinking makes little sense in a country with a history steeped in social and political injustices based along ethno-sectarian lines. It is only natural that some of the responses to ethno-sectarian persecution are ethnic and sect-based responses. And as in other contexts, the salience of identity politics diminishes when structural power imbalances and historical injustices are adequately addressed.

Clerics

3

Shia Clerics in Iraq Haven't Lost Their Authority

Marsin Alshamary

In recent years, many journalists and scholars have claimed that the influence of the Shia religious establishment in Iraq is waning. They point, in particular, to Tishreen movement activists' rejection of religion in politics. But the trajectory of Shia clerical influence in Iraq is more complicated, and the weight of clerics and the seminaries that train them (the hawza) has oscillated over the last two decades. Clerical authority takes at least three forms in Iraq: authority over adherents, direct participation in politics, and informal authority over politics through unofficial channels. Even as one of these channels narrows, others may remain open and vital. While Shia clerical authority in Iraq has changed, it remains a major factor in determining the shape of the country's political future.

"The turbaned man used to be holy," a cleric complained to me. It was winter in the holy city of Najaf, and we were sitting in a sunlit office in one of the newer international religious seminaries.

The cleric, who was the head of the seminary, had his door open as students in traditional clerical garb passed through the halls. It looked, in many ways, like a high school. The students' faces were young and open. They came from countries near and far, foreign, and familiar to the average Iraqi: Lebanon, Iran, Senegal, Pakistan, Afghanistan, and others. When I spoke to the students, they responded in perfect formal Arabic, but often deferred substantive questions to their teachers. They came to Najaf with a mission, hailing from communities where the Shia were persecuted minorities, unlike Iraq today.

Only two decades ago, the existence of such a school would have been impossible. It was a sprawling institution, clearly well financed, and operating freely and even coordinating with government officials to ease visa restrictions for its students. Before 2003, turbaned men used to be venerated by the public, and this veneration made them a threat to the state. Accordingly, the Iraqi government harassed, intimidated, deported, extorted, and executed hundreds of Shia religious clerics. Eventually, the Ba'athist regime under Saddam Hussein attempted to co-opt and capture the religious establishment.[1] Back then, clerics struggled to maintain the very existence of the revered hawza (the Shia religious educational institutions, collectively). But when the Iraqi state was remolded after the U.S.-led invasion in 2003, clerics began to thrive.

Shia Islamists were the overwhelming winners of the first few elections, and they gave the Shia religious establishment and the hawza their freedoms and expanded their resources. The once-predatory and surveilling Ministry of Endowments (Awqaf) was dissolved into several endowment diwans, including the Shia Endowment Diwan, which is state-funded and whose leader is approved and designated by the head of the hawza in Najaf.[2] With state surveillance gone, elite clerical offices collected tithes freely, as the more-open borders allowed pilgrims to flood into the country. For the first time in its history, the hawza was not in a contentious relationship with the Iraqi state. The reversal of fortunes is best described by Abbas Kadhim, who writes: "Suddenly the Ayatullah [Ali al-Sistani], who had been under the strictest house arrest, found himself in a position to make history and that was what he exactly did."[3]

The hawza is essentially an unstructured space of religious learning, an intangible consortium of seminaries, libraries, offices, and mosques. Paradoxically, although it is an unstructured and informalized institution, it produces a rigid hierarchy of religious learning and authority, one that has captured the imagination of many. This includes the Shia Islamists that called on any affiliations with the hawza, whether tenuous or tangible, to bolster their own credibility.

After decades of training, the hawza produces a set of elite clerics that, in theory, have the authority to guide adherents in matters of personal and public affairs. They are then also able to accept the "khums" (meaning "a fifth"), a hefty religious tax that funds their seminaries and offices and that keeps them independent of state financial control. The khums is not strictly enforced (by the state or by the clerics themselves) but is a religious obligation that practicing Shia commit to by annually handing over a fifth of some of their acquired wealth to the religious establishment, to distribute amongst several strands of recipients, including the poor. In this way, elite Shia clerics, bearing the title of grand ayatollah, amass material and immaterial authority. The leaders of the religious establishment, the highest clerics, are referred to collectively as the marja'iyya. It is no surprise that they are either a threat or a potential resource to political authorities, who have vacillated between trying to destroy the institution—the hawza and the marja'iyya—or to control and benefit from it.

But this material and immaterial authority—wealth and public obedience—rests on the faith of adherents and their willingness to bestow it. If, as the cleric from the international seminary feared, the turbaned man is no longer considered holy by his adherents, then the very survival of the hawza is at stake. Without an influential hawza, the political landscape in Iraq will be stripped of an important actor, one that has often served as a mediator at critical junctures.

To reflect on this further, I unpack clerical authority and describe three forms it can take, and I show how those forms have manifested in the Iraqi public sphere over the past few years. The first form of clerical influence is the one described above: the authority a cleric wields over his adherents. The second form is the direct political authority of a cleric who has chosen to formally engage in politics. The last is the informal authority of elite clerics over politics through unofficial channels. In each of these relationships of influence, I ask: Has clerical authority changed in the last two decades, and why? What are the implications of this for Iraq's political future?

I draw on data gathered through months of fieldwork in the hawza, where I spoke to clerics and observed their interactions in their spaces of learning and leadership. I also draw on wider field-work in Iraq, from interviews and conversations with activists, polit-ical leaders, and journalists who are puzzling over the future of the hawza and its place in Iraq.

Rather than subsume all types of authority under one umbrella, I disaggregate based on the three aforementioned channels of influ-ence. These forms are not exhaustive; there are other channels of clerical influence that I allude to in the concluding section. However, these channels of influence are more measurable than others, and are frequently conflated in public discourse, which speaks about the diminishing influence of clerics without delineating which exact *type* of influence is diminishing. Ultimately, I argue that clerical authority over adherents has steadily decreased in the last few years and has now plateaued. Direct clerical authority over politics— at least, such authority that is visible to the public—has become more costly for clerics. Indirect clerical authority, however, continues to function, but is the most difficult to measure. As such, policymakers and ana-lysts should recognize that, as clerical authority over adherents has waned, clerical desire to become visibly involved in politics has also lessened, as a result.

Debating Clerical Influence

Both journalistic accounts of the marja'iyya and scholarly works on Iraq that brush up against the topic of religion tend to paint Grand Ayatollah Ali al-Sistani as a powerful, charismatic, and secluded leader.[4] However, traditional Islamic authority (and not only in Shia contexts), does not premise leadership on charisma, but on scholarly credentials and being able to reproduce the prophetic tradition.[5] Authority is then manifested in a cleric's ability to move an individual to a particular behavior without the use of coercion, due to a claim to scholarly religious credentials. Charisma is the realm of those who cannot make a claim to the prophetic tradition through a reputation of scholarship. It is not the traditional realm of those who inhabit a centuries-old seminary, like the hawza.

Therefore, if an individual loses their Islamic authority, it signifies something much larger than the community's disavowal of an individual: it actually represents the community's disavowal of an entire institution and its ability to be the legitimate interpreter of the prophetic tradition. In other words, if Sistani has lost his ability to influence adherents, then it does not bode well for the hawza as an institution because, as research on the hawza has shown, the institution reproduces a uniform set of socialized individuals.[6] The stakes are great for the loss of the Shia religious establishment's influence over adherents in Iraq. Shia Muslims constitute the majority of the Iraqi population, making Sistani the spiritual leader of millions of Iraqis (in addition to the millions of adherents he has outside of Iraq). For this reason, it is critical that we understand precisely *what* and *how much* of Sistani's influence, if any, is currently in decline.

Public and scholarly discourse over whether Sistani and the religious establishment have lost influence has been brewing for years.

In 2007, Juan Cole wrote an article with a bold title, "The Decline of Grand Ayatollah Sistani's Influence in 2006–2007," which describes Sistani as losing political influence.[7] The essay details Sistani's theological views toward Wilayat al-Faqih ("the rule of the jurisprudent," a theological concept made famous by Grand Ayatollah Ruhollah Khomeini) and his participation in politics in the immediate aftermath of the U.S.-led invasion, when there was a political vacuum. The essay claims that, as of 2007, Sistani's relevance had diminished because the post-invasion political vacuum in Iraq had been filled by other actors. Secondly, the essay claims that the Iraqi public did not listen to his pleas for peace during the sectarian civil war that was roiling Iraq at the time of publication. Sistani ignoring pleas for calm, according to Cole, represented a decline in his authority.

But where Cole saw these events as evidence of Sistani's declining influence, they were, in hindsight, more like evidence of the *limits* of his authority. Sistani could not stop sectarian war—but this fact simply showed the depth of public fear and anger. Sistani's authority did not decline so much as it was insufficient to meet the challenges of a sectarian civil war and a political system with new and ambitious leaders.

Limits to Power

These limits also explain why, years later, Sistani's authority appeared to rise and fall precipitously. In 2014, for example, he issued a religious edict urging Iraqis to join security forces to fight the Islamic State, and commentators perceived his influence to be high: thousands of Iraqis answered the call and flocked to join various security forces, including the Popular Mobilization Units (the disparate armed groups that helped defeat the Islamic State and remain key players in Iraqi politics and the security apparatus). Here again, however, Sistani's success in rallying Iraqis did not show a heightened authority of the religious establishment, so much as it was an example of a religious authority aligning with national security needs during a crisis when other sources of leadership were sorely lacking.

Then, in 2019, when the Tishreen Movement's mass protests brought the country to a standstill, protesters began to heed the Friday sermons that were delivered by Sistani's representatives in Karbala. They followed the sermons closely, as an activist from Baghdad told me in an interview: "As Iraqis, we would wait for the Friday sermons to see if the marja'iyya supported the protestors, or would stand with the politicians."[8] That the protesters followed the religious establishment's messaging while simultaneously calling for removing religion from politics is a testament to the marja'iyya's importance: "Even though I am secular and liberal, I still believe that there is common ground between me and the marja'iyya," another activist told me.[9] That "common ground" was a shared desire for a stable and functional state that did not exploit religious authority. Clerics see these goals as a means to restore their reputation; activists recognize that clerical influence can aid them in their cause and does not necessarily contradict their desire to separate politics from religion.[10]

The religious establishment proved to be a critical actor in navigating a path out of the protest movement through government change. Through its sermons, it acted as a mediator between society and state. It cautioned against the destruction of public property, criticized attacks on media, called for the prime minister to step down, and outlined a path forward through early elections. But the religious establishment had to prove itself to the public and, more importantly, prove that it did not favor the political elite over the protesters. The religious establishment, by 2018, had paid a price for its oftentimes inadvertent association with Islamist parties: the Iraqi street began to distrust the establishment and to doubt that it had the best interests of the country in mind.[11] This association with Islamist parties was rooted in the fact that prominent clerics—like the late Mohammad Baqir al-Sadr and Mohammad Baqir al-Hakim—provided the theoretical and ideological basis of many Islamist parties, as Ali Al-Mawlawi explains in his report in this series.[12]

As Iraq's October 2021 parliamentary elections approached (the sixth such elections since 2003), public sentiment largely rejected what they saw as a corrupted electoral system. Many Iraqis spoke of boycotting, whether out of ideological conviction or out of sheer apathy. It was in this environment, on September 29, 2021, that Sistani issued a statement encouraging Iraqis to vote: "The Supreme Religious Authority encourages everyone to participate consciously and responsibly in the upcoming elections because, although [the elections] are not without their shortcomings, they are the safest way to move the country to a future that is hopefully better than its past."[13]

This statement was not the first time Sistani had encouraged participation in elections or had intervened to direct the electoral process.[14] Sistani played a key role in ensuring elections took place to determine the constitutional assembly and to ratify the constitution in October 2005.[15] And, later, in the second parliamentary election in December 2005, Sistani released a statement (in response to an adherent's inquiry) stating that the election was "not less important than its predecessor [the constitution-ratifying election] and citizens—men and women—should participate widely."[16] That same year, Sistani was criticized for indirectly endorsing the United Iraqi Alliance, an umbrella group for Shia political parties, in the elections. Critics argued that he should have remained politically neutral.[17] Perhaps as a result of this criticism, Sistani urged citizens to vote in 2010 while maintaining the neutrality of the marja'iyya vis-à-vis particular parties.[18] In 2018, Sistani assumed neutrality by leaving the decision to vote to the individual citizen, which many interpreted as permission to boycott. In part aided by Sistani's apathetic stance, Iraq reached an electoral nadir in the 2018 election, with its lowest turnout so far (later surpassed in 2021) and a government that would ultimately be ousted by public protests.

Political versus Cultural Influence

Sistani may have been seeking to avoid another low-turnout election when he released his September 2021 statement urging Iraqis to vote. But for the first time in years, Sistani's entreaty seemed to have little effect. Voter turnout, according to the Independent High Electoral Commission, was 43.5 percent, an all-time low.[19] It's possible that Sistani's statement, shortly before the election and after the voter registration deadline, was simply too late to make a difference. Nevertheless, after the elections there was a sentiment in Iraq that Sistani's influence was waning.

These patterns provide evidence of a declining clerical authority in the political realm. However, they do not necessarily mean that clerical influence over nonpolitical issues has also declined. For example, in the wake of a disastrous earthquake in Iran in 2018, Sistani directed his followers to donate a share of the religious tax toward relief efforts.[20]

What we do know is this: first, that clerics are aware of and concerned about a public reputational shift. It was not just the cleric in the Najaf seminary who recognized the loss of "holiness"; even clerics who are involved in politics, like Ammar al-Hakim of the National Wisdom Movement (also known as Hikmah), admitted in an interview that in 2003 people sanctified clerics ["yuqaddis al-imama'"], but that later, people began to develop "a civil inclination." (Hakim used the word "madani," translated as "civil," which connotes secular political involvement.)[21] However, when I asked clerics about whether they had concerns about decreasing religiosity in the country—which could be a proxy for their decreasing authority in religious matters—surprisingly few of them expressed such a concern. "Quite the opposite," an advanced seminary student and cleric said in a 2019 interview. "It is hard to ask a person to always be religious, 100 percent at all times, day and night. God asks this, but a human cannot logistically do it. There are too many points of weakness. Religiosity is not just praying and fasting. It is a lot of obligations."[22]

Another factor complicating analysis of clerical influence is that public opinion data from Iraq, conducted over various waves by the Arab Barometer, shows that trust in religious leaders has been plateauing, after an earlier drop (see Figure 1).[23]

In other words, between 2013 and 2018, there was a marked loss of trust in religious leaders. However, between 2018 and 2021, levels of trust plateaued. These data—as well as the pendulating pattern of trust in clerics following major events in the last several years, such as the Tishreen protests—suggests that public trust in the religious establishment may yet recover. The religious establishment has aided in this rehabilitation by beginning to differentiate between politicized and non-politicized clerics, whom they have diagnosed to be the root of the clerical decline of political authority.

FIGURE 1. Public Trust in Religious Leaders

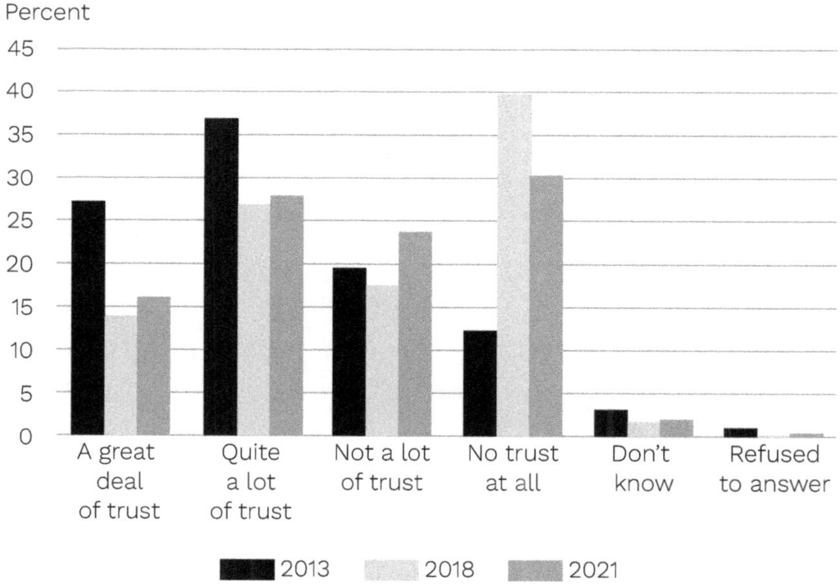

Source: Arab Barometer (Wave III, V, VI).

Direct and Indirect Influence over the Political Class

Nearly every cleric I spoke with bemoaned the Iraqi clerical establishment's fall from grace. In the same breath, these clerics pinned the blame for this fall on politicized clerics who besmirched the reputation of their more academically oriented peers. Ironically, even one of the most politicized clerics, Hakim of the Hikma Movement, made this connection: "There is a decline [in public respect for clerics] because some have gotten involved in politics in an inappropriate manner."[24]

Although Hakim's description of "inappropriate" is vague, it does point to a lack of consensus as to what constitutes legitimate or appropriate intervention in politics. Another cleric from a prominent family, speaking anonymously, was more decisive. "The cleric who gets involved in politics is using his religious legitimacy for the benefit of political parties," he said. "We, as a Najaf entity, do not approve of Ammar [al-Hakim] or of Muqtada [al-Sadr]. I said to myself: if [Khomeini's] Wilayat al-Faqih is right, I will join politics. I found it incorrect and decided against politics. To enter is to become a threat."[25]

What both clerics are describing above is the direct clerical participation in politics through, for example, running for office or taking up a ministerial position. However, neither mentioned the more indirect role that elite clerics can have in politics, when they influence politicians through private meetings and messaging. Given its secretive nature, this latter form of influence is hard to measure.

Direct clerical authority in politics can be measured in a more straightforward manner, and based on voting patterns, does appear to be in decline, with voters giving less support to clerics and Islamist parties generally. (See Figure 2.) The change in the public perception of Islamist parties is also palpable in the Iraqi street, and is exemplified by the views of activists. "In 2003… the population wanted a Shia leader… people used to laugh at [Adnan] Pachachi when he said, 'get a secular leader,'" said an activist from Basra, referring to a veteran Iraqi politician who was famously opposed to the American-led

FIGURE 2. Public Opinion on Religion in Public Office

"Your country is better off if religious people hold public positions."

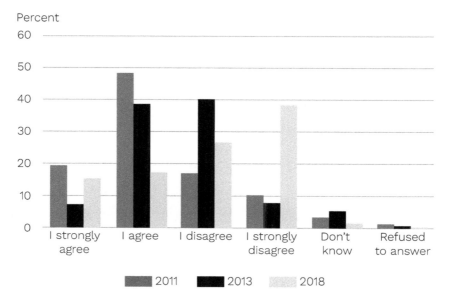

Source: Arab Barometer (Wave II, III, V).

occupation. "Tishreen protests showed that a huge proportion of the population is tired of Islamists and want to live a dignified life; we do not want to suffer under the mistakes of the Islamists."[26]

The electorate has doled out some punishment to clerics in office and of Islamist parties, but this public rejection has been diluted by the electoral boycott. In my conversations with activists, many of those who rejected Islamist parties channeled their rejection into an outright refusal to vote. As a result, the evidence from the ballot box is somewhat ambiguous with regard to the rise and fall of clerics and Islamist parties. For example, while Hakim's movement recently suffered a major loss in the election—going from nineteen seats in 2018 to only two in 2021—the Sadrist Movement gained seats.[27]

It is hard to generalize about the role that clerics have played in Iraqi politics over the years. There are numerous other examples of clerics who took on official positions after 2003 or who ran in elections and won seats in parliament. The first and most prominent example is Ayatollah Mohammad Bahr al-Uloom, who was the president of the Governing Council of Iraq under the Coalition Provisional Authority, first in July 2003 and then again in March 2004. Another notable cleric was Humam Hamoudi, a leader in the Islamic Supreme Council of Iraq (ISCI), who played an important role in drafting the Iraqi constitution as chairperson of the Constitutional Writing Committee. He was elected deputy speaker of parliament from 2014 to 2018. Other examples include Khalid al-Attiyah, who was also deputy speaker of parliament from 2006 to 2010. In addition, Ali al-Allaq, of the Islamic Dawa Party, was a member of parliament for multiple terms. Others from ISCI included Jalal al-Deen al-Sagheer and Mohammed al-Mashkour. Even Iyad Allawi's "secular" Iraqi National List contained, in 2005, a clerical parliamentarian, Iyad Gamal al-Din. Many of these clerics were religious figures during the days of opposition to Saddam Hussein. They either went on to lose in later elections or did not run at all in the latest election in October 2021.

Adapting to Electoral Reality

Some clerics have tried to adapt to their electoral punishment. While Ammar al-Hakim never ran for public office or held an official title, he moved from heading an Islamist party, ISCI, to form the National Wisdom Movement, a nonreligious party.[28] While Hakim maintains the image of a cleric, he is positioning himself in line with Iraqi public opinion. When the National Wisdom Movement performed poorly in the 2021 elections, however, it showed that changing rhetoric does not necessarily soften the imagery of a cleric leading a political party.

But Muqtada al-Sadr, another turban-wearing cleric from a prominent clerical family, may yet show that there is a path for clerics in politics. Sadr has not suffered at the ballot box. On the contrary, his movement won the highest number of seats of any party in the last two elections, in 2018 and 2021. Still, it is difficult to see Sadr as an example of rising clerical power in Iraq, since there are other explanations for his dominance at the polls. In particular, he owes his electoral success to an alignment of three factors: his uncontested claim to his family name and heritage; an electoral boycott; and the new 2021 electoral district law. The law divided Iraq into eighty-three districts (as opposed to the eighteen districts of previous elections) and votes were nontransferable, meaning that the strategy typically used by Sadr's opponents—of flooding the political scene with candidates and amassing transferable votes—was now rendered useless.[29]

Sadr's following is more cult-like than religious, since he lacks traditional religious credentials. This was most recently brought into focus by a statement this year from Grand Ayatollah Kathem al-Haeri, the spiritual advisor to the Sadrists, who criticized Sadr for the chaos he was causing in Iraq, stating that he lacked the scholarly training to be a leader.[30] This statement came after Sadr withdrew his representatives from parliament and took to the streets in protest, frustrated with his inability to form a majority government. Following the statement from his spiritual guide, Sadr announced a withdrawal from politics. In response, his followers resorted to violence and the country was nearly lost to a civil war between the Sadrists and rival Shia paramilitary groups. The next morning, Sadr chastised his followers and ordered them to withdraw. In a display of astounding authority, they withdrew almost immediately.

In other words, Sadr is an outlier. He represents clerical authority in politics, but not the authority of the marja'iyya, which he has no direct claim to. In another report in this series, Ben Robin-D'Cruz argues that Sadrist electoral power comes from four key sources: elite institutional capture, state capture, expertise and social capital, and the aforementioned messianic-charismatic religious authority.[31]

There are signs that other politically inclined clerics who are not outliers like Sadr have learned to navigate public disenchantment with Islamist parties. In the 2021 elections, an intriguing new party—Ishraqat Kanoon—emerged with six parliamentary seats and took everyone by surprise. The party attempts to merge secular civil and Islamic values, possibly in an attempt to appeal to a society that has grown distrustful of Islamists but is still conservative. The party's members have been wary of giving interviews (they politely but firmly declined to speak to me). Despite the paucity of information available about the party, some facts have come to light—including, according to a party member who asked to remain anonymous, that it is supported by the Holy Shrines in Karbala (though not necessarily financially supported).[32] Activists in Najaf and Karbala also claim that the party is tied to prominent clerical families and that it has the implicit support of the marja'iyya.[33] These statements are yet to be confirmed, but if true, reflect the adaptation of the religious establishment to societal changes in Iraq.

The religious establishment has come to terms with the fact that the turbaned man is no longer perceived as holy. And because the marja'iyya obtains its power and money from the public, it will be incentivized to seek ways to ensure the continuity of those resources. This can be reflected through more deliberate distancing from politicized clerics or shifting toward more implicit and less costly forms of intervention, including the so-called Najaf Veto.

The "Najaf Veto"

The so-called Najaf Veto has taken on a nearly fable-like quality, with observers of the Iraqi elections discussing it during every government formation. It is, of course, not a real veto and not an official legal tool. Rather, it is the informal ability of the marja'iyya to reject a candidate for the premiership. It is the norm in Iraq, through informal but entrenched consociationalism, that the premiership is accorded to a Shia candidate; it follows that the candidate must also have the approval of the Shia religious establishment.

Historically, the marja'iyya has exercised its informal veto power in tense moments in Iraqi politics. The earliest example is in 2006 when Ibrahim al-Jafari was adamant on maintaining his position as prime minister, despite the dire situation in Iraq. After the bombing of the Holy Shrines in Samarra, the marja'iyya—through private channels—encouraged Jafari to step down. The same would happen with his successor, Nouri al-Maliki, after the fall of Mosul to the Islamic State in 2014.[34] In both these scenarios, Najaf simply prevented the political process from collapsing, and supported it getting over a hurdle in times of crisis, rather than dictating the precise outcome of the process. In both instances, the Shia political parties reached out to the religious establishment to break the political impasse.

The marja'iyya has flexed its muscles in other, similar ways. During the 2019 protest movement, the marja'iyya encouraged the prime minister, Adil Abdul-Mahdi, to resign—which he did in November 2019. Following him, three different prime minister-designates attempted to form a government; only Mustafa al-Kadhimi, the third and final candidate, succeeded. Kadhimi's success in forming a government—and conversely, Mohammad Tawfiq Allawi and Adnan al-Zurfi's failure to do so—were not caused by the marja'iyya's opinion. Najaf did not push for Kadhimi; they merely did not veto him.

The Najaf Veto falls under a broader range of clerical authority— the informal authority to intervene in high politics. Another variation of this type of authority is the legitimization the marja'iyya gives certain individuals by virtue of agreeing to meet with them or exchange messages with them. Along the same lines, the decision to avoid meeting politicians can be understood as recusing oneself from the process entirely. This has been Sistani's practice for the last few years, where he notably met with only a few Iraqi leaders (like former Iraqi presidents Jalal Talabani and Fouad Masoum) and with some world leaders, like Iranian president Hassan Rouhani, Special Representative

Jeanine Hennis-Plasschaert of the United Nations Assistance Mission for Iraq, and Pope Francis.[35] The evidence points to the fact that the religious establishment is recalibrating its informal political authority, rather than losing it. Najaf's role in legitimizing politicians or vetoing them is still strong. For example, a November 2021 statement from Sistani's office declared that the office was "not a party to any meetings, discussions, communications or consultations regarding the creation of political alliances and the formation of the next government, and there is absolutely no validity to the news that is promoted by certain parties and actors in media and social networking sites."[36]

The publication of such a statement seems intended to protect the marja'iyya from political exploitation and to demonstrate to the public that the religious establishment is not responsible for the behavior of Islamist parties. However, less directly, it also shows that the Shia political class still seeks the legitimacy of the religious establishment. The question remains: if the political authority of the clerical establishment is decreasing, why would the political class still look to it for legitimacy? Perhaps Shia political parties' learning process and adaptation are slower, or perhaps they are willing to exercise every tool at their disposal to remain relevant. The association of the religious establishment with politicized clerics is far costlier for the religious establishment than it is for the clerics themselves.

Recommendations for Policy and Research

The issue of clerical authority, particularly in politics, does not easily lend itself to making policy recommendations. It is both a sensitive topic and, if not addressed appropriately, risks raising the critique of essentialism. After all, why should religious authority matter more in the Iraqi case than elsewhere in the world?

In some ways, this bridge has already been crossed. Sistani's role in politics—past and present—is a favorite topic of analysis, and the question of his succession informs much of the speculation about the future of politics in Iraq. In many of the reports and articles written on the matter—this one included—Sistani's name is synonymous with that of the marja'iyya and even Najaf itself. This should not be interpreted as meaning that Najaf would be irrelevant without Sistani; rather, it indicates that Sistani is a product of the religious establishment. This assertion, along with the reflections on the nature of religious authority, should inform all future decisions made by both Iraqi policymakers and foreign policymakers interacting with Iraq.

The nature of the religious establishment's political authority over its adherents has changed in the last few years. But the rate of decline has slowed. Simply put, policymakers, researchers, activists, and all other parties interested in the role of the religious establishment should not operate on the assumption that it will cease to be relevant in the near future. However, they should also adopt the practice of defining authority and how it is delineated.

Engaging in more public opinion data collection—particularly panel data—could better inform analysts' conjectures and hypotheses about the religious establishment. It is also worth remembering that the religious establishment is ultimately an academic institution, and may also be interested in studying its own influence.

Policymakers, particularly Iraqis, must remember that the hawza is an academic institution and that it can occupy an important position among global religious institutions that will ultimately be beneficial to Iraq. The hawza's influence is not only internal and political. It can also be effective externally as well, given the appropriate environment. An example of the possibilities for international and cross-religious collaboration was Pope Francis's meeting with Sistani in Iraq in March 2021, after which Sistani affirmed his belief that religious authorities like himself have a role in ensuring the security of Iraqi Christians.[37] The meeting was possible because of the improving security environment in Iraq.

As for those policymakers who fear the religious establishment's involvement in politics, this report has shown that the establishment's political influence expands in times of crisis. With good governance and stability, its political role will naturally decline.

Clerical Authority Remains Relevant

To say that clerical authority has diminished in Iraq is to make a sweeping statement, one which there is no evidence to support. What can be said, however, is that the ability of elite clerics to influence politics, through voters as adherents, has indeed diminished and plateaued in recent years. Various forms of evidence point to this: public opinion data, interviews with activists and politicians and, most importantly, the acknowledgement of clerics themselves. But what this presents is not necessarily a reduction in clerical authority overall, but a limitation of clerical political authority.

Future research can inquire as to whether a reduction in clerical political authority has spillover effects onto other areas of influence. It can also inquire whether this reduction caused a decrease in public religiosity, or is a symptom of this decrease—a question as yet unanswered. The reason that Iraqi activists, politicians, and clerics give for this limitation in authority is that once clerics became involved in formal politics—in parliament, for example—their poor performance sullied the reputation of the entire religious establishment.

However, there is little evidence to suggest that elite clerical authority over adherents as politicians has been affected by this shift in public opinion. Quite the contrary, logic suggests that as politicized clerics fall from grace, they will cling ever more tightly to the legitimacy the religious establishment confers. And, in response, the religious establishment will seek to protect its reputation and to more tightly police who can and cannot use its name for political reasons. The marja'iyya is intentionally restraining itself from exerting too much authority on political figures, lest it becomes more implicated in the political system that Iraqis have rejected.

The marja'iyya's restraint leaves many avenues of clerical authority open. Clerics can exercise formal and informal authority over different actors—voters, politicians, activists, and others. They can use religious rhetoric to send direct messages through sermons, or they can hint or suggest their approval and disapproval. They can also utilize public channels to address politicians, thereby broadcasting their involvement in politics and putting politicians in the spotlight. Or they can employ private channels to communicate with politicians. The difficulty in studying clerical authority and in analyzing or reporting on it is that certain types of authority are more easily measurable than others. Moreover, the choice of mechanism with which to relay the message is in and of itself a data point and a valuable insight as to how clerical authority works and is deployed.

This report's methodological weakness is that it is only able to examine publicly available clerical interventions, and some private ones that have become public knowledge, but it cannot present a complete picture. As such, it cautions against a general interpretation of the rise or fall of clerical authority in a context of incomplete data.

This report has examined the direct authority of clerics over adherents who are citizens, which is a category that is of importance to Iraq's political future. The Shia of Iraq constitute a sizable majority with great electoral power and the ability to move them to vote or to stop protesting, for example, has direct political consequences. Therefore, the scholarly and journalistic preoccupation with whether this form of authority is growing or weakening is understandable. However, analysts should exercise caution when drawing conclusions about this question—authority is not only political, and voters are not the only adherents with political power. Future analysis should attempt to detangle and make clear the reach of religious authority. Clerics understand that their authority can be intricate, and their influence both direct and indirect. Researchers must understand this, too.

4

Grand Ayatollah Ali al-Sistani as Guide and Critic, 2014–23

Sajad Jiyad

After issuing a fatwa that helped defeat ISIS, Grand Ayatollah Ali al-Sistani could have leveraged his new influence for more direct political power in Iraq. Instead, since 2014, he has guided from a distance, pushing for better governance and less corruption through his Friday prayer sermons, private meetings, and intermediaries. Although Sistani has never publicly described his political ideology, the last decade illustrates that a pillar of his viewpoint—in marked contrast to the Iranian style of total clerical control—is the sovereignty of the people. Sistani is already the most influential cleric in Shia Islam. His unique approach to political influence also makes him one of the most important guides, or maraji, in history.

As summer turned to fall in 2014, Iraq found itself on some of the shakiest footing of its modern history. The Islamic State had cut through the northern and western countryside with brutal ease, leaving behind a wake of carnage. Its eventual defeat was by no means certain—the immediate focus was simply on keeping the extremist group from capturing Baghdad. At the end of the summer, Nouri al-Maliki was forced to cede the premiership, ending an eight-year term under a cloud of failure.

In this dismal moment, one Iraqi leader stood out for his action and influence. Grand Ayatollah Ali al-Sistani, who is the most prominent Shia religious leader not just in Iraq but in the world, had distinguished himself during Iraq's unprecedented crisis by calling on the citizens of the country to rise up in arms against the Islamic State. His June 2014 call came in the form of a fatwa (a religious edict), but it was directed to Iraqis of all faiths. And it was successful—tens of thousands of Iraqis had enlisted in the country's security forces and in paramilitary groups, and by the end of 2015 were reversing the Islamic State's progress.

Sistani's intervention was remarkable. Unlike the ayatollahs who control Iran and abide by a philosophy of near-total clerical control over government and policy, Sistani believes in a much more indirect approach to politics. While those who follow the Iranian model (known as *wilayat al-faqih*, or guardianship of the jurist) criticize Sistani's philosophy as quietist, the reality is much more complex. As my forthcoming book shows, about Sistani's political life (*God's Man in Iraq: The Life and Leadership of Grand Ayatollah Ali al-Sistani*, New York: The Century Foundation), he is a man of firm ideals who believes that those ideals can only be achieved through the expression of the will of the people. His direct appeal to the Iraqi people to stand and fight against the Islamic State, at a time when the regular army was being crushed, marked a turning point in the then eighty-four-year-old cleric's career, and cemented his position as one of the most prominent *maraji* (religious references, singular *marja*) in the centuries-long history of Shia Islam.

As Maliki departed from office, Sistani voiced other hopes about Iraq's future: he saw an opportunity for Iraq to reset, on the back of international support in its fight against the Islamic State, to rebuild its foreign relations, undertake crucial reforms, and regain trust from the Iraqi people in the political system.

And Sistani could have leveraged his enhanced profile for a much stronger role in Iraqi politics to achieve these aims. True to his long-standing ideology, however, in the last ten years he has chosen a much more careful style of engagement with Iraqi politics. He has subtly pressed for certain changes through his extensive networks, but has never waded directly into the political arena. As such, the last decade has proven definitive of Sistani's legacy.

In this chapter, I document some of Sistani's activities from 2014 to the present, including several of his speeches that have not previously been published in English. These activities show that he is a major Iraqi political actor who has utilized his traditional authority and religious, social, and symbolic capital, without ever abandoning his core principle that it is the people who must push for change. The cleric, now ninety-three, cuts a unique figure in Iraq and in the world, and offers a different perspective on the meaning and potential of Shia power and leadership.

The Political Pulpit

After Haider al-Abadi was sworn in as the new prime minister in September 2014, Sistani began to meet with politicians in the new government in the hope that they would be more willing to listen and make urgent decisions given the seriousness of Iraq's situation. Sistani's representatives in Karbala also regularly met with ministers, government officials, and politicians.

Maliki had resisted giving up the premiership after the April elections, and only finally stepped down after the leak of a private letter from Sistani that urged him to accept the election results. Now, Sistani gave support to the new Abadi government, and even involved himself in Iraq's international relations. In a meeting with President Fuad Masum on November 11, Sistani passed the president a message for the Saudi leadership, whom Masum was due to meet in Riyadh three days later. (Sistani has often favored such indirect modes of communication.) In the message, the ayatollah called for strengthening of relations between the two countries, assuring the Saudis that there was no Shia position against Saudi Arabia.[1] The Saudis responded positively, and this gave the Abadi government the platform to renew the relationship.

In the first six months of the new government, Sistani used meetings and Friday prayer speeches to focus on maintaining support for the war effort while he waited to see what reforms the prime minister was undertaking. Abadi visited Sistani in April 2015 and complained to him that the political elite would not cooperate on pushing through reforms, and that he had struggled to make significant changes. (Sistani had pressed Abadi on a variety of reforms, including reducing the salaries and privileges of senior civil servants, ending the control of parties over ministries and important public institutions, and cutting down on waste of public funds and bureaucratic inefficiency.) Sistani told him to be bold and forthright with the Iraqi people so that it would be awkward for the parties to be seen as blocking reforms.

But the next couple of months passed without much progress, and as the July heat kicked in and the dismal electricity service failed again, protests broke out in Baghdad and several cities in the south. Anger and discontent focused on the poor performance of local governments. Protesters called for corruption to be rooted out.[2] Sistani warned Abadi that blaming previous governments for poor services was not enough, particularly the lack of electricity in the traditional summer heat.[3] After three weeks, Abadi had only limited reactions to the protests, and Sistani once again felt it was necessary to speak out in a very direct manner.

The cleric again chose the Friday prayer sermon as the platform for his intervention. On August 7, he published his most forceful public address to date calling for immediate reforms. He also indicated his continued support for Abadi, but also warned that patience was wearing thin.

The sermon began by making clear who was to blame for Iraq's poor state of affairs: "The political forces . . . [that] hold the reins of power and decision-making through the council of representatives, the central government, and local governments bear most of the responsibility for the past problems and what the country suffers from today, and they must be aware of the danger of continuing in this situation and not developing fundamental solutions to the problems of citizens who were patient for a long time."[4]

The sermon continued by validating people's anger: "The people who endured hardships, defied car bombs, participated in the elections, and chose those who hold power from among the political forces, expect them, and rightly so, to work diligently in order to provide them with a decent life, and to do their utmost to combat corruption and achieve social justice."

Sistani then addressed the prime minister directly—something the cleric had never done before—urging him to strike corruption with an iron fist: "What is expected of the prime minister, who is the top executive official in the country and who has shown interest in the people's demands and his eagerness to implement them, is to be more daring and courageous in his reform steps . . . to take important decisions and strict measures in the field of combating corruption and achieving social justice, and to strike with an iron fist those who tamper with the people's wealth."

Sistani went on to implore Abadi to "transcend partisan and sectarian quotas and the like in order to reform state institutions." He continued: "[The prime minister] should seek to appoint the right person in the right place, even if they do not belong to any of the ruling parties, regardless of their sectarian or ethnic affiliation, and [should] not hesitate to remove those who are not in the right place even if they are supported by some political forces." Sistani concluded by telling Abadi that he should not be afraid of those political forces, but should rather rely on God "and on the honorable people who want this from him and will support and back him in achieving that."

Disappointment

The tone, manner, and instructions of Sistani's August 7, 2015 address are all important. In it, he positioned the marja above the state, as a guide, but in a much more forceful way than might have been expected given his past activities. As it turned out, however, the sermon was the highpoint of Sistani's public interaction with the state, which came at a moment when he felt real reform was possible and his words could give the push needed. But disappointment followed.

Within two days of Sistani's call, the government announced some austerity measures aimed at the political elite.[5] As people welcomed the decisions and momentum continued to build for reform, the parties in parliament felt the pressure to accede to the reforms. They voted to approve Abadi's measures and to give him a mandate to undertake them. Abadi continued to announce more reform measures in the following weeks.

However, these reforms had only limited implementation, and the parties began to push back. At the same time, Sistani said that the measures were not the deep reforms that were required, though he held out hope the measures were a prelude to change.[6] But no real reforms were forthcoming, and as protests disappeared and pressure receded, parliament revoked Abadi's mandate. In the end, many of the reforms that Abadi had announced never happened.[7]

This deeply disappointed Sistani, who sensed that his words were going unheeded, and that Iraq was heading to a disaster.[8] The ayatollah began to limit his direct interaction with politicians. When Abadi visited Najaf on November 5, 2015, the prime minister was able to meet with the other three senior maraji, but Sistani would not grant him an audience.

In a sermon published on January 8, 2016, Sistani went public with his disappointment: "Last year, over a period of several months, we called in our Friday sermons . . . [for] serious steps in the path of real reform, achieving social justice, combating corruption, and prosecuting the corrupt, but the year passed and nothing clear was achieved on the ground, and this is a matter of great regret."[9]

Then came the sermon of January 22, 2016, which Sistani delivered with words of exhaustion and frustration: "Our voices went hoarse, without effect, with repeated calls . . . for officials and the political forces that hold the reins of affairs to be aware of the size of the responsibility placed on their shoulders, and to renounce political differences behind which there are only personal, factional, and regional interests."[10]

By the beginning of February 2016, Sistani had decided that the politicians were not listening and that reforms were not going to happen. He again repositioned himself away from the political elite, refusing to meet with them and even deciding to mostly forgo commenting weekly on current affairs in the Friday prayer speeches.[11] He had returned to his posture of 2011–14, when he had assumed the stance of political opposition to the government, but opposition in the form of disengagement—an effective boycott.

Weeks after Sistani stopped publicly focusing on politics, protests started again, this time with Sadrist backing of the protests and eventually with the participation of Muqtada al-Sadr himself.[12] Even as the protests grew and overran the Green Zone, Sistani was unmoved to comment or intervene. On May 4, 2016, after protesters stormed parliament, Sistani's office simply released a brief statement stating that he was closely watching the situation. The office called on all sides to "think carefully about the future of the people and take serious and tangible steps to get out of the current situation into a better future."[13] The head of the UN mission in Iraq, Ján Kubiš, met Sistani on May 30, 2016. "The marja'iyya is following very, very carefully what is happening and will intervene whenever that is necessary," Kubiš reported after the meeting.[14] For his part, Abadi visited Najaf on June 22, 2016, but was unable to get a meeting with Sistani, a fact that highlighted Sistani's efforts to distance himself from the political elite.[15]

Guiding from a Distance

For the next two years, Sistani did not receive Iraqi politicians and seldom commented on political issues. This stance, from early 2016 to mid 2018, was meant to show his displeasure with the political elite and the lack of reforms. Yet he did not totally ignore state affairs. In sermons, he continued to press for protecting citizens in the liberation effort and respect for human rights when the Mosul campaign against the Islamic State began in October 2016.[16] And after the Kurdistan Regional Government (KRG) organized a referendum on independence in September 2017, Sistani reacted critically.[17] Further, when federal forces retook control of Kirkuk from the Islamic State in October 2017, leading to heightened tensions between the KRG and the central government, Sistani cautioned against a divisive or sectarian view of the events.[18] In another sermon, on December 15, 2017, after the war against the Islamic State was declared to be over, Sistani said: "The battle against corruption—which has been delayed for a long time—is no less ferocious than the battle against terrorism, if not more severe."[19]

The build-up to parliamentary elections in May 2018 saw fragmentation increase within and between parties and political coalitions. Economic conditions had not noticeably improved, and a young population was ever more disenchanted by the political elite and the post-2003 system. Sensing the apathy, Sistani released a long statement for Friday prayers on May 4, 2018, a little more than a week before national elections, outlining his view on the political situation.[20]

First, he explained why he viewed parliamentary democracy as the most suitable choice for Iraq's political system: "Since the fall of the former authoritarian regime, the religious authority has sought to replace it with a system that adopts political pluralism and the peaceful transfer of power by referring to the ballot boxes, in periodic, free and fair elections, in the belief that there is no alternative to following this path in governing the country. . . . The religious authority still holds the opinion that following this path constitutes—in principle—the correct and appropriate choice for the country's present and future."

Next, Sistani described the conditions for elections to work well: "That the electoral law be fair, respecting the sanctity of the vote and not allowing circumvention of it. Including: that the electoral lists compete on economic, educational, and service programs that can be implemented away from personalization, ethnic or sectarian rhetoric, and media one-upmanship." He also cautioned against "external interference in the matter of elections, whether by financial or other support." He added that voters needed to be aware of "the value of their votes and their important role in shaping the future of the country, so they do not give them to unqualified people for a cheap price, or follow whims and emotions, or care for personal interests, tribal tendencies, or the like."

Next, Sistani addressed why apathy had set in among voters:

It is certain that the failures that accompanied past electoral experiences—from the misuse of power by many of those who were elected or assumed high positions in the government, their contribution to spreading corruption and wasting public money in an unprecedented way, distinguishing themselves with large salaries and allocations, and their failure to perform their duties in the service of the people and providing a decent life for the people—was only a natural result of not applying many of the necessary conditions—albeit to varying degrees—when holding those elections.

Sistani went on to talk about the responsibility of voting, though he stopped short of calling it an obligation:

> Participation in these elections is a right for every citizen who fulfills the legal conditions, and there is nothing obligating [citizens] to exercise this right except what they are convinced of in the requirements of the supreme interest of the people and this country. Yes, they should pay attention to the fact that relinquishment of exercising the electoral right gives an additional opportunity for others to have their elected representatives win parliamentary seats . . . but in the end the decision to participate or not remains up to the voter alone."

Despite Sistani's warnings about the repercussions of voter apathy, the elections had a low turnout and the predictable months-long process to form a new coalition government followed. Even though he had made it clear that he did not endorse any party or candidate, popular expectations increased that Sistani would resolve the standoff over who would become the prime minister.

But Sistani didn't choose a winner—at least not exactly. Instead, he withheld endorsements. Abadi's bloc, the Victory Alliance, had fared poorly in the elections, and his chances of continuing as prime minister were slim. But when Sistani's representative criticized the government in the July 27, 2018 prayer speech, Abadi's fortunes were sealed: his term was over.[21] However, Sistani's office also effectively ruled out other senior politicians with a statement on September 9, 2018: "The marja'iyya . . . does not support the next prime minister if he is chosen from among the politicians who were in power in the past years."[22]

Nudging for Reform

Though Sistani generally does not endorse or nominate any politicians for top posts, he sometimes does try to encourage consensus when there is a deadlock. This is especially true when it comes to the issue of the premiership, where the Shia parties compete intensely to gain the post, but mostly settle on a compromise.

According to Sistani's representative in Lebanon, the marja'iyya "intervenes whenever it senses danger imminent in Iraq and the interests of its people, and finds that its intervention is useful in resolving or mitigating intractable crises, and the intervention of the marja'iyya—which is keen not to exceed the legal frameworks— is in various declared and unannounced forms, depending on circumstances."[23]

For weeks after the official election results were announced in August 2018—almost two months after election day—Iraq's parties failed to form a government and select a prime minister. At this point, of the possible choices, Sistani preferred Adil Abdul-Mahdi, with whom he maintained a respectful relationship, and discreetly informed Muqtada al-Sadr, whose party held the crucial seats required, that he would be amenable to such a nominee.[24] So, on October 2, 2018, Abdul-Mahdi was nominated as prime minister, and Sistani once again hoped that a new government would finally deliver positive results in terms of the kinds of reforms he had long sought.

During this time, Sistani continued to refuse to meet with Iraqi officials and kept his political comments limited, but he did receive foreign officials, and he sometimes used these meetings to convey messages to domestic leaders.[25] In a November 2018 meeting with Kubiš, who was now the outgoing head of the UN mission, Sistani said he was "waiting to see the outlines of success in [government] work."[26] On February 6, 2019, Sistani received the new head of the UN Mission in Iraq, Jeanine Hennis-Plasschaert, and used the occasion to urge the government to show quick progress. "If the political blocs do not change their approach in dealing with the country's issues," Sistani warned, "there will be no real opportunity to resolve the current crises."[27]

Yet again, however, the political elite stifled any real improvement in the general situation, by preventing significant reforms, increasing public spending without a clear economic plan, and failing to tackle corruption. In the June 14, 2019 Friday prayer speech, Sistani expressed his dismay:

"The dispute broke out again— at times openly and hidden at others—among the parties that hold the reins, and the conflict aggravated between forces that want to preserve their previous positions and other forces that emerged during the war with the Islamic State seeking to perpetuate their presence and obtain certain gains, and the struggle for positions and positions continues . . . and the rampant corruption in state institutions has not yet been met with clear practical steps to reduce it and hold those involved in it accountable."[28]

Sistani predicted, as he had in 2015, that the popular calls for reform would grow louder: "Those who oppose reform, and are betting that the demands for it will diminish, must know that reform is an inevitable necessity, and if the manifestations of the demand for it diminish for a while, then they will return at another time with a much stronger and broader scope, and it will be too late for regrets."[29]

The Tishreen Movement

The Abdul-Mahdi government turned out to be another disappointment. When protests broke out on October 1, 2019—in what would come to be known as the Tishreen movement—and the security forces reacted violently to them, Sistani responded with a statement in the October 2019 Friday prayer. In the statement, he criticized the government and the political elite, warning them to "rectify matters before it is too late."[30] For the next four months, Sistani returned to using the weekly Friday prayer sermon as his platform to comment on political affairs, as the reaction to protests escalated into a crisis and larger numbers took to the streets. Sistani held the government responsible for the bloody violence: "The government and its security apparatus are responsible for the heavy bloodshed in the demonstrations of the past days," he said in his October 11 sermon.[31] He continued to press for protecting the demonstrations and for the political elite to listen to the protesters' demands, but his words went unheeded.[32]

The violent reaction of the dominant political forces to the Tishreen movement, and the lack of reforms on the horizon, completely disillusioned Sistani in the entire political class. He was resigned to the fact that the state in its current form would not improve its governance, nor would the parties change their behavior. These failures were a deeply painful blow to his aspirations for Iraq. He also felt personally betrayed by those politicians and leaders from whom he had expected so much better, and to whom he had given ample support.[33]

In a November 11, 2019 meeting with Hennis-Plasschaert, Sistani referred to "his repeated warning several years ago of the dangers of exacerbating financial and administrative corruption, poor public services, and the absence of social justice." But, Sistani said, he had not found "ears willing to listen among officials to address this."[34] Sistani went on: "the relevant authorities do not have enough seriousness in implementing any real reform." To reflect his utter disapproval, Sistani even suggested considering other options in dealing with the state. "If the three executive, legislative, and judicial authorities are not able to carry out the necessary reforms or do not want to do so," he said, "then another path must be considered . . . because the situation cannot continue as it was before the recent protests."

The alternative path Sistani alluded to here is a complete change in the political system in Iraq, to a new structure or form of government different from the post-2005 one—though he has not described in greater detail what such a new system might look like, or how it could be achieved. Even today, Sistani continues to warn that the Tishreen protests were a watershed moment, and the political elite cannot continue as if nothing happened.

Islamic Democracy

In the Friday prayer speech of November 15, 2019, Sistani defined his view of the government's authority, in light of what might be called Islamic democracy: "The government derives its legitimacy—in other than tyrannical regimes and the like—only from the people, and there is no one else to grant it legitimacy. The will of the people is represented in the result of a secret general ballot, if it is conducted fairly and impartially."[35] This is perhaps the clearest opinion of a Shia marja on democracy, and is at the heart of Sistani's view on the sovereignty of the people.

Government security forces continued to repress protests and, after a particularly bloody day in Nasiriyah on November 28, 2019, Sistani forced Abdul-Mahdi's resignation by urging parliament to reconsider support for his government.[36] This intervention, which was again made via a Friday sermon, was balanced with a comment on the limits of the marja'iyya and its political role. "The religious authority will remain a support for the honorable Iraqi people," he stated. "It has nothing but advice and guidance as to what it deems to be in the interest of the people, and it remains for the people to choose what they deem to be the best for their present and future without guardianship over them." Abdul-Mahdi announced his resignation the next day.

Instability continued to prevail in the following weeks, and while Sistani kept up his advice and warnings the reality was that they had limited impact on events. In several statements, Sistani had warned about foreign interference in political and security affairs and the need to protect Iraq's sovereignty, but the situation became dangerous in the days preceding and after the assassination of Qassem Soleimani and Abu Mahdi al-Muhandis on January 3, 2020.[37] Sistani was highly critical of the assassination and sent a letter of condolence to Ali Khamenei, Iran's supreme leader.[38]

After four months of protests, repression and violent attempts to end the demonstrations with no new government yet in place, on January 31, 2020, Sistani intervened by calling for early elections. He was recovering from an operation on a broken femur, sustained in a fall at home, but was still forceful in his Friday sermon that day.[39] "It is imperative to quickly hold early elections so that the people can have their say, and the next parliament emanates from their free will and is concerned with taking the necessary steps for reform and issuing critical decisions that determine the future of the country," he stated.[40] The following week's Friday prayer sermon, on February 7, repeated the call for early elections to be held "in a reassuring atmosphere without the side effects of money or illegal weapons or external interference."[41]

The February 7, 2020 sermon was the last Friday prayer sermon to include a political statement by Sistani, and marked the beginning of reduced involvement by Sistani in politics, which continues today. Sistani had begun to feel his words were having little effect and that it was time for the political elite to take full responsibility for their actions without any further advice from him.[42] In some ways, this new attitude is similar to the opposition-through-disengagement stance he adopted in 2011–14.

Political Semi-Retirement

Friday prayers at the Imam Hussain shrine in Karbala were suspended because of COVID-19 on February 28, 2020, and have not resumed.[43] Since the beginning of the pandemic, Sistani has only communicated with the public through rare statements posted on his official website.

In effect, March 2020 was the start of Sistani's semi-retirement politically. For the rest of 2020, Sistani mainly issued directives and rulings on how the COVID-19 pandemic should be dealt with.[44] Sistani's disappointment with Adil Abdul-Mahdi's performance meant that he did not engage with the process of choosing a successor, and he generally kept a distance from the government of Mustafa al-Kadhimi (prime minister from May 2020 until October 2022).

Sistani's representative later explained, in April 2022, why he stopped issuing Friday prayer speeches: "Some political entities were not responding to much of what the religious authority indicated," he said in a statement, and noted that "the supreme marja'iyya does not only want to preach. Rather, it wants the speech to have an impact. And some of [the political parties'] response was very weak, even with the content of the sermon being repeated more than once."[45]

Nearly a year after the October 2019 protests, a date had still not been set for early elections that protesters demanded. When Sistani met with Hennis-Plasschaert again on September 13, 2020, he called for an end to the delay in holding the elections.[46]

Sistani also made several other notable comments in that meeting. First, he insisted that elections be conducted "according to a fair and just law, far from the private interests of some blocs and political parties." These interests had forced parliament to adopt district-level voting in the election law for the first time, against the preference of most parties.

Second, he called for the elections to be "supervised and monitored in coordination with the relevant department in the United Nations mission." This appeal foreshadowed the contestation of election results by the Shia Coordination Framework, a political bloc, in October 2021.

Third, Sistani reiterated the importance of parliamentary democracy. However, he clarified that the goal was not elections in and of themselves, but rather the outcomes they should lead to if conducted properly. "Early elections are not an end in themselves," he said, "but rather the correct peaceful path out of the current impasse from which the country is suffering." These statements repeated his conviction that the people are sovereign, and that parliamentary democracy is the best form of governance for Iraq.

Fourth, Sistani gave the new government some backing and urged it to push ahead with imposing the rule of law: "The current government is called upon to continue and proceed decisively and forcefully with the steps it has taken in order to implement social justice, control the border crossings, improve the performance of the security forces so that they are characterized by a high degree of discipline and professionalism, impose the prestige of the state, withdraw unauthorized weapons from it, and not allow the division of areas in the country into zones that are controlled by certain groups by force of arms under different titles, who do not uphold the applicable laws." (The latter part of this statement was a veiled reference to groups in the Popular Mobilization Commission.)

Cultivating a Broader Appeal

One of the most significant moments in the centuries-long history of the marja'iyya occurred on March 6, 2021, with the visit of Pope Francis to Sistani.[47] It was the first time that a pope had visited Iraq, and his meeting with Sistani emphasized the ayatollah's position as the preeminent religious authority in Shia Islam, as well as his unique influence in Iraq. It also placed greater emphasis on Sistani's role as a leader of faith and a force for better communal relations, rather than that of political referee. The warm meeting, in which the two leaders held hands, was a show of solidarity by Sistani to Iraq's Christians, and highlighted his respect for other faiths and pluralism in general.[48] The pope thanked Sistani "for speaking up in defense of those most vulnerable and persecuted amid the violence and great hardships."[49] The meeting also reinforced Sistani's international credentials as a man of peace. By making the trip to Najaf, Pope Francis showed that in Sistani he had, in the words of a *New York Times* story on the meeting, an "ideal interlocutor . . . holy, credible and powerful."[50] The pope was glowing in his praise of Sistani: "I felt the duty . . . to go and see a great, a wise man, a man of God: only by listening to him do you perceive this. . . . He is a person who has that wisdom and also prudence . . . and he was very respectful in the meeting. I felt honored . . . a humble and wise man, it did good to my soul this meeting. He is a beacon of light."[51]

Ahead of the elections scheduled for October 2021, many in Iraq expected voter turnout to be low. But again, Sistani encouraged "everyone to participate consciously and responsibly in the upcoming elections, although they are not devoid of some shortcomings." As in the past, he admonished voters to "take lessons from past experiences and be aware of the value of their votes and their important role in shaping the country's future."[52]

The election results were intensely contested and, once again, a long period of bitter divisions and heated negotiations over government formation set in. Sistani was adamant that he would not intervene this time, no matter how complicated the situation became.[53] This position was based on his experience and belief that all sides in the political arena were to blame for the country's ills and that none were willing to listen.

Even when Sadrist protests escalated into occupying parliament and, later, into violent clashes with opponents from the Shia Coordination Framework in the Green Zone in August 2022, Sistani refused to publicly intervene.[54] (Though some believe Sistani communicated to Sadr the need to prevent further violence after the events of August 29, 2022, in which at least thirty people were killed, it is unlikely that Sistani did so directly.[55]) Not intervening even at moments of high crisis may point to an evolution of Sistani's strategy to push the political elite to reform—to show that he will no longer work to prevent escalations and leave the politicians (and the public) to deal with their choices, as grave as the consequences may be.

The acrimonious year-long process to form a government validated Sistani's stance: Despite repeated calls from various sides for him to broker a consensus, it turned out that the disputes were so bitter that his intervention would not have helped or been effective. It was better for him to stay out of it completely. His commitment to this approach reflects his desire to protect his legacy and political capital, while also acknowledging that the marja cannot continuously intervene in messy political situations, and that politics and government is primarily the domain and responsibility of politicians. Sistani has made this argument before, and after twenty years of the new Iraq he firmly believes its politicians should be held accountable, and the marja'iyya's need to guide and intervene is much less than it used to be, especially if it falls on deaf ears.[56]

However, Sistani still engages with foreign dignitaries; such engagement reflects the marja's transnational role and its duty of care to Shia communities across the world, in addition to dealing with matters beyond the political confrontations in Iraq. An example of this is Sistani's meeting with the high representative for the UN Alliance of Civilizations, Miguel Moratinos, on December 7, 2022, to discuss interreligious dialogue and the protection of religious sites.[57] Another is Sistani's December 19, 2022 meeting with Christian Ritscher, a UN special advisor and the head of UNITAD (the UN Investigative Team to Promote Accountability for Crimes Committed by Da'esh/ISIL).[58]

Sistani also released a statement on February 7, 2023, concerning the earthquake that hit Turkey and Syria, which shows the continued transnational and humanitarian interests of the marja'iyya.[59] On June 29, 2023, in response to a protest in Sweden in which the Quran was burned, Sistani's office released a letter addressed to the UN secretary-general, António Guterres, urging the UN to take "active steps to prevent the recurrence of such cases and prompting states to reconsider the legislation that allows their occurrence."[60]

The Pillar of the People's Sovereignty

Iraq's next scheduled elections are due to take place by October 2025, and it could be that events until then do not require Sistani to comment or to intervene on political issues. At the time of writing, Sistani is still receiving believers and well-wishers almost daily, but has kept up his boycott of Iraqi politicians and is still seen as a critic of the political elite and as being in opposition to them. Sistani is still assessing the current government of Prime Minister Mohammed Shia al-Sudani, but so far no major criticism of it has emerged from Najaf. For now, Sistani's political role is much less active than it used to be, but he still maintains a close eye on political affairs.

Whatever the next few years hold in store, the decade since Sistani's so-called jihad fatwa—the call to arms against the Islamic State—has solidified his stature in the history of Iraq and in the history of Shia Islam. He has skillfully deployed his charismatic, traditional, and rational-legal authority at various junctures to influence Iraqi affairs, but without ever overstepping the boundaries of his own apparent philosophy of influence rather than control. He is probably the most impactful marja in the last several centuries.

Sistani has never expounded at length on his political ideology, but what he has said—and what we can glean from a careful analysis of his writing, speeches, and activities—underlines that a pillar of his viewpoint is the sovereignty of the people. Several writers who have analyzed Sistani have called this philosophy *wilayat al-umma,* or "authority of the people"—in sharp contrast to the wilayat al-faqih, or guardianship of the jurist, that is the model of Islamist political control in Iran.[61] When asked in August 2003, some five months after the U.S.-led invasion, about what kind of political system Sistani saw as fit for Iraq, his response was: "a system that adopts the principle of consultation, pluralism, and respect for the rights of all citizens."[62]

The post-2014 chapter of Sistani's life and career has shown what this philosophy looks like in practice. That he has not single-handedly solved Iraq's many problems is hardly proof of this philosophy's flaws. Rather, it merely shows that his political influence, like anyone's, has limits—and that, in all likelihood, he prizes the integrity and consistency of his people-first ideology over short-term wins.

Politicians

5

The Sadrist Electoral Machine in Basra

Ben Robin-D'Cruz

Iraq's Sadrist Movement has bested all rivals at the ballot box, non-Islamists and Shia Islamist alike. The secret to its success lies in sophisticated election tactics, capture of strategic networks in the state and civil society, and the charismatic authority of their leader, Shia cleric Muqtada al-Sadr. But the movement also has vulnerabilities linked to the Sadrists' dependency on the personal popularity of their leader, Sadr, as well as weaknesses in the movement's political apparatus that result from its subordination to clerical domination.

Shia Islamist parties have dominated Iraq's post-2003 electoral politics and have taken a controlling share of the country's political system. Among these factions, the Sadrist Movement—led by the cleric Muqtada al-Sadr—appears particularly adept at mobilizing an electoral base and sustaining it over multiple election cycles. Most recently, the Sadrists emerged as the largest single party from Iraq's October 2021 elections. The Sadrists in Basra collected more seats in 2021 than all the movement's Shia Islamist rivals combined.[1] This contrasts with trends in the wider region, where— despite the so-called "Islamist electoral edge"—Islamists have frequently failed to sustain electoral popularity or translate initial electoral success into enduring political hegemony.[2]

At the same time, the power of political Islamism—typically defined as a form of political activism asserting and promoting "beliefs, prescriptions, laws, or policies that are held to be Islamic in character"—appears to be diminishing.[3] For instance, in his forthcoming report in this series, Fanar Haddad argues that "Shia politics" has lost much of its analytical salience for interpreting politics in Iraq, Shia or otherwise.[4] In fact, Islam, and even Islamist ideology, have been decentered in the politics of Iraq's nominally Shia Islamist groups. These parties are increasingly autonomous from religious– clerical leadership, they are transactional in their political alliances with Islamist and non-Islamist groups alike, and their electoral platforms make scant reference to Islamist ideology. Despite their long political dominance, Iraq's Shia Islamists have not sought to create an Islamic state or impose sharia. Where Islamism manifests politically, it tends to do so as a thin veneer, raising the question: what is *Islamist* about Iraq's Shia Islamists?[5]

Here, too, the Sadrists often represent an exception to broader trends. The movement retains strong linkages between religious– clerical and political spheres. Indeed, the formal political apparatus of the Sadrist Movement is largely subordinate to its clerical leadership. Similarly, while other Islamists have moved away from conventional forms of Islamist political ideology in search of alternative sources of legitimation and electoral appeal, the Sadrists have doubled down on religious appeals and their own brand of Islamist ideology—Sadr's ideology of charisma.

How is this Sadrist exception explained? That the Sadrists benefit electorally from a large social base is well known. Yet how the loyalty of this base is maintained, and how it is deployed politically, are not so well understood. In part, this reflects analysts' focus on Sadrist militancy at the expense of the Sadrist base, the movement's "ordinary" followers, and everyday aspects of the movement. As a result, the conventional depiction of the movement tends to highlight its fragmentary nature and lack of internal coherence and discipline.[6] However, shifting attention to the Sadrists as an electoral phenomenon inverts this picture. The puzzle then becomes explaining the remarkable endurance and cohesion of the Sadrist electoral base despite multiple splinters in the movement's religious and paramilitary strata.[7]

The literature explaining the Islamist electoral edge and its fragility has tended to emphasize Islamists' reputation as "political outsiders," and their reputation for effective governance, along with Islamists' provision of nonstate services, the mobilizing power of religious institutions and networks, and the hegemony of Islamist ideology and identity at a societal level.[8] However, these factors do not fully explain Sadrist electoral power. More important have been the Sadrists' capture of strategic networks within both state and civil society, combined with Sadr's particular mode of charismatic authority.[9] These give the Sadrists access to a unique combination of resources. They way that these resources are deployed within a sophisticated electoral strategy ultimately explains the Sadrist exception as an electoral force, both vis-à-vis non-Islamist parties and other Shia Islamist groups.

This report addresses these arguments through a case study of the Sadrists' electoral politics in Basra during the October 2021 elections. The aim is to explain why the Sadrist Movement has proven more capable than both non-Islamists and the group's Shia Islamist rivals at sustaining electoral success over the long term.[10] The report also identifies potential vulnerabilities in the Sadrists' electoral machine. The report ultimately addresses whether the sources of Sadrist electoral power relate to religious and Islamist features of the movement—and therefore whether or not "Islamism," or "Shia

Islamism" remain useful or necessary analytical concepts for under-standing Shia politics in Iraq.

This report draws on the author's analysis of textual and audiovisual materials, such as Sadrist election propaganda, and voting data from the Iraqi Higher Electoral Commission (IHEC). The research is also based on interview data collected by the author during fieldwork in Iraq in the summer of 2016 and spring of 2020. This includes dozens of interviews and more informal discussions with senior and mid-ranking Sadrists in the movement's political, religious, and cultural-intellectual strata, as well as non-Sadrist political figures, activists, and informed observers with first-hand knowledge gained from working either alongside the Sadrists or against them. These data have been supplemented by more recent communications, conducted remotely by the author, with a smaller number of Basra-based observers and Iraqi researchers. In most cases, these sources have been anonymized—either at the request of the interviewees, or on the author's initiative—to protect sources from potential reputational damage or the risk of physical harm. These risks relate to sensitivities around criticism of Sadr and the Sadrist Movement, as well as the illicit or sensitive nature of some of the practices being discussed in the report.

The Sadrists in Basra

The Sadrist role in Basra changed markedly after 2008, when Operation Charge of the Knights (the Iraqi army's campaign in Basra against the Sadrist militia, the Mahdi Army, known in Arabic as Jaysh al-Mahdi) effectively brought a chaotic period of militia gangsterism to an end.[11] Since 2008, a more ordered stability prevailed in the governorate, and the Sadrists adapted accordingly. Sadrist violence previously transacted more directly into financial and other forms of power (for example, via rampant kidnapping for ransom). But post-2008, this violence was redirected through a developing landscape of government contracting, trade, and private-sector commercial activity. For instance, the Sadrists (along with other militia and political groups such as Badr, Asa'ib Ahl al-Haq and the Dawa Party) now provide commercial security services in Basra in the form of private security companies.[12] Sadrist violence was thus "moderated" via its sublimation into the systemic violence of the Iraqi state and its political economy.

One example is the "ikhraj" (or "fixer") companies who manipulate the customs process at Umm Qasr Port, one of the most important economic rackets in Iraq. The ikhraj companies can generate $2–5,000 profit per container, and $10–20,000 on a single transaction, amounting to total revenues per day for this racket in the tens of millions of dollars. The Sadrists operate their own fixer companies alongside other political and paramilitary groups.[13] Where the Sadrists have an economic edge, however, is through their cooperation, with the Beit Shaya'a sub-tribe in al-Faw, to monopolize subcontracting for the Grand Faw Port mega project. The project, which will be completed in phases between 2023 and 2045, hopes to establish the biggest port facility in the Middle East and will cost billions of dollars. In 2019, the Sadrists pushed Asa'ib Ahl al-Haq out of the unofficial economic committee controlling the distribution of these financial flows, becoming the sole patrons of the Beit Shaya'a and turning the Grand Faw Port project into the Sadrists' single biggest revenue stream.[14]

These forms of economic extraction far exceed the value of financial resources that the Sadrists derive from religious sources (primarily religious taxes and charitable donations). Precise figures are extremely difficult to obtain; however, a very rough estimate based on available evidence can be made. Adnan Shahmani, a cleric in Sadr's Najaf office in 2009, stated that the movement collected around $65,000 a month in charitable donations—which, even though it has likely fluctuated over time, seems to clearly represent a small portion of overall revenue streams.[15] Thus, in the Sadrist case, the electoral benefits derived from patronage, services provision, and electoral spending power are linked less to bottom-up resource mobilization through religious institutions and practices, and more to the Sadrists' direct integration with the Iraqi state and civil society.

Strategic Networks

In Basra, the Sadrists have also established strategic networks at ports and border crossing points, as well as several services director-ates and government bodies. These networks are most influential in the electricity directorates, the Basra Health Department, the Basra Ports Authority, and Basra Municipalities Directorate. The Basra gov-ernorate office is also within the Sadrist network, primarily through Deputy Governor Mohammed Taher al-Tamimi, who is a member of the Sadrist Movement.[16]

This form of state capture has extended the Sadrist electoral base in Basra to parts of the professional middle classes, albeit via a highly transactional and fluid logic of affiliation. Consequently, the conven-tional view of the Sadrists as a purely proletarian phenomenon needs to be updated.

In some circumstances, this state capture also allows the Sadrists to act as the state, for example, when issuing legal titles and docu-ments, licenses, and accreditations. The Municipalities Directorate in Basra, largely under Sadrist control since 2010, is one such case. The Sadrists have used the directorate to issue legal titles, and to sell land and property deeds to the movement's supporters at reduced rates and in ways that circumvent planning laws. As a result, cer-tain areas of Basra (Anadalus, the banks of the Khura River, and the so-called Casino Lubnan district) are notorious for quasi-legal slum settlements and business premises that are subject to continual own-ership disputes and attempted demolitions and removals.[17]

State capture works in tandem with the Sadrists' networks in civil society and nonstate social spheres (such as familial and tribal networks). One example is recent protests by the Beit Shaya'a in al-Faw, demanding employment opportunities from the Korean firm Daewoo—which operates the Grand Faw Port project—for local young men. This dispute was mediated by Farhan al-Fartousi, the Sadrist director of the Iraqi Ports Authority in Basra, who brokered a "de-escalation" of the protests. The incident led to Daewoo's rapid creation of several hundred jobs for Beit Shaya'a tribesmen—funded through the Iraqi state via financial transfers from the Ministry of Finance to the Daewoo project. To put this in perspective, at the time of the al-Faw protests, hundreds of graduate students had been protesting at Basra Oil Company offices in the city of Basra for around a year to demand employment opportunities, with much more limited results.[18]

The religious dimension of the Sadrist Movement in Basra is officially governed by a committee comprised of Sheikh Aayad al-Mayahi, the head of the Basra branch of the Office of the Martyr al-Sadr (OMS); the senior Sadrist clerics in the province, Sayyid Sattar al-Battat and Sayyid Haadi al-Dunaynawi, who lead Friday prayers at the most important Sadrist prayer site in Basra (the prayer yard in Khamsa Meel district); and Sheikh Hazem al-Araji, Muqtada al-Sadr's personal representative in the province. Sheikh Hassan al-Husseini and Sheikh Mustafa al-Husseini are the Sadrists' representative and assistant representative for religious affairs in Basra, with the former being particularly well connected in the community. This committee oversees management of the Sadrists' religious and cultural activities, staffing of mosques and hussainiyas (congregation halls), oversight of the khutba al-juma'a (Friday sermon), collection of religious taxes, and distribution of social services. Araji acts as a floating broker, assisting in mediating all manner of religious, political, commercial, paramilitary, and tribal relationships and disputes by leveraging his status as Sadr's personal representative.[19]

This religious structure is critical to the reproduction and political deployment of the Sadrist base. It is primarily at Sadrist hussainiyas and prayer yards that ordinary Sadrists gather and participate in communal worship as an intergenerational and familial community. In addition to the Friday sermon, a Sadrist imam will typically hold smaller and more intimate gatherings after prayers where worshippers can ask direct questions on matters that require religious judgment. This is not primarily a political experience, as questions will typically focus on everyday matters of family life, sexual health, and business practices. Nevertheless, the practice serves to reproduce forms of authority within the movement. Meanwhile, the Friday sermon itself can be a highly political event. The content of the sermon is overseen and controlled by the Najaf OMS. Consequently, if the Sadrist leadership wants a uniform electoral message disseminated within the movement, it can easily do so via the Friday sermon.

These elements all play a role in the formation and reproduction of the Sadrist social base in Basra. This base is not primarily generated or bound together through transactional patronage or utility-based social interactions. Rather, it is fundamentally composed of extended familial networks in which Sadrist identity (which entails varying degrees of religiosity) is intergenerationally reproduced. For instance, one of the most populous Sadrist districts in the city of Basra is known as Hayy al-Hussein (after Hussein Ibn Ali, the third Shia Imam and a symbol of sacrifice and martyrdom), although its earlier name was Hayyaniya. The name change took place around 2006 and reflected the steady transformation of the district's demography due to inward migration from the rural parts of the governorate of Maysan. The change reflected a gradual Sadr-ization of the district, which was effected through familial and tribal networks, producing a community with a high degree of social bonding. Being Sadrist, therefore, is not a primarily "political" identity, as many analysts argue, but rather an identity with much deeper layers of socialization.[20]

Sadrist affiliation also intersects with tribal affiliation where the historic loyalty of tribal leaders to a particular religious reference (marja') transmits through wider tribal networks. However, such affiliations are also fluid and subject to reconfiguration based on more near-term and transactional logics (as in the case of the Beit Shaya'a outlined above). There is rarely an exact overlap between Sadrist and tribal networks. For instance, the Beit Shaya'a in southern Basra follow Sadr, while other parts of the tribe are closer to Dawa or Badr. That said, the tribes in Basra with the most Sadrist representation are Al Furijat, Bani Sukain, Bait Rumi, Al Mariyan, parts of Al Gamarasha (containing a high representation of marsh Arabs with networks involved in arms smuggling and narcotics), and parts of the Bani Malik, Al Bazoon, and Al Shawi tribes.[21]

The Sadrist base is largely urban and rural poor, which continues to give the movement a pronounced socioeconomic class orientation. In the city of Basra, the Sadrist base is clustered in certain poorer districts, which confers important electoral advantages. The areas of Hayy al-Hussein, Jumhuriya, Tamimiya, and Khamsa Meel have been Sadrist strongholds since before Operation Charge of the Knights. Sadrist affiliation in Hayy al-Hussein and Tamimiya is estimated to be at least 85 percent, while Jumhuriya is closer to 70 percent. Khamsa Meel is somewhat lower, as recent rural-to-urban migration has diversified the district.[22] Nevertheless, the main Sadrist prayer yard in the city of Basra is located in Khamsa Meel, with the second most significant prayer yard being in Kut al-Hajaj (close to the districts of Hayy al-Hussein and Jumhuriya). All these districts, with the exception of Tamimiya, fell within the city of Basra's District One electoral district, making this district highly competitive for the Sadrists.

Sadrist Election Strategy and Tactics

Understanding how these networks and resources are mobilized for elections requires considering the strategic dimension of Sadrist electoral politics. At the national level, Sadrist electoral strategy in

2021 took shape as a form of Sadrist exceptionalism. The movement eschewed its previous attempts to build broad-based pre-election alliances, and relied entirely on mobilizing its own core base. Election posters exhorted supporters to elect a "pure Sadrist."

Campaign rhetoric contained the usual platitudes about corruption and reform, but these were placed within a religious frame: Sadr's unique and sacred mission to guide Iraq back to power, prosperity, and sovereignty. This was overlain with explicitly religious appeals to "return Iraq to the correct religious path" and to restore "obedience to the hawza" (referring to the seminary that establishes Shia doctrine).[23]

This messaging sought to energize the Sadrist base around a religious obligation. In this sense, the Sadrists did not present the politics of reform and anti-corruption as a matter of practical policy prescriptions, but rather as a form of ethical action without a strong sense of political instrumentality. Reform was elevated into a religious endeavor. Secondarily, Sadrist electoral discourse sought to prevent bleeding at the edges of the base in the form of votes lost to the protest parties—those parties established in the wake of the Tishreen movement that began in October 2019—or to abstentions, by trying to associate the protest movement with religious deviance and moral corruption.[24]

The Sadrists feared the pull of the Tishreen movement on Shia youths.[25] In fact, internal polling by the Sadrists ahead of the election raised concerns among the leadership, prompting Sadr to consider alternative strategies, such as an election boycott.[26] Recent survey data commissioned by Chatham House has indicated the surprising depth of sympathy for the Tishreen movement among ordinary Sadrists, despite a recent history of antagonism between the two camps.[27]

However, the Sadrist election strategy was assisted by three contextual factors. First, a new electoral law that was finalized in 2020 shifted Iraq to a form of "first-past-the-post" voting system. The law subdivided each governorate into several electoral districts returning three to five members of parliament based on the number of votes each candidate obtained, rather than a proportional system with centrally managed party lists and transferable votes.[28] The new system advantaged groups able to mobilize a core base and with the internal discipline to strategically distribute votes among their candidates. This new system played directly into Sadrist exceptionalism.

Second, the failure of the rival Fatah Alliance to adapt to the new system caused internal fragmentation and an incoherent election strategy that undermined the multiparty coalition's votes-to-seats ratio.[29]

And third, the Tishreen movement's partial boycott of the election amplified the Sadrist electoral edge in the context of low overall turnout. This was particularly true in Basra, where Tishreen groups offered no political platform to contest the elections.

The Sadrists took full advantage of this opportunity by adapting swiftly to the new electoral system. This effort was spearheaded by Walid al-Karimawi, a professional political consultant and one of the few non-hawza figures in Sadr's "inner circle." Karimawi has headed the Sadrists' electoral file for multiple election cycles, is highly experienced, and Sadr trusts him. He wields considerable central control over the movement's electoral strategy and operation.[30] He also plays a key role as a broker and negotiator in the Sadrists' postelection government formation negotiations.[31]

Karimawi implemented a four-tiered electoral strategy based on a careful assessment of the Sadrists' strength in each electoral district. The strategy determined how many Sadrist candidates were deployed in each constituency, with a maximum of three (usually two men and one woman) in districts with the highest density of Sadrist voters. Crucially, the Sadrists were also able to control how their vote base was distributed among the movement's candidates within each electoral district. This was achieved by dividing up each district into sectors, each assigned to vote for a specific candidate.[32] This was visible in Basra, where electoral posters for Sadrist candidates promoted different candidates in different neighborhoods without any overlap or direct competition.[33]

No other political party could match this degree of control. The ultimate effect was remarkable efficiency in translating votes into seats, with each Sadrist seat in Basra costing fewer votes, on average, when compared to the seat-cost ratio for the movement's rivals. In fact, the total number of votes cast for Sadrist candidates in Basra fell by around 20,000 between the 2018 and 2022 elections, while the total number of parliamentary seats won increased from five to nine. (There is further discussion of the Sadrist electoral performance in Basra below.)

The Sadrists also masterfully utilized Iraq's parliamentary gender quota system, which requires that a quarter of seats go to women. Of the ninety-seven women elected to parliament in 2021, twenty-four were Sadrists. The Sadrists secured more seats via the gender quota than Fatah's total number of seats. The Sadrists' advantage within the quota system relates to the distinct way in which the Sadrist vote base is mobilized (explored more below). Women running for parliament in Iraq typically garner fewer votes than men, and tend to lack comparable bases of local popular support. This affects women Sadrist candidates less than those of other parties or independents, because they rely on the strategic distribution of votes by the Sadrist electoral machine, rather than their own, autonomous support base.

Moreover, the threshold of votes required to win a seat through the gender quota is significantly lower, making this a highly efficient investment of votes per number of seats gained. In fact, in districts where the Sadrists had a very low representation, they were still able to gain a seat by focusing all their votes on a single woman candidate. This worked even in a small number of "Sunni" districts in Baghdad.

The success of the Sadrist strategy depended on accurate information about the geographic distribution and demographics of the movement's core support and discipline and control over its mobilization. The Sadrists had a further advantage because the movement's base was mainly structured around familial networks, which meant that the base tended to be clustered in specific districts that were easily recognizable as Sadrist strongholds.

However, the Sadrists also benefited from two innovations. The first was Bunyan al-Marsous, or "Solid Foundations," a project launched by the movement several months ahead of the elections. Ostensibly, Bunyan al-Marsous was pitched as an internal reorganization of the movement's activities and how it interacts with its followers. The project promised to provide Sadrists who registered with their local OMS access to a range of services including a form of health insurance, assistance finding employment, and microloans for economically insecure families or small businesses. However, the registration process also gave the movement detailed data on the distribution and demographics of its support base, including residential addresses and contact phone numbers, allowing the Sadrists to coordinate election instructions at a micro level.

The second innovation was the launch of the Sadrist election mobile app. This was the first of its kind in Iraqi politics and provided Sadr's followers with useful information about candidates and which polling stations to vote at. The app included GPS functionality to help navigation to polling stations and thereby ensure higher turnout. (As the new election system divided governorates into multiple subdistricts, it had become important to know which polling station to visit to correctly register a vote.)[34]

The final element of the Sadrist electoral strategy was the tactical use of independents to split or squeeze out their rivals. In several Basra districts, Fatah candidates lost out to independents who were rumored to have secured tacit agreement from the Sadrists to run in areas of high Sadrist representation.[35]

Selecting Sadrist Electoral Candidates

The Sadrists have a distinct approach to selecting their electoral candidates. Prospective members of parliament do not apply for the role, nor are they assessed and selected via democratic or competitive party-political mechanisms. Rather, one of Sadr's representatives within the provincial OMS directly approaches potential candidates to scope their interest in standing. If the individual shows willingness, they are then sent to the Najaf OMS for further vetting and to receive Sadr's approval and direction. The process is centrally managed by Karimawi and the Political Committee of the Najaf OMS.

Social profiling of Sadrist candidates in Basra indicates that experience and skill as political activists are not qualities that the movement prioritizes in choosing candidates for parliament. Rather, the main criteria are prospective candidates' track record of Sadrist activism, loyalty to the movement, and willingness to follow orders. Also crucial are prospective candidates' familial ties and other forms of social connectivity to the movement (such as tribal connectivity).

The Sadrists tend not to recruit significant local personalities with their own popular bases of support. Consequently, Sadrist electoral candidates are often relative unknowns with less public profile and political experience than candidates fielded by other groups. Candidates' possession of certain types of cultural and social capital is also desirable. For instance, the Sadrists often recruit university professors and other professionals, seeking to benefit from the social prestige of these professions. Strong local tribal links can also make a candidate more attractive.[36]

There are exceptions to this general pattern. For instance, in more competitive districts Sadrists may want to tap into the additional mobilizing power of certain actors with more personal popular appeal. In such cases, it is more likely to find prominent Sadrist figures from Saraya al-Salam, or those with a significant national profile, selected as candidates.[37]

Religious Authority

Sadr's religious-charismatic authority has several important effects in an electoral context. To begin with, it has reduced the movement's dependence on Islamist political ideology as a mobilizing and legitimating resource. This has insulated the Sadrists electorally from the declining popular appeal of Islamist ideology in Iraqi politics, allowing the movement to short-circuit the causal dependence between effective governance and legitimation that has damaged the Sadrists' more purely political Islamist rivals.

The political strategy of the Sadrists is mainly geared toward tactical positioning in the contest to dominate elite politics, and not toward advancing an ideological or programmatic version of Islamist politics. This positioning is facilitated by the primacy the movement places on religious authority over political ideology, which in turn explains the Sadrists' ability to assume multiple and often contradictory political stances, and to engage in a wide variety of electoral strategies, without suffering a critical loss of credibility with the movement's base.[38] In other words, the primacy of religious authority results in greater flexibility in political contexts, allowing the Sadrists to swiftly adapt to shifting opportunities and threats. Being religiously centered has also helped prevent internal schisms over ideological disputes when compared to rivals such as the Dawa Party, or to Lebanon's Hezbollah.[39]

As noted above, the Sadrist Movement chooses its candidates for parliament for their proven loyalty to Sadr and historical ties to the movement, and not because they possess their own strong bases of local support. They also tend to be lay activists without a religious background in the hawza. This approach maintains a clear divide between the religious and political figures in the movement, and ensures the subordination of the latter to the former.

As such, Sadrist politicians are largely expendable, and Sadr has sometimes replaced entire swathes of his movement's members of parliament from one election to another with no detrimental impact on the Sadrists' electoral performance.[40] This system instills discipline on the Sadrist political apparatus, helping to ensure that key political decisions taken by Sadr and the leadership translate smoothly into the desired political action.

Finally, if religious institutions and networks play a bonding function, amplifying solidarity and mediating organizational capacity at the local level, then it is Sadr's charismatic religious authority that transcends the local and lends greater mobilizing power and coherence to the Sadrist base as a national electoral phenomenon.

Sadrist Electoral Vulnerabilities

The sources of electoral power outlined above explain the Sadrists' dominant electoral performance in Basra in October 2021. The movement won the most seats (9), and the most votes (87,399). In fact, the movement won more votes than those of the entire Coordination Framework combined (which includes the Fatah Alliance, State of Law, Nasr, Hikma, Fadhila, and others). However, drilling down further into the electoral data at the provincial level reveals potential vulnerabilities for the Sadrists, particularly when thinking about the movement's longer-term electoral prospects.

The Sadrists saw an overall decline in the vote tally of its electoral platform in 2021. However, this has been somewhat overstated since then, although the Sadrists obtained only 885,310 votes in 2021, down from 1,493,542 in 2018; the 2018 figure includes the votes for non-Sadrist candidates (the Iraq Communist Party and other leftist and liberal parties) who participated in the Sadrists' Sa'iroun Coalition. While few of these candidates won seats themselves, they nevertheless contributed votes to the total of the Sadrist coalition in 2018.

A closer look at Basra helps clarify what has happened to the Sadrist base in recent years. Here, the Sadrist vote tally between 2018

and 2021 fell from 121,103 to 87,399. However, of the 50 candidates Sa'iroun ran in Basra in 2018, 12 were from secular parties,
who contributed 10,147 votes to Sa'iroun's total. Consequently, the
decline in the Sadrist-only vote tally was just 23,557.[41] This number is still significant, particularly given the high rates of population growth. However, it should also be considered against a general
decline in voter turnout, with around 2 million fewer votes cast in
2021 compared to 2018.

Nevertheless, it was the 2018 election, and not the 2021 vote,
that represents the anomaly in terms of Sadrist electoral success.
This can be attributed to two main factors. First, in 2018 the Sadrists
were able to lead a multiparty coalition rather than relying entirely
on their own core base. And second, in 2018 the Sadrists launched
their electoral campaign on the back of several years of sustained
engagement in pro-reform protest activity. This was a marked contrast to the stance of the movement heading into the 2021 vote,
when it was geared toward propping up the administration of the
prime minister, Mustafa al-Kadhimi, after Sadrist forces assisted in
violently suppressing the Tishreen movement.

Overall, the example of Basra suggests that, while the Sadrist
base has not dramatically shrunk, it may have peaked in 2018 and
is now undergoing a period of stagnation or slow decline. The 2018
experience indicates that, to reverse this trend, the Sadrists would
need to reenergize a younger generation of voters through a more
authentic antiestablishment protest politics, and also reconnect with
non-Sadrist factions to form a coalition that would add votes from
other parties, or independents, to the core Sadrist base.[42]

The Basra data indicates other potential challenges for the
Sadrists. Only one Sadrist candidate was among the top five in the
governorate in terms of total votes, and only three were in the top
ten. If Tasmeem (the alliance of Basra governor Assad al-Idani) had
joined up with the Coordination Framework, their combined votes
would have easily outstripped the Sadrist total. In fact, Idani's vote

total alone would have pushed the Coordination Framework above the Sadrists. Tasmeem's leader, Amer al-Fayaz, was a Fatah member of parliament in 2018 and he scored the fourth-highest overall vote total in Basra in 2021.[43]

In other words, the Sadrist electoral dominance in Basra was partly a reflection of the fragmentation of its Islamist rivals and their inability to distribute their votes more strategically. However, these are likely non-repeatable factors from which the Sadrists will not benefit again, with the Coordination Framework either changing the election law prior to a future vote, adapting to remedy the mistakes it made in 2021, or both. (See Figure 1 and Figure 2.)

FIGURE 1. October 2021 Election—Basra—Vote Blocs

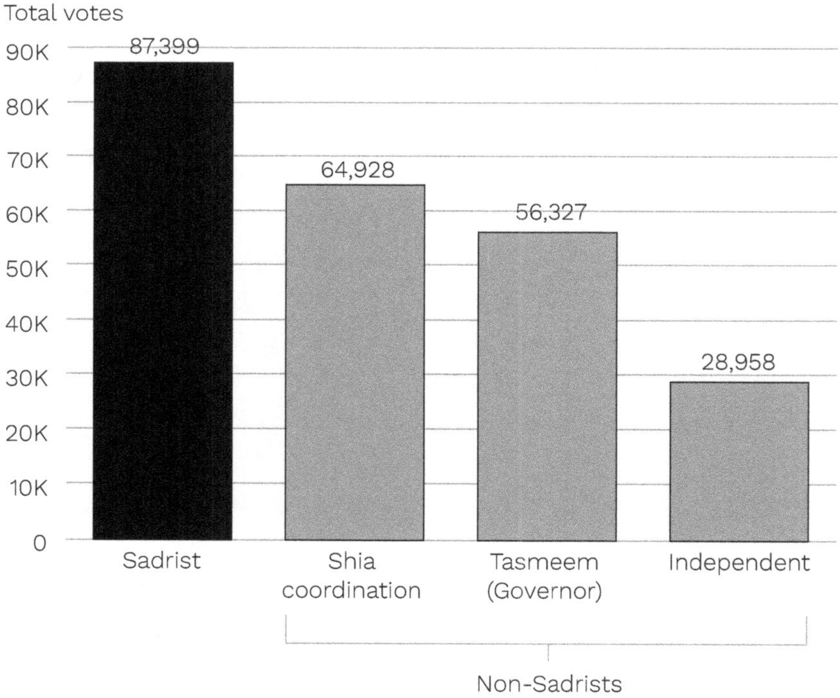

Total votes

	Sadrist	Shia coordination	Tasmeem (Governor)	Independent
Total votes	87,399	64,928	56,327	28,958

Non-Sadrists

Source: Author's tabulation from the official election data report by the Iraqi Higher Electoral Commission.

FIGURE 2. October 2021 Election—Basra—Vote Tallies of Successful Candidates

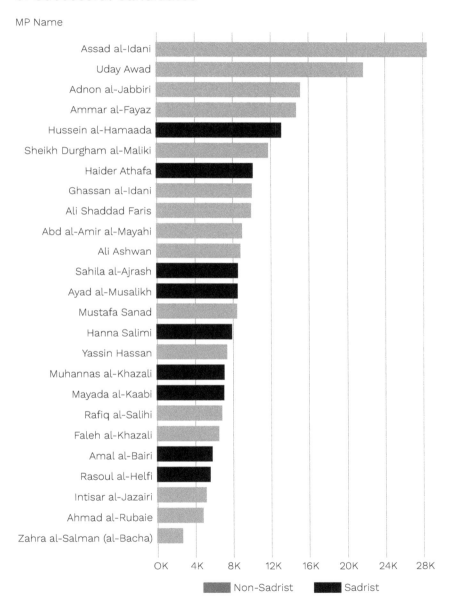

Source: Author's tabulation from the official election data report by the Iraqi Higher Electoral Commission.

The most popular candidates in Basra were big local personalities—such as Governor Idani, Fayaz and Asa'ib Ahl al-Haq/Fatah politician Uday Awad—with proven track records of effective campaigning on local issues. The success of Awad, who scored far more votes than any individual Sadrist candidate, points to the potential local strength of Fatah. Awad's popularity in Basra is not primarily explained by the Fatah brand or the ideological appeal of Islamism, Asa'ib Ahl al-Haq, or "resistance" politics. Rather, Awad has built his own popular base by campaigning on more mundane issues such as lobbying in Baghdad on behalf of Basrawis embroiled in various employment disputes.[44] If Fatah adapts to the new election law, a consolidation of its ranks around dominant local personalities like Awad is likely to pay dividends at the next election.

Another example that shows the local strength of Fatah is Durgham al-Maliki, another Basra candidate who performed well in the 2021 election. Maliki is well connected to Nouri al-Maliki and State of Law, is a sheikh of the Bani Malik tribe, and the second-most senior figure in the tribe after the tribe's leader, Sheikh Abdul-Salam al-Maliki. Already a member of parliament, Durgham al-Maliki gained further popularity in Basra for his support for Tishreen protesters after October 2019 (illustrating how the complexities of local politics in Iraq do not always conform to the broad brushstrokes of national-level political narratives).

In contrast to popular local candidates like Idani, Awad, and Durgham al-Maliki, Sadrist candidates rely heavily on the popularity of a single national figure—Sadr himself. This reliance places the Sadrists on the opposite side of an emerging trend in Iraq's electoral politics toward more locally empowered candidates, whose constituents believe are capable of fixing local issues and delivering practical benefits for their communities. Being less capable of competing in this type of politics may hamper the Sadrists' prospects in future elections. However, this will also be determined by how far, and in what direction, the political class opts to change the electoral reform law.

Explaining the Sadrist Exception

The Sadrists represent a fascinating case study of Islamist electoral politics in part because the movement's sustained success over almost two decades breaks with broader trends in the Arab world. In this broader trend, a focus on Sunni Islamism and its failure to turn initial electoral victories after the Arab uprisings into enduring political hegemony has tended to dominate the narrative. Meanwhile, Iraq's Shia Islamist parties have followed a different, and often overlooked, trajectory by securing their position at the heart of a political system. This Islamist political dominance has been sustained despite the waning popular appeal of Islamist political ideology and Iraqi Islamists' poor governance record across virtually all typical metrics.

The Sadrists are perhaps the most important part of this apparently paradoxical story of Islamist electoral success in Iraq, providing the state and its electoral politics with connectivity to a popular social base of support that has elsewhere diminished. Yet the Sadrists are also an exception within this picture of Shia Islamist political dominance in Iraq. As an electoral base, the Sadrists have remained remarkably cohesive and disciplined, while the rest of the Shia Islamist bloc has fragmented into a proliferating number of parties and militias. The Sadrists have also remained a religious-political movement in which clerical authority is tightly connected to political activity, at a time when the electorate in general has become more critical of the role of religion in politics.[45] The Sadrists also appear uniquely insulated from the reputational damage of poor governance.

Consequently, the factors normally thought to explain the Islamist electoral edge—reputational status, provision of nonstate services, the mobilizing power of religious institutions and networks, and the hegemony of Islamist ideology and identity at a societal level—do not capture the full story of the Sadrists' electoral power. Nor do they explain variation between the Sadrists and other Shia Islamist factions in Iraq, or between those factions and the broader Islamist scene.

The Sadrists' electoral success reflects a sophisticated use of election strategy and tactics, allowing the movement to outmaneuver its rivals. This strategic sophistication is linked to the long-term continuity in senior personnel involved in the Sadrists' development and implementation of election strategy, allowing these actors to accumulate considerable experience, social capital, and practical know-how in their specific field of expertise. This contrasts with a common misconception about Sadr's operational style in which he is said to have weakened the movement by continually cycling senior positions and demoting his most capable associates.

As this report has shown, state capture and Sadrist penetration of civil society underpin the tactical and strategic aspects of Sadrist electoral politics. State-capture—facilitated by Sadrist connectivity to civil society (as in the case of the Beit Shaya'a)—generates much more financial revenue, and extends the scope of patronage networks much further, compared to more bottom-up processes and resources that draw from religious institutions and practices. At the same time, state capture has allowed Iraq's Islamist groups, including the Sadrists, to set the rules of political competition in advance, gaining a crucial electoral edge against those excluded from the strategic networks in elite institutions such as the judiciary.[46]

What sets the Sadrists apart from their Islamist rivals, however, is not only their greater connectivity to civil society, but also Sadr's distinct form of charismatic ideology. This report has detailed the multiple electoral benefits of this religious factor, ranging from how it has insulated the Sadrists from the reputational damage of poor governance and the waning popular appeal of Islamist political ideology, to how it results in great discipline and cohesion within both the Sadrist political apparatus and the movement's social base.

This religious authority also speaks to conceptual discussion about the salience of "Islamism" and "Shia Islamism" as analytical terms for interpreting Iraq's Shia politics. While the "Islamist-ness" of the Shia political scene in Iraq is increasingly difficult to discern, a powerful religious-political linkage remains in the Sadrist case. Nevertheless, the distinct nature of Sadrist Islamism means that this exception does not disprove the thesis that Islamism as a political ideology or identity is losing traction in Iraq. Rather, the Sadrist exception highlights the variety in forms of Shia Islamism and the diversity of ways in which religion and politics can intersect. These complexities are not captured by simple binaries such as quietism versus activism, Najaf versus Qom, or by the subsuming of Shia political Islam into the meta-category of Khomeinism (also known as Wilayat al-Faqih).

Implications for Policy and Elections

From a policy perspective, the Sadrists' circumvention of the relationship between effective governance and legitimation is particularly striking. The literature has often taken the quality of governance and normative legitimation of political systems to be bound together and to be fundamental to both sustained electoral power and political stability. The Sadrists, however, illustrate how the governance-legitimation link can be broken by showing there are ways Islamists can build electoral bases and secure political power without necessarily delivering quality governance over the long term. Western analysts have perhaps not fully grasped this fact, due to the tendency of Western secularist discourses—both academic and policy—to apply rationalist and utilitarian frames to political life. This type of discourse has often reduced religion to a tool of political ends, and failed to explore how religion and politics can mutually constitute each other, and how politics can also serve religious purposes or modes of action (for example, an ethical form of action based on duties and sacrifice rather than instrumental or transactional logics).[47]

Finally, the religious nature of the Sadrist Movement also points to future electoral challenges. The Sadrists prioritize loyalty, discipline, and the maintenance of clerical control when it comes to the movement's political wing. This means it is rare to find Sadrist politicians with their own large bases of popular support. The electoral performance of candidates for parliament is often precariously tied to the popularity of Sadr himself. Moreover, Sadr is continually at risk, through his political participation, of having his charisma diluted and becoming a routine politician. Consequently, Sadr must always seek to strike a balance between staking out positions in the state and political field, and the need to revivify his authority through forms of activism with more utopian and messianic qualities (for example, certain forms of militancy or protests).

The circularity of this practice can be expected to produce diminishing returns over time, and could be an explanation for the gradual erosion of the Sadrist base among Iraqi youths. The need to combat this erosion could push Sadr and his movement into more radical political positions in the future, as the group shifts from a focus on the tactical management of elite politics to a greater focus on the management of its own base of support.

6

Men of Dawa: How the Personalities of One Party Shaped Iraq's New Politics

Maria Luisa Fantappie

The Islamic Dawa Party, a Shia Islamist political movement, has had unparalleled influence in defining the written and unwritten rules of power in Iraq since the 2003 invasion. Three of Iraq's five post-2003 prime ministers have been Dawa members: Ibrahim al-Jaafari, Nouri al-Maliki, and Haider al-Abadi. The three Dawa prime ministers were unable to transcend the practices that helped the party survive in exile. Instead, during their terms Iraq's system of rigid ethno-sectarian appointments and quotas became ever more entrenched, at the expense of state efficiency. One revealing way to understand the role of the Dawa Party in Iraq's post-invasion politics is through the biographies of leading Dawa figures and the network of relations they built and maintained.

Since the invasion of 2003 that toppled the regime of Saddam Hussein, no political party has been more central to Iraqi politics than the Islamic Dawa Party. Three out of Iraq's five prime ministers during this tumultuous period have been members of the Dawa leadership. Several more senior Dawa members have served as ministers, governors, and security officials.

As Saddam Hussein's regime fell, the party had little popular base inside the country. But, unlike other parties, the Dawa Party comprised members of the educated middle class. During their exile in Iran, Syria, and the United Kingdom, Dawa members networked with opponents of Saddam's regime of all backgrounds. Its cadres were well connected with the incoming political class and therefore particularly well suited to navigate post-invasion politics.

Dawa members' influence in defining the written and unwritten rules of power in post-invasion Iraq has been unparalleled. Under their lead, Iraq's consociational system took shape, with resources and government positions being divided up by ethnicity and sect. This new system enabled political parties and personalities to seek power and best their rivals by trading the security, economic, and symbolic capital of state positions. Kurdish, Sunni, and Shia parties were thus consigned to an intra- and intercommunal struggle over resources to monopolize leadership within their respective communities.

Each of the terms of the three Dawa prime ministers marked an attempt to define Shia rule over the Iraqi state as distinct from the experience of Iran's Islamic Revolution of 1979. Yet, ultimately, all three Dawa prime ministers were unable to transcend the practices that made the party successful as an underground and exile organization, but were inimical to building a functioning state. Ibrahim al-Jaafari (prime minister in 2005) enabled the rise of an ethno-sectarian state that entrenched communal divisions. Nouri al-Maliki (prime minister 2006–14) promoted a centralized state sustained by a network that reported to him personally and only benefited his loyalists. And Haider al-Abadi (prime minister 2014–18) attempted to rebuild state institutions, but found only a few allies across the Iraqi political spectrum; his objective remains unaccomplished.

Several detailed accounts exist of the Dawa Party's history, structure, and ideology. However, this report breaks new ground by investigating the role of the Dawa Party in Iraq's post-invasion politics, through the lens of leading Dawa figures' biographies, which have, until now, not been available in English. The specific ways that each of these Dawa men's terms played out are also a result of their personalities and the network of relations they built and maintained over time.

The three men also represent three distinct generations of Dawa activists—generations with different defining experiences, connections to other Shia political forces, and relationships with the Iraqi national identity. Jaafari, from a working-class trading family, governed as a conflict-averse negotiator, entrenching ethno-sectarianism. Maliki, shaped by deep attachments to his tribe and region—and by years in exile—attempted to rule Iraq almost entirely through his personal networks. Finally, Abadi had a vision for professionalizing the Iraqi state—but lacked the personal ambition and networks to do so.[1]

The Trader: Ibrahim al-Jaafari

Born in 1947, Ibrahim Abdul Karim Hamza al-Eshaiker was among the early militants of the Dawa Party. Later, during the years of his militancy, he took the nickname of Abu Ahmed al-Jaafari, and is today known in Iraqi politics as Ibrahim al-Jaafari. In 2005, Jaafari became the prime minister of the first elected post-invasion Iraqi government. During his premiership, the Dawa Party acquired power by balancing rival forces, brokering intra-Shia consensus, and shaping the ethno-sectarian system that still governs Iraq.

The young Ibrahim grew up in remote rural areas neglected by the state in the countryside outside of Karbala. In the 1950s, fast-paced urbanization and population growth had deepened the gap between the main urban centers and the provinces. People of the rural Shia districts of Basra, Karbala, Diawniya, Hilla and Kut—where nearly 50 percent of the total rural population lived—increasingly aspired to move into urban hubs and receive an education. Baghdad and Basra doubled in size. Mosul's population increased by a third.[2]

Jaafari was one of fourteen siblings (eleven brothers and two sisters). His father died when he was four, and he spent most of his youth in the streets of Karbala, working at the central market while attending school. The souk taught him the spirit of adaptation and negotiation skills. "The souk was my veritable school of politics," he told an interviewer.[3]

Jaafari's introduction to Shia political Islam came through the library of his hometown and in nearby mosques. He officially joined the Dawa Party in the late 1960s (about a decade after the party was founded, sometime around 1957).[4] Enrolled at the medical school of Mosul University, he was responsible for the Dawa Party's branch on campus. Islamism attracted members of the pious bourgeoisie of southern Iraq, who aspired to the education of the urban middle class. Most such students were enrolled in the medical and engineering schools and, like Jaafari, could afford attending universities but felt discriminated against due to their provincial origins. In the political Islam of the Dawa Party, they found a path to claiming their identity in opposition to the urban, largely Sunni middle-class elites, and an alternative to the secularism of the Iraqi Communist Party.[5]

Jaafari was among the early followers of the Dawa Party, but was too young to be part of the party's core leadership.[6] He never met Muhammad Baqir al-Sadr, the prominent cleric who was the Dawa Party's ideological leader. The period 1964–68 has been called the

Dawa Party's "golden age", and the party enjoyed a certain margin to act inside Iraq, as the Ba'athist government was preoccupied with a crackdown on the communists.[7] During this time, the Dawa Party increased its followers in the universities and among the intelligentsia.[8] It opened religious centers and libraries across Iraq and tasked a group of emissaries (*wakala*) to run them. It organized students' processions (*mawkib al-talaba*) to commemorate the martyrdom of Imam Hussein.[9] Students would become sympathizers to the Dawa Party through word of mouth, and could only become members following background checks on their families and networks of friendships. Libraries, local mosques across the south, and universities in Basra, Mosul, and Baghdad were hubs to attract younger recruits.

But the Islamic Revolution in 1979 in Iran marked a dramatic turn in the party's trajectory—and in Jaafari's life. Events in neighboring Iran reinvigorated the spirit of the Shia Islamist militants of the Dawa Party, who became convinced that a well-organized revolution could succeed in overthrowing the Iraqi regime. The euphoria around the Islamic Revolution pressured Muhammad Baqir al-Sadr to openly support it—even though he may not have been convinced that the conditions in Iraq were right to support an Iran-style success. But with Sadr openly supporting the revolution in Iran, the Saddam Hussein-led Ba'ath Party grew fearful of a spillover into Shia Iraq.

Saddam redoubled efforts to repress Dawa militants.[10] The Dawa Party's core leadership was put under arrest, executed, or forced into exile. Religious centers were closed down, ceremonies commemorating the martyrdom of Imam Hussein banned, and students of the *hawza*—the Shia seminary—closely monitored by security forces.[11] In April 1980, the Dawa was banned, and party membership became punishable by death. Saddam arrested and executed Muhammad Baqir al-Sadr and his sister, Amina Sadr bint al-Huda.

Dawa activities within Iraq now had to be conducted in absolute secrecy.[12] "Keeping a beard was enough to get arrested," Nouri al-Maliki later recalled in a television interview.[13] Jaafari fled with his wife and two sons, first to Syria, and then to Iran.

Exile in Iran

The 1980s was the decade of the party's dispersal (*intishar*). With its founders assassinated, its rank-and-file exiled, and its cells scattered and disconnected from one another, the Dawa Party was "a body without head," as Maliki later said.[14] Some members escaped Iraq and took refuge in Iran's southern province, Ahwaz, where the Islamic Republic hosted and organized affiliated armed groups.[15] Others temporarily relocated to Damascus, where they nurtured ties with other members of the Iraqi opposition. London was a hub to nurture relations with the West.

Jaafari survived purges and escaped imprisonment. He spent the 1980s in Ahwaz and in Tehran, working as a medical doctor.[16]

Jaafari's reasons for relocating to Iran were more practical than ideological. Syria had only been a temporary base, a transition point. In Syria, families of Iraqi exiles had no legal permit of residency nor access to education and medical care.[17] Iran provided exiles with housing, medical assistance, and education for children.[18] Clerics and militants with a link to Ayatollah Ruhollah Khomeini, Iran's new supreme leader, could offer social services to Iraqi refugees and prisoners of war, and recruit them to fight Iraq's regime from Iran. (The Iran–Iraq War ran from 1980 to 1988 and killed half a million people.) These exiles would join operations conducted by the Iranian Revolutionary Guards Corps, and enjoyed its backing and training.[19]

The Islamic Revolution challenged the Dawa Party's Islamist credentials and called its strategy into question. Sadr had theorized the path to the establishment of an Islamic state as a process of many gradual phases (*marahil*). This included participation in politics through elections, decision-making that involved consultation between clerics and party cadres, and the rejection of violence. The Islamic Revolution challenged this gradual approach. It elevated clerics—*al-fuqaha'* (sing. *faqih*), or "the jurists"—as the ultimate decision-makers. Non-clerical laymen had only a minor role.[20]

Questions haunted many of those who spent the years of exile in Iran as the Iran–Iraq War raged on: "If a revolution is happening in Iran," Jaafari said, "why not in Iraq, where Baqir al-Sadr theorized Shia Islamism, had lived, and made disciples?"[21]

Trying to Remain Iraqi

In exile, the Dawa Party strived for its ideological and organizational independence from the Islamic Republic. "Iraq's Shia like to grow things from their own soil," a Dawa militant said at the time.[22] But the leading Dawa clerics had been co-opted by the Iranians, its fighters mobilized into competing Shia militant bodies. The Dawa newspaper, *Al-Risala,* was banned in Iran.[23] Tensions grew deeper between those clerics and laymen who had grown close to the Iran-based opposition, and others based in Damascus and London. Those cadres in Iraq advocated for the Dawa Party's organizational, theological, and political independence from Iran, and advocated a return to Sadr's philosophy. "We knew political Islam before the Iranians," said Sadiq al-Rikabi, a former Syria-based cadre, and a Dawa leader.[24]

Jaafari stood in the middle of the ideological, geographical, and social divides of Iraq's Shia oppositions. From his modest two-room flat in Ahwaz, he engaged with other Iran-based exiles to piece together the tatters of Iraq's Shia Islamist opposition. He established, with eleven others, the Supreme Assembly of the Islamic Revolution in Iraq (SAIRI)—rebranded in 2007 as the Supreme Council of the Islamic Revolution in Iraq (SCIRI)—an umbrella group of Iraqi Islamist oppositionists under the patronage of Khomeini.[25]

Jaafari was on good terms with all sides of the Iran-based opposition cadres and armed militants. He enjoyed the support of Iran, credibility within his own party as a veteran, and credibility among exiles as a long-standing member of the opposition. Proximity to Sadr's disciples won him credentials as a repository of Sadr's thinking and a point of reference for the party's leadership. He shuttled messages between Iraqi opposition meetings in London and Tehran.[26] He also had solid connections with Abdul Aziz al-Hakim, the lead cleric of SCIRI, and its armed branches. Jaafari later recounted friendly conversations with Kurdish opposition leaders Masoud Barzani and Jalal Talabani, who supported his successful candidacy for vice president of the Iraqi Interim Government led by Ayad Allawi in 2005.[27] He also met with future members of the Coalition Provisional Authority and the Iranian ambassador to Iraq.

Even though Jaafari enjoyed a broad network among exiles, the Dawa Party lacked an armed following and a popular base inside Iraq. It did not have an organized armed wing such as SCIRI's Badr Corps. It was rather unknown inside Iraq. In the 2005 provincial and legislative elections—the first since the invasion—the Dawa Party won only 42 out of 275 seats at the national level, third among Shia parties. None of its members were appointed governors. When attempting to gather people in Nasiriyah to protest against the occupation forces, only a thousand people showed up.[28]

Nonetheless, after the 2003 invasion, Jaafari leveraged the Dawa Party's strong connections in the ruling class as much as he could. He balanced power between the domestic Shia opposition, led by Moqtada al-Sadr (the son of Mohammad Sadeq al-Sadr, first cousin of Muhammad Baqir al-Sadr), and SCIRI. Moqtada al-Sadr enjoyed a large popular base in Shia-populated areas, and SCIRI had an organized armed branch to hold on territory. That, alongside support from Iran and his extensive connections with Iran-based exiles, paved his way to become the first prime minister of Iraq in 2005.

Cutting Deals

As a skilled mediator, Jaafari brokered the bargain between Kurdish and Shia groups to allocate state positions according to communal identities. Kurdish parties wanted regional autonomy. They got their wish, and Shia parties, in return, got Kurdish support for having a Shia politician in the premiership in Baghdad. Both wanted the Sunnis and old regime cronies out of power. Jaafari was the intermediary of this and many other transactional exchanges.

In Baghdad, the newly elected Jaafari balanced the interests of rival Shia parties by trading state positions and resources among them. Through him, Iraqi members of the Iran-based opposition replenished the ranks of the new Iraqi state. Badr commanders put on police uniforms in middle-ranking positions of the Ministry of Interior. Fighters affiliated with Moqtada al-Sadr transformed into regular soldiers on the Ministry of Defense payroll. Dawa members who were close to Iran took on senior security roles.[29]

In the governorates, Jaafari emerged as a kingmaker between Shia rival factions, such as—in Basra—Fadhila, Dawa splinters, and SCIRI. While allying in governorate councils with SCIRI (which already controlled most of the governorate councils in the mid-Euphrates and southern governorates), Jaafari also allowed the Sadrist militias to grow more powerful by appointing Sadr-affiliated army commanders. During Jaafari's premiership, the government acquiesced to the Sadrist militia, the Mahdi Army, controlling neighborhoods of key urban centers, including in Baghdad.

Jaafari's term left a heavy legacy on Iraqi and Shia politics. The Shia–Kurdish formula of ethno-sectarian representation ended up excluding the Sunnis, fueling an insurgency and undermining the already meager prospects of salvaging functioning state institutions from the ruins of the former regime. Power-sharing in Iraq was reduced to dividing the share of state positions and resources among political forces, which fueled intra- and intercommunal sectarian competition. Sectarian tensions peaked in February 2006, as al-Qaeda militants bombed the Al-Askari Mosque in Samarra, leading the Shia forces to seek another candidate for the position of prime minister, who could put an end to violence. [30]

Strongman with a Weak State: Nouri al-Maliki

With Nouri Kamal al-Maliki's eight-year-long premiership (2006–14), the Dawa Party attempted to leave behind its legacy as an opposition party, and govern the new Iraqi state. While less ideological and sectarian than his critics believed him to be, Maliki was unable to overcome the legacy of his past—as a man from the southern governorates, and as an oppositionist. Obsessed by control and driven by mistrust, he only managed to sustain the build-up of a patronage network that reported to him personally, which ultimately weakened institutions, helped the rise of the Islamic State, and finally fractured the Dawa party itself.

Born in 1950 in a remote village of the mid-Euphrates, Maliki is a man of his region. He was deeply rooted in his village—Janaga—his family, and his tribe. As a young man, Maliki never traveled abroad. By the age of thirty, he had visited Baghdad and Najaf only for day trips.[31] By 2003, he had been in the West only once, for a human rights meeting in Brussels, and "stayed in the hotel and saw nothing of the city," as a former Iraqi lawmaker later said.[32]

In his twenties, he became exposed to Islamist thinking by attending a mosque in Hindiya, a town near his village. Soon, he became an undercover militant, preaching Shia Islam to members of his family and distributing pamphlets during religious holidays. He was well connected to a diverse array of locals through his job as a bureaucrat at the education department of Hilla, the city nearest his village, and counted among his colleagues Ba'ath members and members of the Iraqi Communist Party. In the early 1970s, Maliki had to remain vigilant. "I knew when to keep a low-key [profile]. Others, who didn't, were arrested or executed," he recalled in interviews he gave to Al Iraqiya television.[33]

But in 1979, Maliki's membership in the Dawa Party was about to be discovered, and he was forced to flee. He escaped to Jordan, crossing Sunni-dominated Anbar governorate for the first time along the way. From Jordan, he went on to Damascus, where he would spend the next twenty-three years organizing and networking in the Iraqi diaspora.[34]

Maliki's early years of exile were unrewarding. In 1980, he relocated to Sayyida Zainab, a poor Shia suburb of Damascus, where the Dawa Party's militants and clerics began organizing. Maliki was far from his family and arrived with just $200 to his name. In Syria, President Hafez al-Assad left him and his Dawa comrades only a small margin for their political activities. Maliki has told an interviewer that, on the day that Muhammad Baqir al-Sadr was executed in April 1980, Dawa activists in Syria could barely organize a protest in front of Iraq's embassy in Damascus, because of the stifling political atmosphere.[35]

Two years later, as the Iran–Iraq War raged, Maliki relocated to Ahwaz, Iran, near the Shahid al-Sadr camp, the only Dawa-affiliated military training center. Daily life was tough. Rockets fell in areas neighboring his modest house. His wife cooked for fighters crossing in and out of Iraq.[36] The neighborhood he lived in was nearly deserted. He attempted to support the establishment of an armed wing for the Dawa Party, but the initiative was short-lived. Eventually, the Dawa Party's senior cadres, Jaafari included, handed over the camp to the more Khomeini-friendly Badr Corps. Frustrated, Maliki went on to Tehran and spent the next decade shuttling between Iran and Syria doing the party leadership's bidding.

The Uprising of 1991

In 1991, months after Saddam was defeated in the Gulf War, Iraq's southern governorates— alongside many others—revolted against Saddam. The moment marked a turning point for Maliki and his peers. The Ba'ath Party began explicitly referring to protesters by their communal identity: "There will be no Shia after today," went one Ba'athist slogan. This actually boosted the Shia identity of the anti-regime protests.[37] Resentment grew among members of the

Dawa Party against other Iraqi Shia opposition groups based in Iran, which attempted to claim ownership of the uprising and provoked a backlash from the regime.[38] Saddam doubled down on his repression.

Meanwhile, Saddam's ill-conceived invasion of Kuwait had changed the attitude of the United States and international community toward Baghdad. The exiled Iraqi opposition began looking more to the West, rather than Iran, for infrastructure and support. Iraq's Shia political Islam began to have an identity of its own, distinct from that of Iran's Islamic Republic. The "Declaration of the Shia of Iraq," penned in 1992 by Mowaffaq al-Rubaie, a member of the Dawa Party, alongside other secular Shia dignitaries, was a milestone in elaborating the political vision for Iraq in the post-Saddam era—a vision that moved past Shia transnational ideology. The declaration envisioned an Iraq ruled by the principles of democracy, federalism, and respect for community rights.[39] The opposition began to feel that the end of Saddam's regime was in sight, and what to do next became a "recurrent question."[40]

The turn away from Iran, however, did not mean that every exiled opposition member grew enamored with the West. Maliki was disappointed with the West's lack of support for the popular revolts of 1991.[41] In interviews, he criticized the American administration of George H.W. Bush as an enabler of the crackdown on protests, as being responsible for the suffering of average Iraqis under sanctions, and for plotting to control the Iraqi opposition through Western-friendly personalities, such as Ahmed Chalabi.[42]

As the opposition's center of gravity shifted away from Tehran, new safe havens emerged for Iraqi exiles. Syrian president Hafez al-Assad opened space for the opposition, and Maliki kept in contact with Syria's security services.[43] Dawa members in Damascus stopped looking to Iran's revolution for inspiration and, by the early 1990s, the party seemed increasingly focused on a political agenda rather than one centered around Islamist ideology. It abolished the "jurist's council" (majlis al-faqih) that it had relied on for guidance, and expelled clerics and laymen with close ties with Tehran. It refined its internal organization to coordinate between scattered cells of exiles and what remained of the domestic opposition. The party developed an internal electoral system in charge of electing a leadership. A conference (*mu'tamar al-da'awa*) was set up to periodically gather members of local committees, electing an assembly (*sh'ura*) and leadership (*qiada al-amma*).[44]

Inside Iraq, party cells continued to operate, but in absolute secrecy. Only one delegate of each local cell (consisting of a maximum of four members) handled external communication with other cells.[45] Through a Joint Coordination Committee, the party connected with non-Shia members of the opposition, and advocated against Saddam throughout Europe and in Gulf countries.[46]

At the time, Maliki was responsible for media relations.[47] "We worked on building a leadership for the opposition," Maliki told an interviewer.[48]

Guided by Distrust

Despite these efforts, the Iraqi opposition was far from united. Maliki and comrades remained distrustful of other regime opponents—Kurdish parties, Chalabi, and Ayad Allawi—who held frequent consultations with U.S. officials.

Maliki's distrust was nothing new; for much of his life he had only warily engaged with U.S.-backed and non-Shia opposition groups. Throughout Maliki's career, his mistrust periodically pushed him back into an unenthusiastic alliance with other Shia groups, and thus under Iran's wing. A similar distrust dominated the relationship between the exiled and the domestic opposition. Each one claimed to be the authentic opponent of Saddam.

One node of domestic opposition was building around the charismatic cleric Muhammad Sadiq al-Sadr (first cousin to Muhammad Baqir al-Sadr) and his Friday prayers inside Iraq. Maliki dismissed the scale of the cleric's growing popularity—"nobody knew Sadiq al-Sadr among exiles outside Iraq," he told an interviewer.[49] Muhammad Sadiq al-Sadr was assassinated in 1999 (likely by the regime), but his followers maintained a covert network across the south. And after 2003, masses mobilized around Muhammad Sadiq al-Sadr's son, Moqtada al-Sadr.

After the 2003 invasion, Maliki lacked grassroots support, and focused on building a network of contacts inside the palaces of Baghdad. In 2005, he was elected to parliament, and was also a member of the committee that drafted Iraq's new constitution. His networking paid off: when Jaafari was voted out, the Dawa Party supported Maliki for prime minister; they hoped he could ensure the party's continued relevance among the Shia and in Iraqi politics more broadly.[50] Other Shia forces supported him because they perceived him as nonthreatening.[51] American officials trusted his credentials as a nationalist, since he spent his exile in Syria rather than Iran.

Winning against Shia Rivals

As soon as he took office, Maliki ended Jaafari's opposition-centric politics. He struck allegiances with former enemies—the Ba'athists—to prevail against his former comrades—other Shia Islamists groups. Borrowing a page out of Saddam Hussein's book, he won Ba'ath cadres' allegiance through a combination of threats and rewards. His trusted contacts in Hilla, Karbala, Nasiriyah, and Basra ran background checks and built files (*malaffat*) on former Ba'athists: their families, hometown, tribes and past careers. He uncovered their pasts to threaten them with disqualification. He won their allegiance by rewarding them and their families with positions, turning them into his trusted emissaries across state institutions, including the army, the police, special forces, provincial councils, and the judiciary.

Overall, Maliki used de-Ba'athification as an instrument to build power and not as an instrument to take revenge against past oppression.[52] For Maliki, former Ba'athists were simply members of society who had fallen in line with the dominant power at the time. As such, most of them could switch sides and pledge allegiance to the new ruler—the Dawa Party. All that the Dawa Party needed to do to gain this allegiance was guarantee that such individuals would be reinstated in their ranks and social status.[53]

Thanks to this strategy, Maliki could, by 2007, rely on a network of former army generals with a past in the Ba'ath to prevail against his Shia competition—including from within his own party. The Iraqi army defeated the Mahdi Army in the Battle of Basra in 2008, undermining the Sadrists' credibility as a national resistance against the U.S. occupation. Maliki then dethroned SCIRI, sacking its affiliated governors and police chiefs over incompetence and corruption cases.

Meanwhile, Maliki replaced the old guard within the Dawa Party with younger, more secular cadres. This younger generation hailed from families of Dawa exiles in Europe and the United States. They were educated abroad, spoke foreign languages, and had worked as traders, investors and doctors before returning to Iraq. Tired of their junior position within Dawa and being criticized for their lack of Islamist credentials, these younger cadres found in Maliki a vehicle to senior roles in the state hierarchies.

By 2009, Maliki had become the symbol of the party, and the center of its new networks.[54] The 2009 provincial elections granted Maliki's loyalists positions across Iraq's governorates and across the state institutions. Loyal officers rose to top positions within the army, the police, and other security services. Loyal Dawa cadres became governors of governorates with large decision-making powers in security, recruitment of civil servants, and private investments. In the same year, Maliki's networking earned him an appointment as secretary general of the Dawa Party.[55]

With oil prices peaking as high as $140 per barrel, Maliki went on a government hiring spree, and employed members of the southern tribes in the police.[56] Maliki understood how to rebuild the bureaucracy—which was in shambles after Saddam's fall—to reward his allies.[57] He issued laws codifying public sector grades and systems of bonuses, and satisfied civil servants' ambitions for perks, including stable pension.[58]

Maliki now had a network of informal contacts reporting to his office, which circumvented the formal legal framework. While this personal network helped Iraq project the image of an efficient state, it was actually fueling personality politics at the expense of efficient institutions. Maliki has described his years as prime minister as being constantly on the phone, micromanaging his networks. He spent time compiling files of corruption and terrorism that could incriminate his rivals, and disbursing promotions and wealth to keep allies.

The more Maliki grew powerful, the more he grew suspicious. His Dawa comrades, especially those with a history of exile in the West, described Maliki as increasingly paranoid, and vulnerable to conspiracy theories that often misguided his decision-making.[59] Paranoia and impulsiveness eventually led him to take the wrong decisions.

Limited Networks

Gradually, the Dawa Party aborted its nascent national project and reentered its alliance with Iran-affiliated Iraqi Shia groups. In the run-up to the 2010 parliamentary elections, Maliki established the State of Law Coalition, running separately from other Shia parties, which included candidates with no history in the Dawa or Shia Islamism. "He wanted to cash in on . . . his hard work and grow more powerful than other Shia leaders," a former Iraqi lawmaker said.[60]

But Maliki's constituencies remained limited to the mid-Euphrates and the south. Sectarian stereotypes remained unaddressed. Dawa members, Maliki included, had rarely visited Sunni-majority areas, and kept nurturing grievances against those areas' middle classes, who they thought had enjoyed privileges during Saddam's reign.

They still viewed Sunni constituents with suspicion, seeing them as complicit in the rise of al-Qaeda, and ready to do anything to return to power. Only a few Sunni commanders, politicians, and tribal leaders were able to enter the Dawa Party and Maliki's circle of trust—often at the price of betraying their tribe, abusing the population of their hometown, and persecuting anti-government activists.

Nor did the Dawa Party provide a vision for dealing with Iraq's neighbors or other international actors after the United States exited the country in 2011.[61] As the civil war in Syria unfolded, Maliki antagonized the Gulf monarchies and Turkey, which increasingly forced him back into depending on Iran.

Eventually, the government failed to consolidate its fragile national credentials. In the 2010 parliamentary elections, the State of Law narrowly lost to Ayad Allawi's Iraqi National Movement (also known as the al-Iraqiya List), which had forged an alliance between secular groups, including both Shia and Sunnis. The loss inflamed Maliki's obsession with control. He deployed a network of informants and security agencies in the governorates to dismantle al-Iraqiya's networks. Police chiefs and governors were sacked, and tribal leaders were intimidated or detained as potential terrorists.

Maliki tried but failed to overcome the boundaries of Shia communal politics. Demonstrations in Sunni areas of Iraq and the arming of a Sunni-dominated opposition in neighboring Syria validated and amplified Maliki's suspicion that a Sunni regional plot was at play in Iraq to threaten him and Shia rule, which pushed him closer to Iran. He quickly returned Badr commanders to senior security roles in intelligence agencies and across the southern governorates. Iran-affiliated paramilitaries were allowed to move freely in Baghdad and send their members to fight in Syria, to prop up the regime of Bashar al-Assad.

Iran loyalists became the source of intelligence Maliki trusted the most, guiding his decisions on domestic and regional politics, from repression of demonstrations in Sunni areas to breaking ties with neighbors in the Gulf, which he suspected of funding Sunni extremism across Iraq and Syria.

Maliki also stepped up cooperation with Iranian Revolutionary Guard Corps commanders and former members of the Iran-based opposition, and supported clerics in Najaf against Ayatollah Ali al-Sistani, one of the most important clerics in Shia Islam. There was some irony in this new turn—Maliki had opposed Iran's influence on Iraq's Shia opposition during his youth, but now he suddenly became an ardent collaborator with Iran.

As the Islamic State swept across Iraq in 2014, it only served to further confirm the suspicions that Maliki had accumulated over a decade. For Maliki, Iran emerged as the only regional ally that the Shia of Iraq could rely on, and Shia-populated areas became the only viable ground for Dawa political support.[62]

The Story of the End: Haider al-Abadi

The summer of 2014 was a grisly and unnerving season in Iraq. Among numerous other atrocities, the Islamic State massacred more than a thousand Iraqi cadets, mostly Shia, at Camp Speicher in June. By the end of the summer, the extremist group controlled some 70 percent of Anbar governorate, and had advanced to the outskirts of Baghdad. Then, the American military intervened just three years after its vaunted withdrawal in 2011.

Maliki's premiership felt, to most, like a failure, and actors from multiple political sides became set against him holding the position for a third term. The West held Maliki accountable for the corruption and the sectarianism that enabled the Islamic State to rise. Shia forces he had undermined during his mandates were eager to see him departing. Those pro-Iranian Shia forces who were still on his side stopped defending his personal whims.

The near fall of Iraq to jihadist militants came as a shock to the Dawa Party. "We failed to build a state," said Fahad al-Shammari, a senior Dawa member I interviewed in 2015.[63] Dawa members with a more secular orientation saw the rise of the Islamic State as a warning that the time had come for Shia political Islam to move past ideology, forge cross-sectarian alliances, reform the state, and invest in balanced relations with Iraq's neighbors, regardless of their sect.[64] "The Dawa is a Shia and an Iraqi party. . . . It went too close to Iran, and we lost our independence," said a younger member of the Dawa, in an interview in 2015.[65] "The reform of the state ought to be at the top of the party's agenda," Shammari said.[66]

Other Dawa members had a different, and almost opposite, reading—a difference of opinion that would soon lead to a significant political divide. If anything, the rise of the Islamic State showed that Iraq owed its survival to Iran. Iraq's Shia parties' attempt at governing Iraq in cooperation with Kurdish and Sunni parties had failed. Such members viewed intra-Shia solidarity, in the model of Iran's revolutionary experience, as being the key to resilience. This thinking held that Baghdad would have fallen to the jihadists, had it not been for Sistani's fatwa calling the population to arms, Shia religious clerics' intervention in politics, the Iranian Revolutionary Guard Corps' support, and transnational Shia military mobilization.[67] Thus, Iraq could only exist if it was willing to be the vanguard of the Shia transnational movement.

Sadiq al-Rikabi summarized the evolution of the party's dilemma: "In 2004, we focused on how to succeed in Baghdad. In 2008, how to succeed in the provinces. By 2010, we were optimistic we could cross the sectarian boundaries. But the rise of [the Islamic State] gave us no other option but to stand with Iran."[68]

Thus, in July 2014, as Maliki's fortune and credibility were at their lowest point, the Dawa Party put Haider al-Abadi forward as its candidate for the prime minister. The nomination was an attempt at a fresh start—and to ensure that other Shia parties didn't capture the premiership. Abadi was a nonthreatening technocrat, and the Dawa Party also hoped he would be palatable to the West, since Iraq was desperate to have a partner in the fight against the Islamic State.

And yet, Maliki stubbornly held onto his chair, the prime minister's residency, and his affiliated security forces, pointing to the fact that his State of Law coalition had prevailed in the parliamentary elections earlier in April.[69] Finally, Sistani wrote a letter suggesting that a change of prime minister would be advisable to solve the political crisis. Only then did Maliki agree to step down. [70]

A Break from Ethno-Sectarianism?

In the spirit of a fresh start, Abadi spent his years as prime minister (2014–18) trying to leave behind ethno-sectarianism as well as personal power politics, and reinvest in the state. Ultimately, however, his enterprise was limited by a lack of solid allies among Shia forces, and by the legacy of his predecessors. Iraq's institutions were stacked with public servants who remained personally connected to Maliki. At the end of his term, Abadi's project remained incomplete, and divisions within the Dawa Party have since gradually led to its demise as the epicenter of Iraqi and Shia politics.

Abadi was of Maliki's generation of the Dawa Party, but with a different upbringing and history of party activism. Born in Karrada, a central district of Baghdad, Abadi left Iraq in 1976—not as a fugitive, as Maliki did, but as a student, to continue his studies in Manchester, UK. Abadi is a well-traveled member of Baghdad's urban middle class. This is in sharp contrast to Maliki, a southerner of provincial origins.

In another contrast with Maliki, Abadi worked as a professional in the West while also being a Dawa activist.[71] He speaks English fluently, and in the run-up to the invasion he had frequent meetings with Western government officials. A minister of communication in

Iraq's Governing Council (2004) and a lawmaker, Abadi operated as a member of the party's leadership.

With Abadi as prime minister, the Dawa began to rethink how Shia political Islam fit in a democratically elected state. During Jaafari and Maliki's terms, the party and its leaders had approached the state as a form of capital, whose positions could be traded with other political forces to consolidate leadership over the country.[72]

But now, the Dawa Party wanted to invest positively in reforming the state and its institutions. This goal meant that the state needed to retain (or regain) command and control over coercive agencies, including the Popular Mobilization Units (PMU) that had answered Sistani's call to fight the Islamic State. It also meant moving past Shia communal politics and forging cross-sectarian alliances; diversifying international relationships to include not just Iran but also non-Shia neighbors (such as Turkey and Saudi Arabia); and balancing its relations between Iran and the West. Parliamentary politics and alliances with other moderate Iraqi Shia parties would help build cross-sectarian alliances and move past personality politics.[73]

The Maliki–Abadi Divide

The Maliki–Abadi divide mirrored a deeper fissure among Iraq's Shia powerbrokers in religion, politics, and the security forces. As the struggle against the Islamic State unfolded, a feud grew over the succession to Sistani (who was already eighty-four years old in 2014). Some clerics argued that whoever succeeded Sistani should stay out of politics; others supported clerical guidance in politics.[74] Abadi and the Dawa moderates heavily relied on Sistani's teachings and affiliated clerics, who argued that clerics should refrain from openly intervening in politics.[75]

Maliki tapped into ideological differences to advance his cause. He supported rival clerics, and tried to tilt the succession toward scholars advocating for the *wilayat al-faqih* (the guardianship of the jurist)—a system, like Iran's, in which clerics have a much more direct role in state affairs. But Maliki's opposition to Abadi and his Dawa supporters was driven more by self-interest than by ideology. "Maliki does not believe in the wilayat al-faqih," a cleric in Karbala told me in 2015. "He only believes in his own interest."[76]

These rival clerics included Ishat al-Fayyad (a relative of a Dawa Party veteran, Hussein Shahrestani) and Mahmoud Shahroudi. "Much of the future of the course of Shia Islam depends on the succession to Ali Sistani," Mowaffak al-Rubaie, the senior Dawa cadre, told me from his house in the Kadhimiya neighborhood of Baghdad in 2015.[77]

Even as Abadi was prime minister, Maliki was the Dawa secretary general, and power within the Dawa Party remained split. Party members describe this as a moment of confusion and crisis. Abadi has even called it a "*fitna*," a concept used in Islamic tradition to describe sedition.[78]

Maliki and Abadi's differences couldn't be solved within the Dawa Party structures. In 2015, attempts to establish a committee for reconciliation between two party wings failed.[79]

During Abadi's term, the intra-Dawa Party split polarized Shia politics as a whole. In the lead-up to the 2018 elections, Iraq's Shia politics gathered around two clusters advocating for different visions of Shia political Islam. Ammar al-Hakim, who had a new movement that had splintered away from Badr, and the Sadrists supported Abadi and advocated for the integration of the Popular Mobilization Units, or PMU, into state control. (The PMU are armed groups that rose up to fight the Islamic State in 2014.) At the opposite end, the heirs of the parties and movements with a shared experience of fighting alongside Iran's Islamic Revolutionary Guard Corps (such as the Badr Corps—now the Badr Organization—Asa'ib Ahl al-Haq, and the Hezbollah Brigades) bet on transnational Shia ideology. These actors worked to establish the PMU as an institution independent from the state. "Iraq is a line of defense of Iran's revolutionary experience," said a member of Asa'ib Ahl al-Haq.[80] Even the PMU was divided according to these new poles. One branch, the Hashd al-Walay, followed Iranian supreme leader Ali Khamenei, while the other, the Hashd al-Marja'iyya, followed Sistani.

In the 2018 parliamentary elections, Abadi and Maliki competed in rival blocs: Abadi's Victory Alliance and Maliki's State of Law. Both blocs lost, and a compromise government was formed under Adil Abdul-Mahdi, with the backing of all the major Shia factions, including Muqtada al-Sadr's Sa'iroun coalition. This government proved short-lived; Sadr withdrew his backing for the government during the 2019 popular uprising in Iraq, known as the Tishreen movement.[81] Abdul-Mahdi resigned and brought to power another fleeting government under Mustafa al-Kadhimi. Early parliamentary elections in October 2021 delivered another victory for the Sadrists, but they were unable to secure enough votes in parliament to form a majority government. This led the Sadrists to withdraw from parliament, allowing Mohammed Shia al-Sudani—the current prime minister—to win the premiership under the aegis of the Coordination Framework, an alliance of non-Sadrist Shia political parties that includes Maliki's State of Law coalition as well as Abadi's miniscule Victory Alliance.[82]

In 2019, Maliki was once again elected secretary of the Dawa Party as the leadership council met in Karbala. Eight members of the leadership boycotted the meeting, criticizing the mechanism used to conduct the election and Maliki's previous commitment not to put himself forward as a candidate.[83] "The Dawa leadership council in Karbala reminded me of the Ba'ath Party Conference in 1979, when Saddam Hussein consolidated his grip on the party and annihilated all mechanisms of consultative decision-making," a member of the Dawa Party leadership told me. "That marked the end of the Ba'ath Party."[84]

Aftermath

There has not been a Dawa prime minister since Abadi. Today, while the Dawa Party has not officially disbanded and none of its notable members has officially left it, the Dawa leadership is geographically dispersed and ideologically split. Party veterans have left Iraq and retired to London. Cadres of Maliki's generation of activists—most of whom are in the party leadership—have either withdrawn from politics or are too disillusioned to attempt a reunion.[85] Younger cadres are sympathetic to a moderate and reformist view, but are still beholden to Maliki's power, position, and influence within the state. At various points, members of this younger generation have attempted to put themselves forward as candidates for the prime ministry. The Dawa Party headquarters in the Green Zone have been reduced to a place for social gatherings of minor party figures who are still in Iraq. Ultimately unable to shape a vision for their own Shia community and for the state in post-invasion politics, the Dawa Party is dying out.

And where it was once a mediator of Shia politics, the Dawa Party has become the symbol, if not the driver, of the divisions in Shia politics.

The divisions within the Dawa Party track a debate about Shia political Islam that remains unresolved. Should Shia political Islam coexist with non-religious political institutions, as envisioned in the 1992 "Declaration of the Shia of Iraq"? Or, alternatively, should Iraq follow Iran's revolutionary model of religious clerical guidance? Iraq's Shia political parties have battled with this dilemma since their time in exile, trying to carve out space for their own version of Iraqi Shia politics.

The outcome of this debate depends on a number of unpredict-able variables. One is the succession to the senior clerical leader-ship (known as the *marja'iyya*) of the ninety-two-year-old Sistani.

Another is the future of Iran's Islamic republic. These variables will be defining factors guiding the course of Iraqi Shia politics. In a similar way, the ability of the Iraqi Shia street to change the course of institutional politics remains an unknown but determinant variable. Moqtada al-Sadr's movement is the only one with a popular constituency that is able to challenge, through street mobilization, the ethno-sectarian system that allowed Maliki and his allies to prevail.

At the time of writing, Sadr has failed in such attempts. During the summer of 2022, his decision to withdraw Sadrist lawmakers from parliament in spite of having won more votes than Maliki in the parliamentary elections undermined Sadr's chances to select the prime minister. Sadr also lacked sufficient Iraqi political allies. Kurdish and Sunni politics remained anchored to the post-2003 system, dominated by communal concerns and powerful personalities. What's more, they continue to find in Maliki a helpful ally.

While the debate around Shia political Islam remains open, Iraqi politics is likely to unfold alongside some predictable patterns, shaped under the influence of former Dawa prime ministers. Any prime minister will have to deal with the legacy that fifteen years of Dawa politics has left. The ethno-sectarian system that dominated Iraq's post-invasion politics under Jaafari is likely to continue, guiding the process of selection of prime minister. The selection of Sudani is a testament to such resilience, since he is a compromise between personalities monopolizing representation of the Kurdish, Shia, and Sunni communities.

Personality politics—perhaps the heaviest legacy of Maliki's time in office—are also likely to dominate representation within each community, reducing space for political parties to play an active role. The prime minister, regardless of his or her affiliation, will have to balance between the rival trends of Shia politics, and relationships with Arab and non-Arab neighbors, the West, and the Global South. Yet, any prime minister will be caught in the Catch-22 of having to play politics according to the established rules, while struggling against these same rules in order to address the mounting governance challenges that Iraq faces.

Above all, the competition between competing strands of Shia politics—which three Dawa prime ministers could neither placate nor resolve—is more relevant than ever, and will continue to shape Iraq's political system.

Protest

7

Young Revolutionary Parties Are Still Iraq's Best Hope for Democracy

Taif Alkhudary

The Tishreen movement that began in October 2019 marks an unprecedented development in indigenous democratization in Iraq. The movement has revealed an alternative way of doing politics, based on a unitary Iraqi national identity, rather than the system of ethno-sectarian apportionment that has dominated Iraq since the U.S.-led invasion of 2003. However, fragmentation and ideological immaturity have prevented political parties that emerged from the Tishreen movement from acting effectively in political opposition. The incentives—and fears of violence— that have long shaped Iraqi politics have proven difficult to overcome. The revolutionaries' attempts to engage Iraqi institutions to create change still hold great promise—even if they have not yet delivered major success.

In the first issue of the revolutionary Iraqi newspaper *Tuk Tuk,* published in November 2019, journalist and long-time activist Ahmed Abd al-Hussein argued that, since 2003, the Iraqi people had been expected to endure all manner of indignities in support of a corrupt bargain. Poverty, the collapse of essential services, violent coercion, foreign interference—everything had to be tolerated simply to prop up the political system. The supposed alternative to that system was chaos, bloodshed, and, ultimately, the loss of democracy.

Abd al-Hussein compared this bargain to the concept of a "foolishness contract" in Islamic jurisprudence: an agreement that is so plainly indecent that it is invalid. The weeks preceding the first issue of *Tuk Tuk* had made this indecency clearer than ever. State security forces, under the watch of Prime Minister Adil Abdul-Mahdi, had killed more than a hundred peaceful protesters.[1] And the Iraqi revolutionaries in the street were, at last, rejecting the poisonous and deceptive trade-off. "The youth revolution came in October 2019 to try this foolish contract and to hold those who benefit from it and who implemented it to account," Abdul-Hussein wrote.[2]

In this report, I argue that the revolution that began in Iraq on October 1, 2019 represents an indigenous democratization movement that has deeply criticized the type of putative democracy that arose in Iraq after 2003. This revolution ruptured the political status quo and suggested an alternative way of doing politics based on a unitary Iraqi national identity. However, fragmentation and ideological immaturity have prevented protest parties that emerged in the aftermath of the revolution from engaging in effective opposition politics.

I begin by examining the problematic development of Iraq's system of ethno-sectarian apportionment, known as *muhassasa,* as a project for a post-Saddam democratic Iraq. Next, I turn to the Tishreen movement, arguing that the violence used by the dominant Shia parties against predominantly Shia demonstrators shattered what had been, until then, a common-sense belief perpetuated by the sectarian political elite that loyalty to sect- or ethnicity-based community was the only way to ensure protection in Iraq. In place of this social contract based on ethno-sectarian division, protesters called for a civil state based on a unitary Iraqi national identity. However, the political parties that emerged out of the Tishreen movement have been unable, so far, to propose a strong alternative vision for Iraq—a symptom of their splintering and ideological infancy.

I end my analysis by briefly drawing on Chantal Mouffe's notion of agonistic democracy to argue that the Tishreen movement can be seen as a counter-hegemonic movement, which—contrary to popular interpretations—does not totally reject institutions. Instead, it has engaged directly with institutions, with the aim of profoundly altering the power relations at the heart of Iraqi politics and creating a more egalitarian state.

This report's analysis is based on interviews with fifteen protesters and members of protest parties carried out between February 2020 and May 2022. Most interviewees are middle class, with eleven based in Baghdad, two in Nasiriyah, one in Diyala, and one in Najaf. (Unless otherwise noted, I have kept interviewees' identities anonymous to protect their security and enable the most forthright responses.) I supplemented these interviews with informal conversations and several research workshops held during the same period, as well as several visits to Baghdad's Tahrir Square—the central public space of the Tishreen movement—in December 2019. This report also draws heavily on the writing of journalists and protesters published in *Tuk Tuk* in November 2019—the newspaper forms one of the most cohesive and comprehensive records of the thoughts and aims of protesters.

Outsiders Design Iraq's "Democracy"

Long before the U.S.-led invasion of 2023, the vision for a democratic post-Saddam Hussein Iraq began to take shape through a series of conferences in Europe and the Middle East, convened by exiled Iraqi politicians and their Western allies in Europe and the Middle East. Among the most important of these conferences was one held in Salahaddin in October 1992 and attended by 234 exiled politicians.[3] It is there that the idea of "sectarian apportionment" (*al-muhassasa al-ta'ifia*) began to be developed. The meeting formed an executive committee, composed of twenty-five members of the opposition, and an advisory council. These positions were allocated according to meeting participants' perception of the proportion of each sect in the country.[4] In addition, the conference formed a tripartite presidential council composed of a Sunni, a Shia, and a Kurd.[5] Taken together, this collection of councils and committees was supposed to represent a provisional government-in-waiting.[6]

Later, in the run up to the 2003 invasion, a series of additional conferences were held in London. In July 2002, a conference held at the Imam Al-Khoei Foundation in New York produced a document titled "Declaration of the Shia of Iraq" with the stated aim to "elucidate a Shia perspective on the future of Iraq."[7] The document, which was signed by exiled Iraqi politicians who would later go on to hold various senior government positions, presented Iraqi society as being divided between Shia and Sunnis and saw Shia Islamist movements as the principal vehicle through which equality for the Shia population would be achieved. In December 2002, some 350 exiled politicians attended a conference called "To Save Iraq and Achieve Democracy" in the Hilton Metropole Hotel on Edgware Road in London.[8] While continuing to view Iraqi society as divided along ethno-sectarian lines, they reverted to the original principles agreed on in Salahaddin.

During the December 2002 conference, the political elite deployed several key narratives around democracy, rights, and victimhood to justify the imposition of ethno-sectarian apportionment. The conference's closing statement asserted that the opposition aimed "to save Iraq from dictatorship and to create a pluralist democratic regime, where rule is decided through the ballot box."[9] In this way, it emphasized the importance of elections for installing democracy in Iraq and giving Iraqis control over their political representatives. In addition, throughout the conference the political elite emphasized the non-sectarian nature of this proposed new regime— but while constantly falling back on the language of ethno-sectarian division. For example, Mohammed Baqir al-Hakim, then head of the Supreme Council for the Islamic Revolution in Iraq (the precursor to today's Islamic Supreme Council of Iraq), wrote in a statement read out during the conference that the "new Iraq" would be built "in the interest of the Iraqi people, not the interests of factions, sectarianism or groups and on the basis of respect for national, religious and ethnic specificities."[10] Crucially, by giving representatives of all of Iraq's ethnic groups and sects a say in governance, the exiled politicians presented the new system as the only one that could right the wrongs of the previous regime—which had persecuted the majority-Shia population and the Kurds—and provide reparations for the harm that had been done to those groups.[11]

After March 2003, all the occupying forces needed to implement this vision of democracy and to give it a veneer of legitimacy was the right group of political elites to act as representatives of the different ethnic groups and sects. To this end, the U.S.-led occupation created the Iraqi Governing Council in July 2003, a body of twenty-five opposition politicians and tribal leaders—selected according to their ethno-sectarian identities—which was supposed to give voice to Iraqis during the occupation. The system of ethno-sectarian division was then used to form the Iraqi Interim Government in June 2004 and in the five elections that followed. In the first of these elections, in January 2005, the politicians who had been empowered through international intervention leveraged their visibility from involvement in the first two post-2003 governing bodies to present themselves as the only viable political actors.[12] These elections marked the beginnings of the dominance of Iraqi politics by Shia Islamist parties.

Ethno-Sectarian Metrics for Legitimacy

In the new politics of Iraq, the concept of "representativeness" became a shorthand for legitimacy. For the exiled politicians and their allies, representativeness was equated with having so-called representatives of different sects and ethnic groups within the new government mechanisms they had set up. Moreover, the occupying forces defined representativeness, without any cross-country discussion about political identity.[13] The system of ethno-sectarian apportionment, then, worked to entrench ethnic and sectarian identities by making them the core organizing factors of politics. It took for granted that, as long as members of the elite from each group were included in government, then they would represent the interests of the ethnic group or sect to which they belonged. These developments marked the beginnings of the new status quo—a set of power relations on which politics in Iraq would be based after 2003. This status quo naturalized identity-based divisions as the only way that politics could be done. The alternative, according to those who endorsed the new system, was a return to dictatorship and the kind of oppression that the Shia and Kurds were subjected to under Saddam Hussein.

However, as some at the time already recognized, Iraq's sectarian power-sharing system could only lead to further instability and periodic outbursts of conflict.[14] Power-sharing systems such Iraq's habituate warring parties to violence by guaranteeing them a place at the governance table.[15] The new status quo of ethno-sectarian apportionment was directly responsible for the civil war that gripped Iraq from 2006 to 2008 and resulted in the deaths of hundreds of thousands of civilians.[16] The war was largely sparked by competition between rival elites who either wanted to increase their stake in, or to overthrow, the post-2003 political settlement.[17] Six years later, the rise of Islamic State was largely fueled by sectarian politics pursued by Nouri al-Maliki, which left a substantial number of Iraqis alienated and disenfranchised.[18] The fight against the Islamic State led to the rise of a network of rivaling paramilitary groups (known as the Popular Mobilization Units), which entered formal politics in 2018. These groups used their weapons, resources, and political influence to violently suppress any opposition to the system of ethno-sectarian apportionment and their place within it.

Further, the system of ethno-sectarian division introduced in 2003 has allowed establishment parties to capture the state and systematically rob Iraqis of public goods. After each election, political leaders engage in protracted negotiations using an informal set of rules to divide the country's ministries between themselves in governments of "national unity." This practice has allowed the dominant post-2003 parties to place civil servants loyal to them in key positions within ministries, to siphon off state resources to fund party activities.[19] This practice is so widespread that some estimates put the amount of money lost to corruption since 2003 at $150–300 billion.[20]

This corrupt system has deprived ordinary Iraqis of a functioning state, and denied even their most basic rights and service provisions. Thus, despite having the fifth-largest oil reserves in the world and making more than $60 billion in oil revenues in the first half of 2022 alone, the poverty rate in some areas of southern Iraq is over 50 percent.[21] What is more, government electricity provisions are practically nonexistent, with households sometimes subjected to total power outages at the peak of summer, when temperatures frequently exceed 120 degrees Fahrenheit in much of Iraq.[22] In addition, the youth unemployment rate is over 27 percent, a figure that continues to rise as thousands of young people enter the labor market every year. Yet young people have few opportunities for employment unless they are affiliated with one of the dominant post-2003 parties.[23]

This all adds up to massive discontent, especially among the youth. And all aspects of this discontent have their roots in the ethno-sectarian system that the 2003 occupation and its allies imposed.

The Revolution Reclaims Democracy

When protests first started on October 1, 2019, they were primarily demonstrations against the lack of services and unemployment. However, when the political elite responded to the protests with violent suppression, the protesters began to undertake a systematic critique of the post-2003 political system. In an article published in the first issue of *Tuk Tuk,* activist and journalist Ahmed al-Sheikh Majid wrote that part of the reason the protesters changed their focus was that it was dominant Shia parties who were attacking Shia protesters. As such, the notion that only loyalty to a sect could provide security—so crucial to the maintenance and legitimacy of the post-2003 political system—was revealed to be untrue. He wrote:

> A lot of the protesters also think that "the snipers were Iranian and not Iraqi.". . . This is a new change in awareness that goes beyond the story of similarities in sect that in the past resulted in total political surrender. The narrative of terrorism and fear of the ghost of the Ba'athists no longer affects the youth. This generation has entered into the battle of rights . . . in the face of the crisis faced by the Shia parties—both those close to, and those not affiliated, with Iran. This is the issue that is always justified through the narrative of the continued threat to the "sect's fortress."[24]

In previous protest movements in 2011 and 2015, Maliki had accused demonstrators of being Ba'athists and later of being affiliated with Islamic State, as a means of stoking sectarian fears, inciting violence against demonstrators, and ensuring that mass gatherings subsided. But Sheikh Majid wrote that attempts to resurrect this type of accusation against the 2019 protesters now rang especially hollow, since they were, themselves, largely from Shia areas.[25] Instead, the indiscriminate violence unleashed against the protesters made it crystal clear that sect and ethnicity didn't matter when someone mounted a direct challenge to the political system—the political elite were prepared to attack to protect their stakes in it. In this way, what had been made to seem like a common-sense justification for the current political order and the place of the political elite within it was ruptured. In turn, this allowed protesters to see that there could be other ways of doing politics and convinced them of the compelling need to transform the political system.

As the Tishreen protests continued, its critique of the political system developed into a broader grappling with the type of democracy installed in Iraq after 2003. Activists argued that, although elections had been held every four years, Iraqis were not granted the rights they had been promised when the new system was ushered in. As another protester explained, writing in *Tuk Tuk* under the pseudonym Abu al-Tuk Tuk, these deficiencies also became abundantly clear through the authorities' use of violence against demonstrators:

> Since 2003, the ruling authorities have impressed onto themselves all the accessories of . . . democracy. This began when they made the ballot box the iconic evidence of democracy, leading to limited freedom of expression [and the empowerment] of the bayonets of militias, which have covertly taken control of the streets and the media in most cases. The storm of [the Tishreen protests] blew away the authorities' makeup and their mask of democracy, the source of which is America. And here is the regime in its naked truth, just a domineering dictatorial regime, that borrows the worst of Saddam Hussein—oppression, torture and mass executions—and from their Iranian master, the worst of its characteristics—snipers, treachery, and a devilish edict.[26]

The writer seems to suggest that democracy in Iraq after 2003 has been little more than a facade maintained through the holding of elections. This facade was imposed through foreign interference and has seen the reemergence of oppression in new forms—as the use of violence to suppress the demonstrations showed. In this "democracy," Iraqis had only limited rights to freely express themselves.

A State of Parties

For the Tishreen protesters, another example of this facade of democracy is the way that the dominance of Islamic parties since 2003 has led to the creation of a "state of parties" that represents the interests of the ruling elite, as opposed to those of its citizens.[27] This idea was developed in another 2019 article in *Tuk Tuk* written by Mohammed al-Mahmoudi. Iraqi elections, he wrote, are simply a chance for Iraqis "to choose the face who rides in on the horse of sectarianism," in a farce ordained by the election law and sectarian elites. "What the youth are doing now is an attempt to return life to . . . democracy, which is clinically dead because of quotas, sectarianism, and corruption."[28]

Mahmoudi seems to suggest that all the key organs of a functioning democracy in Iraq have stopped working, but the system of ethno-sectarian apportionment is kept alive because it serves the interests of the political elite. The electoral commission and elections laws enable this status quo while sectarian elites rally for votes through convincing people that it is sectarianism that will protect them and their interests.

Demonstrators attempted to restore some form of functioning democracy to Iraq through their critique of sectarianism, the ethno-sectarian quota system, and corruption. Moreover, protesters argued that the political system implemented after 2003 has only allowed the development of a procedural form of democracy, which gives power to a variation of the same political elite and does not allow for substantive change. Thus, in another article by Abu al-Tuk Tuk, the author argued that "opiates like elections no longer have any effects on the body of the young Iraqi citizen."[29] In other words, elections are no longer tools through which the public can be numbed and made to accept that the established political system is the forum through which political change will come about.

A prominent activist from Nasiriyah provided a more detailed account of why he thought that the electoral system did not provide a real opportunity for Iraqis to influence decision making.

> Democracy is not a piece of paper and a ballot box. This is not correct at all. . . . In democracy there are basic conditions so that it can be called democracy—there needs to be electoral equality. It is not possible for an emerging party to compete with a party that carries arms outside of the confines of the state and has access to the resources of the state and even uses public funds [to fund itself]. . . . This is a sham, not democracy. What we see in Iraq is not a democracy. . . . These are cosmetic and not democratic elections.[30]

In this activist's view, Iraqi elections do not allow for real competition because nontraditional actors, lacking access to the coercive and material resources that the dominant post-2003 parties control, cannot compete.

The Need for Institutions

In different contexts all over the world, academics have criticized consociationalism for promoting a limited form of democracy, as it guarantees positions in government to elites and undermines the ability of citizens to use elections to hold their leaders accountable.[31] As a result, consociationalism promotes a form of "sectarian authoritarianism" that limits the competitiveness of elections by allowing a variation of the same politicians and parties to stay in power, and provides no real alternatives to the political status quo.[32]

The protesters recognized that in the context of Iraqi consociationalism, democracy was at best limited, and at worst, clinically dead. They expanded their key demands to include the government stepping down in favor of a temporary caretaker government made of independent actors who had never held political positions and had no political aspirations; a new elections law; and the implementation of the 2015 Political Parties Law, which has never been enforced.[33] Activists saw these measures as the only way to ensure that new and independent faces could enter parliament. They also insisted that, as the Political Parties Law requires, the establishment parties reveal their sources of funding and wanted to ban them from having armed wings. As another protester from Nasiriyah explained:

> The Political Parties Law is still ink on paper today, and is not implemented. Today, the factions that are around are the same factions that have arms and are registered with the Popular Mobilization Units as armed wings. The same factions run in elections. . . . One of the demands that we have [is] that any armed wing or militia should not have any role in the political process. Why? Because arms affect the safety of elections and [prevent] elections from being held in the correct way. Since 2018, big parties have entered in the name of Popular Mobilization Units, and . . . we rejected this process. We knew that [these parties' entrance] would take the country to . . . revolution, because they are one of the reasons for the destruction of this country. . . . [The Tishreen movement is] pushing with great force for a country of institutions, so that the Ministries of Defense and Interior are the only ones that have weapons.[34]

According to this view, the Popular Mobilization Units' involvement in elections has skewed the playing field, and opened the political arena to the possibility of heighted violence, like what occurred during the 2019 protests. The possibility of violence influences both who is willing to run for election and the outcome of elections. The protesters' call for a "country of institutions" is a bid to bring arms under the control of the state.

The desire to reconfigure institutions is also evident in protesters' demand for a presidential system in Iraq, which they argued would give them more control over politics by allowing citizens to directly vote for the president. (Currently, the Iraqi president is elected by parliament, and has limited powers.)

The interest in making politics channel popular opinion was also evident in the way that the demonstrators organized in protest squares. Protesters organized themselves into teams that undertook specific tasks, with logistics tents that would give out food to those sleeping in the squares, groups to clean protest spaces, and tents for the provision of legal services and medical assistance, among other initiatives.

But political decisions in the squares took a more horizontal form. A young protester from Baghdad explained how he organized both within Tahrir Square and with activists in protest squares in the south of the country:

> A long time after the protests began—maybe two or three months [into them]—the youth in my tent and I were able to put in place a mechanism where we brought together 650–850 tents. . . . We said, Don't worry, guys, we're not going to have a leader. We'll issue statements that represent this collective, and the statements will not be issued without a gathering of the representatives of the different tents. . . . A statement would only be issued with the agreement of everyone.[35]

This protester went on to explain that ensuring that everyone was involved in decision-making was necessary because in 2015 Sadrists co-opted the protest movement and protesters no longer trusted the idea of having leaders. This form of horizontal organizing allowed protesters to consider how social relations could be made more emancipatory, including through refashioning them in a way that gave individuals more control over decision-making.

"We Want a Country"

The desire to change institutions so that they better serve the Iraqi people is perhaps best exemplified by the key slogan of the 2019 protests: "We want a country." The slogan implicitly condemned the status quo—a state of parties and sects, in which a citizen's rights are only protected if they are affiliated with one of the dominant post-2003 parties and abide by those parties' sectarian vision of Iraq. Sheikh Majid articulated this critique clearly:

> The youth came out of the Shia areas and were faced with bullets against their bare chests, without any symbol apart from the Iraqi flag and the slogans "Here to take my rights" or "We want a country.". . . The protests were totally Iraqi, and they used nationalist slogans in the face of a non-nationalist government. . . . The authorities did nothing but respond to the dreams of the youth with bullets in their chests or heads.[36]

Sheikh Majid seems to suggest that protesters were not making demands based on their sect or ethnic group—even though most hailed from Shia areas. Rather, they made their claims as Iraqi citizens, who were then attacked by a government that did not believe in a unitary Iraqi identity. This shift away from sectarian politics and toward a "state of citizens" is further exemplified by protesters' rejection of foreign interference, and in particular of the United States as the source of "sham democracy" in Iraq, and of Iran as the state whose interests are being served by the post-2003 political parties.

But despite the use of the slogans emphasizing a unitary national identity, protesters did not necessarily try to erase all differences. Indeed, those brandishing nationalist symbols such as the Iraqi flag were accompanied by others painting murals with references to Western pop culture—in other words, the kind of iconography that many young protesters had grown up with since 2003, following the opening of Iraq after the sanctions period. At the same time, there were protesters who carried religious symbols such as images of Grand Ayatollah Ali al-Sistani and Shia imams.[37] And while some saw, in acts of charity in the protest squares, the spirit of the Shia rituals of Ashura and Arbaeen, others interpreted them as demonstrating that "civic duty" was not dead in Iraq.[38] Protesters used all these varied symbols as part of a critique of Islamist parties in Iraq and to call for a civil state (dawla madaniya).

This openness to difference worked to dispel the idea of homogenous ethno-sectarian communities on which the post-2003 political system was built. It demonstrated that there were different currents and beliefs within any ethnic- or sect-based community. In this way, protesters demanded that the social contract that had been imposed on them from the outside be rewritten on their terms and refashioned it in their image using cultural references relevant to them.

The Aftermath of Tishreen

The aftermath of the Tishreen movement saw the emergence of several new political parties affiliated with the demonstrations. Among the most significant of these parties was Emtidad, which emerged from the south of the country to win nine seats in the October 2021 elections. The name Emtidad means "extension" and is meant to signal the continuation of protests in a new and more institutionalized form. The other key party to emerge, also from the south, was the National House (al-Bayt al-Watani), a name meant to confront the divisive rhetoric of the "Shia House," a term that Iraqi politicians have long used to urge Shia solidarity. Both parties have tried to devise strategies to challenge the current political order. However, I argue that their vision for an alternative Iraq beyond the system of ethno-sectarian apportionment remains underdeveloped.

Both Emtidad and the National House have suggested that the alternative political framework they are developing is one based on unitary Iraqi nationalism. A member of Emtidad from Baghdad asserted that the party's ideology is underpinned by "loyalty to Iraq, not loyalty to muhassasa," as well as the notion that "we are Iraqis, and we belong to Iraq regardless of where we come from."[39] In speeches delivered by the party since entering parliament, it has also called for the creation of a "state of citizens."[40] This call has been echoed by the National House, as a party member from Nasiriyah explained:

> The National House emerged from Tishreen. During [those protests], we wanted to get rid of the political class and the muhassasa system, which destroyed Iraq. We believe that Iraqis should be one, and we believe in a united national identity. We reject the ethno-sectarian apportionment and suggested citizenship [mawatana]—the regime of citizenship—as an alternative to it. We think that the democratic process in Iraq is disfigured, and in order to fix this disfiguration, a political party with a national identity needs to emerge. This party should include all components of Iraq, from the north to the south. No party has done this before us.[41]

The party member seemed to suggest that the National House wanted to create an Iraqi state where citizens are represented as "Iraqis"—and not by their sect or ethnicity. Or, as several National House members have repeatedly said, they want to be represented based on their belonging to the "Iraqi *ummah*," or nation (using a term often associated with the expansive notion of an Islamic nation) as opposed to their membership in a particular sect or ethnic group.[42]

These party members envisage the needs of citizens being placed before the narrow interests of party, sect, or individual politicians. The National House is attempting to implement this vision, in part, by having a presence outside of Shia-majority areas in the south, and has branches in Mosul and Salahaddin.[43]

An Ideology Still in Its Infancy

However, the notion of a unitary Iraqi national identity remains underdeveloped. For example, when speaking about the party's success during the October 2021 elections, the same member of Emtidad suggested that those who voted for his party were looking to punish other parties. "We were not elected on the basis of a program; we don't know what our vision is," he said. "We don't know who we are."[44] As a consequence, the only vision for an alternative to the system of sectarian apportionment that Emtidad has so far been able to propose is a promise to stay out of the customary division of public resources between the dominant post-2003 parties, and act as an opposition. Thus, Emtidad has not necessarily been able to produce an alternative way of doing politics. Its strategy seems to be limited to an act of negation.

Similarly, several members of the National House have stated that the ideology that underpins their vision of a politics based on unitary Iraqi nationalism is "liberal democracy."[45] They were unable to elaborate on what this would mean in practice, apart from respecting the rights of others and implementing liberal economic policies. On the one hand, this demonstrates that the protesters' call to really transform power relations has been blunted by the realities of party politics. On the other, it shows how, by trying to move away from political language that described Iraq has comprising ethno-sectarian "components"—language that has been so vital to sustaining Iraq's post-2003 political system—these parties have gone to the other extreme, utilizing the language of liberal individualism. This shift attests to how the imaginations of this once radical movement have been neutralized and limited by Iraq's consociational regime, where the only type of citizen they can imagine in the state is a liberal individual. However, these limitations are perhaps unsurprising given that many of the demands that protesters made at the height of demonstrations were also based on individual rights claims.[46]

Furthermore, because the notion of unitary Iraqi national identity is in its infancy, it has become difficult for the new protest parties to come up with a common ideological basis on which to build alliances both among themselves and with other entities, such as trade unions and civil society. This lack of alliances has weakened their attempts to challenge or alter the political system. The lack of a clear ideological underpinning also means that party members and supporters are not loyal to the party itself and the ideas that it stands for, but rather to key figures within these parties. Protesters and party members interviewed for this report attributed these problems to the way that the dominant post-2003 parties—the Sadrists chief among them—have conditioned the electorate to vote for individual leaders as opposed to ideas or programs. This lack of a clear ideology underpinning the vision of a form of Iraqi politics based on unitary nationalism and civic principles has led to the rapid fracturing of the new protest parties, with many prominent members publicly resigning very soon after their formation.[47]

The fragmentation of protest parties is also the result of accusations that they have been co-opted by the dominant post-2003 parties. For example, some five hundred members left the National House, and its offices in Babil and Najaf closed, after the party's general secretary supported Mohammed al-Hadi—who ran as an independent alongside Sa'iroun in 2018—for the position of governor in Dhi Qar.[48] Hadi's initial promises that he would support the party's calls for reform have not materialized, and instead the party's general secretary, Hussein al-Ghorabi, was accused of corruption, leading to his temporary suspension.[49] Emtidad has experienced similar public resignations, with seventeen prominent members leaving the party in protest over the decision to vote for Mohammed al-Halbousi as speaker of parliament.[50] The divisions intensified when, months later, five sitting members of parliament left Emtidad, accusing its general secretary, Alaa al-Rikabi, of having sided with the Tripartite Alliance (a short-lived alliance between the Sadrists, the Kurdistan Democratic Party, Mohammed al-Halbousi's Progress Party, and a faction from Khamis al-Khanjar's party, Azm) and betraying the principles of the Tishreen movement.[51] At the time of writing, Rikabi had also been suspended.

The rapid disintegration of the protest parties demonstrates that, because power is so fractured within Iraq's power sharing system, it becomes difficult to take concrete political steps, such as forming allegiances or developing policy programs, as there is always a possibility of being accused of supporting a particular side. This has worked to prevent protest parties from developing broad-based alliances that might be capable of mounting a fatal challenge to the political status quo.

Agonistic Democracy

The broader significance of the history and arguments traced in this report can be illuminated by considering the analyses of political theorist Chantal Mouffe's work on what she calls "agonistic democracy."

Agonistic democracy, for Mouffe, includes movements that seek to overturn "hegemonic practices." She defines these as practices through which any particular order is given meaning.[52] These practices are always necessarily temporary and susceptible to change, and predicated on the exclusion of other possibilities. In this way, they always articulate a particular configuration of power relations. What is taken to be a natural order is in fact the result of "sedimented hegemonic practices."[53] The order does not represent a deeper external objectivity apart or removed from the practices that brought it into being. As a result, every order is susceptible to being challenged by counter-hegemonic practices.

According to Mouffe, then, radical politics consists of creating a different form of hegemony. Radical politics is a "'war of position" whose objective is not to create a society beyond hegemony, but is rather a process of radicalizing democracy—the construction of more democratic, more egalitarian institutions."[54] Mouffe argues that democratic politics does not consist of overcoming the "we/they" opposition, but rather changing the way that this opposition is configured.[55] In other words, democratic politics is not just an attempt to replace those in power, not merely a competition between elites, but also an attempt to question the dominant hegemony and to profoundly transform the relations of power with a view toward creating a different kind of politics. In addition, she suggests that maintaining difference is important because it allows for an assessment of power relations within a given group, as well as a "political analysis of the complex configuration of power forces that need to be challenged to create a more just and democratic society."[56]

Mouffe argues that, while activists who call for a total withdrawal from institutions might lead to calls for alternative ways of doing politics, this can only be the beginning of the struggle. It is important to engage with institutions to transform existing political hegemony. By doing so, leftist projects are able to provide real alternatives to citizens and to make institutions "vehicle[s] for the expression of popular demands."[57] If protest movements refuse to engage with traditional institutions, then the radical potential of such movements will be substantially weakened.

Mouffe's work is concerned with Western liberal democracies facing the rise of right-wing populist movements. While she does not consider consociational power-sharing regimes like the one implemented in Iraq after 2003, I find that her work is nevertheless useful in the Iraqi context. It sheds light on the way that the post-2003 political system in Iraq attempts to erase difference through creating an overly consensus-based model of democracy, which erases power relations by positing ethnic- and sect-based communities as externally bounded and homogenous entities. In addition, it allows for a reading of the Tishreen movement as a counter-hegemonic movement that refuses to accept the system of ethno-sectarian apportionment as the only way that politics can be done in Iraq. As one political activist put it, the revolution "saw a breaking of the divinity of certain parties and political figures. People were no longer scared to criticize politicians."[58] In other words, for the first time, the revolution allowed people to see that there was no *natural* order and that the politics and politicians that had been in place since 2003 could be challenged.

In addition, Mouffe's theory allows us to think about how, contrary to what some commentators have suggested, the Tishreen movement was not nihilistic or marked by a total rejection of institutions.[59] Rather, as this report has shown, the Tishreen movement has encompassed both a street struggle and organized political opposition, which has not only sought to replace those in power, but also to profoundly transform the power relations on which the system of ethno-sectarian apportionment is built and sustained. The Tishreen activists have done this through a direct engagement with institutions. This engagement is captured in the famous slogan "We want a country," which does not call for a withdrawal from institutions, but rather seeks to create a state that works for ordinary Iraqis. The engagement is also evident in calls to implement the Political Parties Law, rewrite the Elections Law, and shift to a presidential system, among other demands. The engagement with institutions is perhaps most profoundly evidenced by the creation of protest parties that have sought to provide real political alternatives to Iraqis and to channel their demands *through* and *against* traditional institutions, as a means of creating a more egalitarian and democratic state.

Tishreen's Ideals May Yet Prevail

Iraq's Tishreen movement represents an indigenous democratization movement. In its attempt to alter the power relations at the core of Iraq's system of ethno-sectarian apportionment, it engaged with Iraqi politics, in Mouffe's terminology, agonistically. Both the protesters and the new protest parties that emerged out of the Tishreen movement have sought to make a shift from a political system dominated by Islamist parties to one based on a form of unitary Iraqi national identity. Under this new system, constituents would be represented on the basis of their "Iraqiness"—in other words, simply by virtue of their citizenship—as opposed to their belonging to a particular sect or ethnicity. The revolution worked to rupture the notion that the system of ethno-sectarian apportionment is the only way that politics could be done in Iraq. However, the new protest parties have been unable to fully articulate their alternative vision for Iraq, beyond vague assertions of the Iraqi nation.

Nevertheless, the extent to which the Tishreen movement and the protest parties that came in its aftermath have threatened the dominant post-2003 status quo should not be underestimated. The threat to the system was evident in the unprecedented use of indiscriminate and excessive violence against protesters. More recently, the influence of the Tishreen movement could be seen in the way dominant Shia parties positioned themselves as championing substantive political reform during the government formation negotiations following the October 2021 elections. Three examples of this are worth mentioning at length.

One, Muqtada al-Sadr insisted on the formation of a "national majority" government and the breaking of the parliamentary norm of consensus, resulting in political stalemate and the breaking up of the "Shia House" due to Sadr's refusal, up until the new government was formed in October 2022, to include Maliki in the new government.

Two, the Victory Alliance, a grouping within the Coordination Framework (a coalition of pro-Iran political parties) attempted to create a rhetorical difference between "agreement" and "consensus," in an apparent attempt to appease Tishreen protesters. The Victory Alliance has argued that it does not want to participate in the division of public goods between parties according to the norms of a "consensus" government, but does want to be included in decision-making. But the new vocabulary hasn't translated into any meaningful changes to the system of ethno-sectarian apportionment.[60]

Three, and finally, both the Coordination Framework and its rival Tripartite Alliance sought to position, at least rhetorically, independent members of parliament and protest parties as the key groups for ending Iraq's ongoing political deadlock.[61]

These brief examples of the way that Shia parties have positioned themselves following the elections attest to their understanding that, in order to maintain relevance and draw legitimacy from the Tishreen movement, they need to appear to be pushing for the substantive institutional change that protests called for. They are indicating a willingness to move beyond identity-based politics through demands for a "majority government," as opposed to ethno-sectarian apportionment; "agreement" but not "consensus"; and appearing to endorse independent candidates. Ironically, while these gambits point to the influence of the Tishreen movement, they are also clear attempts to exploit the political moment created by the protests—exploitation that is made possible because protest parties' conception of what an alternative political system might look like remains underdeveloped.

Of course, it will not be the post-2003 parties who mount a decisive challenge to the power relations at the heart of Iraq's system of ethno-sectarian apportionment, or who create a more egalitarian order. These parties have captured and gutted the state, reducing it to a fiefdom for the promotion of their own interests.

To succeed in their challenge, the new protest parties need to be supported in strengthening their institutionalization. This might include working on developing the content of a unitary Iraqi identity so that these parties can cultivate loyalty, among their members, to the principles they stand for, as opposed to charismatic leaders. Such an ideological development will prove crucial to ensuring the parties' longevity. The new parties also need to work on building coalitions—with other parties, civil society, and unions. These coalitions are needed to be able to better decipher the complex power relations at play, and to explore all the different ways that these relations need to be challenged.

In addition, the parties must continue to create a foundation for themselves beyond those areas dominated by Shia parties, in order to put the notion of the "Iraqi ummah" into practice with nation-wide party membership. This, along with alliance-building, will also allow the parties to further incorporate different segments of Iraqi society, and ensure that voters' loyalty is to the party as opposed to individuals within it.

The ultimate test of the Tishreen movement's ideals, however, will be whether these parties survive the gravity and power of Iraq's system of ethno-sectarian apportionment, and overcome resistance to it over the current electoral cycle. If the parties are able to do this and can show that they are trustworthy vehicles through which change can be enacted, then perhaps they can—in the long term—profoundly alter the power relations on which the post-2003 political system is built. Then, finally, they might build a system that serves the interests of the Iraqi people, as Iraqis, and that can create the country that the people have long demanded.

Systemic Constraints

8

The Logic of Intra-Shia Violence in Iraq

Renad Mansour

Since 2003, violence has been an important tool in the competition for state power in Iraq. Elites have used "politically inclusive violence" to cement their public authority. The same logic has undergirded state-aligned violence against the Islamic State and the Tishreen movement—one a violent extremist group, the other a largely peaceful grassroots mass mobilization. Iraq's coercive apparatuses—including its various state forces and hybrid actors—are prone to fragmentation. But they coalesce to protect the political system when it is threatened, regardlss of the source of that threat. This analysis implies that, while it may be possible to keep the Iraqi system from its worst violent excesses, it is unlikely that Shia armed groups can be integrated into the state in the near future.

In the late hours of the evening of November 7, 2021, an explosive-laden drone hit the residence of Iraqi prime minister Mustafa al-Kadhimi. The assassination attempt injured several security guards but left Kadhimi unhurt. As details of the attack came out, it became clear that the strike was not a genuine attempt on the life of the prime minister, but instead a message. Armed networks linked to the Popular Mobilization Units (PMU)—a government umbrella organization of paramilitary groups—had been deployed in response to the October 2021 elections in which the PMU's political wing, the Fatah Alliance, had lost considerable seats to its Shia rival, the Sadrist movement. In response, Fatah had sent protesters to occupy part of Baghdad's fortified Green Zone, a fortified area in the city center which houses government offices and international representations. Security forces clashed with protesters, several of whom were killed. This violence set the stage for the assassination attempt, which the Kadhimi administration blamed on PMU factions—although the attackers have yet to be identified.[1]

The government formation process following the October 2021 election was the most violent since regime change in 2003. Beyond the strike on the prime minister's residence, it included attacks on political party offices and tit-for-tat assassinations in southern Iraq.

But this violence followed a logic built into the post-2003 Iraqi state. Since 2003, violence has been an important tool in the competition for state power. It has been a key to the elite's public authority. If a side has not won enough votes and suffers a loss in political capital, it can still lean on its access to arms and coercive capital—the utility of violence—to keep its seat at the negotiating table.

The post-2003 Iraqi state has been based on an elite bargain between the opposition Shia Islamist and Kurdish nationalist groups. Iraq's new leaders, many of whom were returning to Baghdad for the first time in decades, had a specific vision for how violence would fit into the new political system. Their priority was to prevent another military strongman like Saddam Hussein from emerging again. In addition, private access to arms could ensure that the new leadership acquired and maintained state power. As such, they refused to completely integrate their forces into government structures, whether Shia armed groups into the central government or the Kurdish pesh-merga fighting forces into the Kurdistan Regional Government.

This type of politically inclusive violence in the new Iraq has been designed to serve two primary functions: to negotiate politi-cal power and to protect the consensus-based political settlement against internal and external threats. Such politically inclusive vio-lence is different from violence that goes against the system, such as insurgencies and groups like the Islamic State. It is also different from a civil war, because it still seeks to maintain the elite bargain. Perpetrators of politically inclusive violence have instead used it to keep the elite's place in the system.

A Bloody Logic

This report focuses on the emergence of armed Shia Islamist factions following 2003. These groups had long histories dating back to the origins of the opposition against Ba'athist Iraq. The simplest way to categorize them is to go back to two Shia networks: the Mohammad Baqir al-Hakim network, which began in the 1980s and was close to the Islamic Republic of Iran, and the Mohammad Sadiq al-Sadr network, which emerged in the 1990s inside Saddam's Iraq. Both these networks would become key players in building the new Iraqi system after Saddam.

The key Shia group not linked to these networks was the Islamic Dawa Party, which was often historically opposed to developing its own militia. However, when Dawa leader Nouri al-Maliki became Iraqi prime minister in 2006, he realized that his power in the state required him to have direct access to arms. In lieu of a strong militia, he took personal control over parts of the government, including the Counter Terrorism Service (CTS) and other parts of the army, which became known as *jaysh al-Maliki*—Maliki's army.

In the post-2003 order, the role of armed groups was normalized into the process of state competition. Shia Islamist factions in every contested transfer or shift of governing power have resorted to this violence, which is not intended to overthrow or weaken the state, but rather, to secure a faction's share within it. However, it took some time for this logic to solidify and the new system to crystalize.

Muqtada al-Sadr's insurgency against the Iraqi government, which started in 2004 and resulted in a civil war, challenged this logic. The Sadrists were the main group excluded from the political system drawn up by the Iraqi opposition and its American backers. Their exclusion led to the civil war, which ended in 2008 with Sadrist defeat. Since then, the Sadrists have been included in the state and have therefore not resorted to violence. Despite the many predictions over the years that Iraq is again heading toward civil war, such a conflict has never materialized: a majority of the violence has been *part* of the system, and not against it.

Ultimately, following the 2021 vote, violence as a political tool for power worked. Sadr's attempt to build a majoritarian government that excluded parts of Fatah failed. Instead, Fatah stayed in government and eventually played a leading role in the emergence of the next prime minister, Mohammed Shia al-Sudani.

Violence meant that the ruling elite could be more powerful than the government. A few weeks after the October 2021 Iraqi national election, I was in Baghdad's Al-Zaqura Palace, a government building, for a meeting with the senior advisors to Kadhimi (prime minister at the time). As we discussed the latest developments, a group of demonstrators from the PMU thronged outside to protest the election result. They occupied parts of the Green Zone without government permission.

As our meeting in the palace began, the noise from outside made it difficult to hear or speak, agitating the prime minister's advisors. They closed the windows, but the noise went through. We laughed at the irony: they were the government. They wished they could just remove the protesters who were occupying a crucial part of the city. But they knew that they couldn't. They were powerless. We just had to speak louder in our meeting.

The moment symbolized the reality of state power in post-2003 Iraq. I was sitting in a remarkable palace built by the Ba'ath Party in 1975 to show off power. But on that day, the government's most senior officials struggled to conduct meetings. Power was no longer only vested in the concrete walls of the palace. Instead, it was also with those armed protesters outside.

Politically Inclusive Violence

During the government formation process in 2021, the Sadrists sought to use their electoral victory to move against the consensus-based system that had governed Iraq since 2003. They formed a tripartite alliance with the Kurdistan Democratic Party (KDP) and unified Sunni bloc (Siyada) to form a "majority government," which called for the unprecedented exclusion of major Shia elite figures—namely, former prime minister Nouri al-Maliki and parts of the Fatah Alliance. This move was a direct provocation against the post-2003 political settlement, and it invoked responses in various sectors, including violence. Fatah's networks of violence—including vanguard groups loosely linked to the PMU—were deployed against the members of the tripartite alliance. Erbil, the capital of Iraqi Kurdistan, became the soft spot for numerous rocket attacks linked to resistance militia groups. Siyada leader Mohammad al-Halbousi's house was attacked by groups from this network.

Facing the prospect of exclusion, Fatah and its networks used violence to maintain the consensus that governed Iraq after every election, and their place in it. In other words, it was politically inclusive violence, understood as part of the distribution of power within the state. Scholar Clionadh Raleigh and her coauthors argue in a 2022 paper in the *Review of International Studies* that "in states with high levels of ethnic inclusion, if representatives of large or wealthy communities fail to acquire a due share of ministerial positions, higher levels of political violence are expected."[2] Fatah was under threat of losing its due share, and as such, had to leverage its coercive capital—its capacity to force its will, with violence if necessary. This process is part of a "competitive clientelism," Raleigh and coauthors write, in which "groups and their elite representatives use political *violence against the state* and each other to secure access to authority, positions, and proximity to the leader."[3]

This report looks specifically at Shia armed groups as a case study to understand the relationship between violence and the post-2003 Iraqi state. But the same logic applies across the board, including, for example, to the KDP peshmerga and the rival Patriotic Union of Kurdistan peshmerga. Rather than an anomaly against the state, the proliferation of armed groups loyal to political parties and not the Iraqi government was built into the design of the new state.

Politically inclusive violence does not aim to bring down the system or provoke a civil war. In contrast, Sadr's majoritarian push following the October 2021 election initially went against the logic of the consensus-based system. His attempt to exclude Maliki and parts of the PMU risked the outbreak of violence outside the confines of politically inclusive violence as armed Shia networks threatened escalation through the use of inclusive violence—from protests to assassination attempts. However, in 2022, Sadr ultimately backed down when he was faced with an altercation—unlike in 2006, when he launched an insurgency against the system. He did not take violence to the next step. On August 29, when he sent his protesters to invade the Green Zone, he immediately withdrew as soon as the death toll exceeded thirty. Over the years, the parameters of violence within the system had become clear, and the system had crystalized its ability to constrain civil war.

The Historical Origins of Shia Armed Groups

When the Islamic State conquered Mosul in June 2014, Grand Ayatollah Ali al-Sistani issued a religious edict (*wajib al-kifae fatwa*) calling for men to enlist in state security forces to defend Iraqi territory. Answering his call, Iraqis rose up. But they were not signing up with the government's failed armed forces. Instead, most new recruits were joining the newly formed PMU (known in Arabic as al-Hashd al-Sha'abi). Only a few days after the edict, Prime Minister Maliki drew on Sistani's call for recruitment to issue an executive order that created the PMU commission—a legal body for the PMU directly under the Prime Minister's Office.

Far from new, Maliki was gathering and legitimizing a group of preexisting militias that were part of the post-2003 Iraqi system. The original seven groups of militias included the Badr Organization, Asa'ib Ahl al-Haq, Kata'eb Hezbollah, Kata'eb Sayyid al-Shuhada', Harakat Hezbollah al-Nujaba, Kata'eb al-Imam Ali, and Kata'eb Jund al-Imam.[4] Maliki had even, on occasion, referred to this loose network as a "popular mobilization," which deployed against "Ba'athists" and "insurgents" to bring down protests and unrest in Sunni areas as well as in Syria, where some of these groups supported the regime of Bashar al-Assad in the civil war that erupted in 2011. These groups had strong relations with Iran, which became a major patron of Maliki's second term (2010–14). The other major Shia militia, Muqtada al-Sadr's Peace Brigades (Saraya al-Salam), remobilized and also joined the PMU. As such, the PMU has been a fluid network deeply embedded in the Iraqi state, and integral to how violence has been deployed in the post-2003 political system. How the PMU operated in the security, political, economic, and general social space reveals the type of organization it truly is.

The origins of these PMU networks reach back to before 2003, to two Shia networks: the Mohammad Baqir al-Hakim network and the Mohammad Sadiq al-Sadr network.

The example of the Hakim network offers a case study in how violence was mobilized as part of political competition in post-2003 Iraq. Stemming back to the early 1980s, Mohammad Baqir al-Hakim established the Supreme Council for the Islamic Revolution of Iraq (SCIRI) in Iran, where he spent over two decades in exile. SCIRI formed its own armed wing, known as the Badr Corps (Faylaq Badr). The General Command of the Iranian Armed Forces paid around $20 million per year to Badr to pay salaries and purchase weapons, food, vehicles, and equipment.[5] According to Iraqi sociologist Faleh Abdul Jabar, "Despite SCIRI's talk of the Badr Army as an Iraqi organization, the force was under Iranian command. The commander of the force was an Iranian colonel."[6]

Badr's key power brokers were Hadi al-Ameri, its chief of staff; and Abu Mahdi al-Muhandis, its assistant commander. In the 1990s, Badr was an underground militant force with bases throughout Iraq. Its southern axis was on the Iran–Iraq border between al-Ahwaz, in Iran, and al-Huwaiza, an Iraqi marsh area in the Maysan governorate. Its middle axis was on the border between Dahlaran and Muthana governorate. Its Baghdad axis was in the Bakhtaran area between Baghdad, Wasit, and Diyala. Its northern axis was in Sulaimani.

Despite Ameri's institutional superiority in the organization, Muhandis was a key network broker. The two competed for influence in Iraq. Muhandis managed to gain a stronger role in managing the underground networks in the four axes, while Ameri handled more of the centralized administrative affairs.

Smaller groups also existed at the time. For example, Kadhim "Abu Zeinab" al-Khalesi commanded Badr's fifth brigade (the al-Mustafa Brigade) inside Iraq. However, he was also connected to the underground Dawa Party and Sadrist networks that were not allies of Badr. In 1991, he formed the Islamic Movement in Iraq and its armed wing, Kata'eb Jund al-Imam, to reach out to these non-Badr Iraqis in the south. In this way, Khalesi was simultaneously in the Badr network, but also a key network broker across the opposition.

Negotiating with Violence after 2003

Following the U.S.-led invasion, Badr moved some 10,000 fighters into Iraq and established itself along the eastern governorates bordering Iran, from Diyala to Wasit, where it had its main axes.[7] But Badr became more than a military force. As Ameri took control—due to his close relationship with SCIRI leader, Hakim, who was close to the Americans—he used Badr as a vehicle for SCIRI political negotiation.

In 2004, following a Coalition Provisional Authority (CPA) order called for the dissolution of militias. Rather than causing the militias to disappear, the CPA's order actually presented an opportunity for Badr to compete for political power inside the government. The Badr Corps rebranded itself as the Badr Organization. From 2005 to 2008, it sent its members into the Ministry of Interior (although some merged into the Iraqi security forces). Many joined the Iraqi Federal Police. Taking control of large parts of the ministry, Badr now had its own minister, deputies, and directors general. The goal was to acquire state power through gaining influence over the crucial ministry. As was the case for all parties in the new Iraq, those who were sent into the ministry answered to the Badr leadership, and not necessarily to their superiors in the ministry or the wider government.

Eventually, the other ruling elite—the Kurdish and Shia parties—recognized how Badr and ISCI had gained power in the Ministry of Interior. They then entered this competition, sending their representatives to become senior officials in the ministry. Andrew Rathmal, a former advisor to the ministry, writes that the plan "to retain in place powerful Daawa, Badr and Kurdish (KDP) deputies" rested on an underlying idea:

> By appointing a relatively weak minister and giving him three key deputies who were powerful players in their parties/militias, the intention of the governing alliance was to

ensure that the [Ministry of Interior] could not become the armed wing of any one party. The intent was for each of the key parties to ensure that they could make use of the patronage and coercive assets available to them via the ministry, but also to ensure that their rivals did not become too powerful.[8]

Despite the pretense of integrating into the Ministry of Interior, Badr did not give up its private access to arms. Instead, it maintained tens of thousands of fighters outside the ministry. Retaining these fighters allowed the party to remain powerful, and to compete for power. Badr also maintained its relationship with other parts of the historic Hakim network. For instance, Muhandis had long ago split to form Kata'eb Hezbollah. Kata'eb Hezbollah did not play Iraqi government institutional politics, and it rejected the U.S. occupation. Despite this split, however, Muhandis remained a key broker in the Iran-aligned networks and worked closely to provide Badr with leverage when needed.

Access to arms gave Badr crucial capital in the negotiation for the state.[9] For instance, when Maliki needed support to fight off the Sadrist insurgency during the civil war—he was, at the time, a weak compromise prime minister—he turned to Badr. Ameri deployed his fighters to support Maliki, who eventually won the Battle of Basra in 2008. In return, Maliki awarded Ameri and Badr with state positions. Ameri eventually became minister of transportation, and Badr officials would continue to lead the Ministry of Interior. Maliki even made Ameri the military governor of Diyala (al-masoul al-amani) in 2014.

Ameri's access to violence led to his successful rise in the Iraqi state. This example reveals the nature of the state as designed after 2003. Violence became an important bargaining chip that helped the new ruling elite compete for government institutions and gain state power.

Violence to Protect the System

Violence in post-2003 Iraq has also had to protect the consociational power-sharing system from internal and external threats. The move to stop Sadr's majority government bid was an example of how this violence can be deployed to defend the system. Having performed well in the elections, one member of the elite bargain—Sadr—saw an opportunity to exclude others, and as such, change the nature of the system from consensus to exclusionary. However, the PMU networks that had lost some political capital from the vote could still resort to violence, which was what they did to protect Fatah and Maliki's place in the system, as well as the consensus nature of the state.

The Islamic State represented an external threat to the post-2003 system. Its insurgency conquered one-third of the country. The PMU fought alongside divisions in the Iraqi army, Ministry of Interior units, the CTS, Kurdish peshmerga, and local tribal mobilization units in the governorates of Anbar, Salahaddin, Nineveh, Diyala, and Kirkuk. The response saw the institutionalization of several militias in Iraq, as Maliki (then the prime minister) put them into the National Security Council under the Prime Minister's Office (PMO). This institutionalization strengthened the system and its ability to defend itself.

Other threats to the system came from inside. The October 2019 Tishreen movement, which erupted in Baghdad and much of the southern governorates, did not call for the end of a specific leader or party, but rather for the end of the system. In response, the agents of violence that protect the system collectively responded by killing more than six hundred protesters and wounding tens of thousands. It was a system response that included Ministry of Interior armed groups such as the anti-riot police, the National Intelligence Cell, SWAT, and PMO armed groups, such as the PMU and CTS. Violence that underlined the elite bargain was designed to maintain it.

It is strange indeed to consider, but in a certain sense the Islamic State insurgency and the October 2019 revolution are in the same category of threats. The Islamic State is a violent challenge against the Iraqi state from the fringes of society. In contrast, Tishreen is a major, grassroots, predominantly nonviolent movement from within the Shia society in Baghdad and southern Iraq. But these two phenomena do have a key similarity: they both push for structural change to the post-2003 system and, as such, both are met with violent resistance from the forces created to protect that system. The responses to both the Islamic State and the Tishreen movement reveal the connectivity of agents of violence to the Iraqi state network. The violence against protesters showed that, even as Iraq's coercive apparatuses—including the PMO, the Ministries of Interior and Communication, and even Iraq's judiciary—are prone to fragmentation, they coalesce to protect the political system when it is faced with existential threats.[10] In short, understanding the network—rather than looking at state-versus-nonstate, or formal-versus-informal spaces—provides a more realistic explanation as to how the PMU has been able to serve as a coercive agent in the post-2003 Iraqi state.

Rethinking the Nature of Violence

Each time violence flares up from Shia armed groups in Iraq, the usual coterie of analysts predict an imminent civil war.[11] However, the country has not seen an internal Shia war since 2008. But that has not meant there has not been intra-Shia violence. In the most recent iteration, both Fatah's protests and the Sadrists' protests against the 2021 election and government formation process led to violence and even deaths, sparking the most recent predictions of impending civil war.[12] But a civil war never erupted. Instead, the elite bargain underlining the system has created violence that is designed to be politically inclusive. In the post-2003 system, each Shia party can use its coercive capital to contest for state power, but is less able to use it against the state.

And indeed, instead of fighting the state, the Shia Islamist parties have developed their coercive capital to defend the system. The formation of the PMU is testament to this fact. In 2014, as the Islamic State took over large swathes of Iraqi territory, the different groupings that historically made up the Shia military networks all came together to form a response to the threat. Years later, when the threat came from inside, as Iraqi youth—many of them Shia—called for revolution, these groups again came together with the state to protect the system. At this point, the PMU was deeply embedded into the Iraqi state, under the National Security Council.

Many international policymakers working to stabilize Iraq have focused on security sector reform. Guided by a neo-Weberian understanding of the monopoly over legitimate violence, their efforts have tried to integrate the historic networks of Shia armed groups into the government. The United States and other international organizations, such as the European Union and NATO, have worked in Baghdad attempting to integrate the PMU armed groups in a unified Iraqi government command structure. None of these attempts have succeeded, because they have run counter to the logic of the post-2003 Iraqi state.

Policy interventions should be designed with the understanding of the state outlined in this report. Integrating Shia armed groups into the government will not work, because it would require changing the very nature of the system. Instead, given how the system has solidified, policy should focus on holding to account the system, to keep it from its worst excesses, as Iraq's ruling elite lean more on coercive capital to defend the state against an increasingly disillusioned population.

9

Iraq's Sectarian Relapse: Lessons of the "Shia House"

Thanassis Cambanis

Many Iraqis say they are tired of sectarianism and desire a national politics of common interests. The Tishreen movement that began in 2019 seemed to open a promising new chapter of trans-sectarian vision in Iraq. Nonetheless, sectarian and identity politics continue to dominate Iraq through institutional advantage, communal ties, and the effective use of violence. In the political crisis of 2021–22, an alliance of Shia parties doubled down on such strategies in a sobering rebuke of the trans-sectarian spirit—a "sectarian relapse." Still, Iraqis are increasingly organizing along political and ideological lines rather than ethno-sectarian, and the next phase will pose a serious and welcome test for sectarianism in Iraq.

After the U.S. invasion and the collapse of Saddam Hussein's regime in 2003, Iraqi politics coalesced around the identity groupings of the exile opposition: Shia Arabs, Sunni Arabs, Kurds, and smaller minority groups. As factions competed for power during the following two decades, rivals in each community never even tried to distinguish themselves by politics or ideology. Nor did any significant faction successfully reach across identity divides to recruit leaders or constituencies from other communities.

Iraqis have repeatedly tried to challenge sectarian modes of power, but sectarian factions have successfully defended a system in which identity trumps all other axes of political affiliation. What's good for sectarian factions is not the same as what's good for a population that lives in mixed communities whose security and livelihoods depend on national stability. The persistent sectarianism of Iraq's political factions contrasts with the apparent preferences of many Iraqis, perhaps a plurality, who want effective services and security on a national, not communal basis.

If so many Iraqis are tired of sectarianism and identity-based politics, and yearn for better governance, how has sectarian and ethnic factionalism so completely swallowed ideological and programmatic politics?

The factions with the most resources after 2003 found ethnosectarianism the easiest route to power. In the ensuing decades these factions have defeated increasingly sophisticated challenges to the ethno-sectarian system, aided by an electorate whose fears often, justifiably, have an ethno-sectarian character: armed groups often threaten Iraqis on the basis of their identity, and factions distribute resources on a community basis.

Sectarian and ethnic parties dominate for three primary reasons: their use of violence, structural advantages in the political system they built, and their continuing appeal with a significant share of the population who seek protection from persistent extremist attacks from sectarian groups such as the Islamic State.

In this chapter, I first tour the post-Saddam Hussein political history to demonstrate that many schools of anti-sectarian and non-sectarian politics have competed against sectarian factions for power, but have failed to make serious inroads. Then, I look in detail at the most recent episode in which sectarian politics was enforced, the 2022 confrontation in which the Shia Islamist factions in the Coordination Framework overturned a trans-sectarian grand bargain and imposed the logic of each sect for itself. I characterize this imposition of identity politics as a "sectarian relapse." Finally, I venture some possible explanations for the political success of reductive sectarian disciplining.

The Sectarian Paradigm

Iraq's sectarian relapse is all the more striking and puzzling in light of the widespread frustration with identity-group politics and factions that profess no discernible political or ideological program.

Political factionalism, based on sectarian and ethnic identity, has successfully dominated Iraqi politics and the distribution of power, despite the widely expressed popular contempt for sectarianism. Identity politics, sectarian or ethnic, have emerged as a dominant norm, crowding out programmatic politics based on ideology, policy, or more plastic group affiliations.[1]

The desire to reduce or minimize sectarianism, however defined, does not remove it as a factor. Today, there is a struggle between Iraqis who want to marginalize sectarianism, or remove its sting, and those who find sectarianism the ideal tool to mobilize followers and mete out violence. That struggle is perhaps more visible than before because the anti-sectarians have gained strength. As a result, there is now a viable nationalist narrative, which holds that after the rise of the Islamic State, Iraqis of all identities banded together and sacrificed their lives to liberate the mostly Sunni Arab areas conquered by the extremist group. According to the nationalist, anti-sectarian narrative, the government of Haider al-Abadi (prime minister 2014–18) and then the Tishreen protest movement represented a widespread yearning for a coherent state and better governance. Abadi briefly won accolades from Iraqis who wanted the state to work on behalf of citizens rather than for a cartel of sectarian factions. One of the main slogans of the Tishreen movement was "We want a nation."

The sectarian counternarrative, perhaps cynically but with some truth, holds that even when Iraqis are done with sectarianism, sectarianism is not done with them. Groups like the Islamic State kill and displace on sectarian (and sometimes ethnic) grounds. While sectarian leaders might seek to erase nuance and complexity, they draw on genuine wells of affinity and fellowship that, for example, unite Shia around common rituals and clerical teachings, or make it hard for Kurds to fully disavow the pull of *kurdayeti* ("Kurdishness"), or which in today's Iraq require Sunni Arabs who seek the trust of mixed company to preemptively disavow the Islamic State.

In times of sectarian strife like the 2006 sectarian war, the later years of Nouri al-Maliki's premiership, and the rise of the Islamic State, sectarian identity and loyalty are—tautologically but nevertheless truly—the first although not the only markers of whom to trust. As the quick overview of Iraq's last half century suggests, identity politics in Iraq form as much in reaction to genuine outside threats, like the genocidal campaigns of Saddam and the Islamic State, as they do in response to communal solidarity and the machinations of identity demagogues within communities. Even the protest parties that won seats in parliament in the October 2021 elections mobilized within communal lines. In the drama of 2021–22, the Shia parties banded together to impose sectarian discipline on Iraq; but during that crisis, every faction in Iraqi politics, including movements representing Kurds, Sunnis, and smaller identity groups, operated in the illiberal, ethno-sectarian paradigm—each group claimed members from only one identity group, and none of the factions possessed even a trace of internal democracy or transparent decision-making.

The terms themselves serve as important signals. In the early years of Iraq's transition from Saddam to a post-U.S. occupation political order, the ambitious returned exile Ahmed Chalabi used the term Shia House to describe an inchoate coalition of Shia factions, including his own Iraqi National Congress.

Since then, the term's use waxed and waned. In 2005, a grand alliance of Shia factions campaigned as the United Iraqi Alliance, but some politicians in the grouping referred to it as the Shia House. Influential cleric Grand Ayatollah Ali al-Sistani denied that he supported the coalition, but did not stop it from using his image in its campaign.

During various periods of conflict with his rivals, Muqtada al-Sadr invoked the Shia House as an ordering concept, suggesting in 2018 that, in Iraqi political negotiations, the Shia had to sort out their competition first, before engaging with parties from other sects.

In 2021, Shia politicians made explicit the Shia-first formula that had hitherto been implicit. As in Lebanon, leaders in Iraq followed the sectarian ordering of top government positions, without such an order anywhere being written in law. A new way of selecting the prime minister was proposed by Qais Khazali, an important Shia factional head and militia leader who represents an Iraqi nationalist constituency as well as a maximalist strain close to Iran's Islamic Revolutionary Guard Corps. Instead of negotiations between competing Shia blocs, *all* Shia blocs would have to come together and choose a consensus candidate.[2] Over time, Khazali and other Shia leaders—even those who disagreed with the proposal—began to refer to it as the Shia House. And while "Shia House" entered public discourse as a common term, the grouping's ethno-sectarian counterparts did not adopt similar formulations. Politicians spoke of "the Sunnis" and "the Kurds" as political groupings, but not of a Sunni House or Kurdish House— perhaps testifying to the enduring effect of early political formulations after Saddam's ouster from power.

Anti-sectarianism and Relapse

During the quarter century that Saddam Hussein dominated Iraqi politics, identity played an inescapable role in Iraqi life, although it was not the sole determinant of status and security. Saddam built his power on overlapping networks: familial, tribal, regional, and ideological.

The Ba'ath Party, in the abstract, transcended identity. In practice, Saddam's regime accorded special privileges to members of his clan, and, over time, proved especially advantageous to Sunni Arabs from tribes and communities that served Saddam's interests. The regime singled out Kurds and Shia Arabs for genocidal persecution, although it inflicted repression and violence on Iraqis from every identity group if they were perceived to oppose the regime.

Yet while Saddam's closest aides tended to come from his family, tribe, or region, his regime drew on support from loyalists from every community. So there was truth to the claim that Saddam's regime was not sectarian, or not solely sectarian, just as there was truth to the claim that Saddam targeted Kurds and Shia Arabs, on the basis of their identity.

Exile politics reflected the regime's ambiguous sectarianism. Groups like Chalabi's Iraqi National Congress and Iyad Allawi's Iraqi National Accord fashioned themselves as nationalist movements that happened to be led by non-sectarian Shia. (Allawi proved to be anti-sectarian over time, whereas Chalabi eventually embraced a sectarian role.) Kurdish exile groups tended to reflect the divisions within Kurdish politics. Meanwhile, groups like the Dawa Party and the Supreme Council for Islamic Revolution in Iraq defined themselves as Shia Islamist. Most of the exile groups worked together, united in their opposition to Saddam and their support for the U.S.-led invasion in 2003.

U.S. policy first embodied and then entrenched a lazy sectarianism. The U.S. military and then the occupation authority classified Iraqis first and foremost by identity group, rather than by any other affiliations or agendas.[3] The practice might have begun as a convenient shorthand rooted in ignorance, but also in prejudices shared by some Iraqis; but U.S. actions quickly elevated ethno-sectarianism to the prime organizing principle of politics and armed groups.

At the prompting of exiles who benefited from a sectarian power-sharing system, the U.S. occupation authority chose to allocate seats in the inchoate Iraqi government by sect and ethnicity, rather than by political party, social class, region, gender, or literally any other more complex formula.

The sectarianism of American occupiers and Iraqi exiles functioned as a self-fulfilling prophecy. American officials held power directly from 2003 to 2005, and continued to exercise outsize influence until the withdrawal of most U.S. troops in December 2011. Occupation officials inaccurately conflated Saddam, the Ba'ath Party, the Iraqi military, and Sunni Arabs—an essentialist recipe that guided poor policy decisions, in particular the choices to disband the military and to adopt Chalabi's vague but broad approach to de-Ba'athification.[4] Americans in the early period accorded privileges to Kurds, Shia Arabs, and small minority groups, while treating Sunni Arabs with suspicion. On a local level, U.S. military officers and provincial occupation officials formed transactional local alliances with more nuance.

By the time of the U.S. withdrawal in 2011, ethno-sectarianism had become simultaneously more entrenched and at the same time increasingly muddled. Every single significant militia and political faction had an ethnic or sectarian identity, and drew its members almost exclusively from a single community. At the same time, these formations assembled in ethno-sectarian terms held views about sectarianism and nationalism that were widely divergent, and frequently contradictory. Kurdish parties freely allied with all manner of federal Arab factions, and seemed to simultaneously advocate incompatible frameworks: federalism *and* nationalism, Kurdish autonomy *and* Kurdish independence. Sunni Arab communities spawned sectarian extremists like al-Qaeda and the Islamic State. But repentant Sunni Arab sectarians also formed the Sunni Awakening, which turned against *takfiri* ideology to ally with the United States and with the Baghdad government. There also emerged Sunni Arab nationalists and reformers. Shia factions included outright Islamists, hybrid Islamist-nationalists, and militia-factions distinguished by their views about territory, economic control, and security rather than any discernible differences on identity and policy.[5] Notably, despite major cleavages among Shia factions, all invoked nationalist rhetoric and all made efforts to partner with non-Shia factions, even though none made a convincing effort to recruit a trans-communal membership or serve a trans-communal constituency.

Ultimately, all Iraq's factions supported the status quo created by the Americans and exiles: a sectarian power-sharing system in which positions were allocated first by identity (Shia, Sunni, Kurd, and so on) and only secondarily by faction. Security and services, at the individual level, were always distributed by factions from the same identity group as their constituents.

Complex People, Rigid System

This sectarian power-sharing system preyed on the insecurity created by the U.S. invasion, which shattered the remaining institutions of state and then put in place policies that prevented the reemergence of coherent and effective state institutions.

In 2003, Iraqi communities were even more intertwined geographically than they are today. Different areas might have had predominant demographic groups, but neighborhoods and governorates were mosaics of ethnicity, sect, and class. Families, tribes, workplaces, and institutions were mixed—as they remain today. Kurds who were subjected to the Anfal campaign and Shia Arabs in the south who suffered the 1991 regime crackdown experienced Saddam's regime as heavily ethno-sectarian. Other Iraqis, especially those who enjoyed favorable transactional relationships with the regime, might have described Saddam's rule as authoritarian rather than sectarian. I do not mean to suggest that pre-2003 Iraq was a sect-blind utopia or melting pot—only that, for some Iraqis, ethno-sectarian identity was but one of many indicators of profession, politics, and status.

After 2003, raging identity violence reframed the lived experience of sectarianism for many Iraqis. Sunni takfiri groups targeted and murdered Shia communities with a degree of brutality that shocked Iraqis already steeped in the horrors of dictatorship and war. The takfiri groups (al-Qaeda, the Islamic State, and lesser-known formations) also made a point of disseminating propagandistic depictions of their violence, which had the effect of spreading the takfiri sectarian narrative. During the same period, Shia death squads invoked sectarian iconography while pursuing a revenge campaign against their (usually Sunni) enemies. Iraqis with fresh memories of genocidal campaigns against Kurds and Shia Arabs sought protection from a reprise of recent, painful history. Whether or not Iraqis individually aspired to live in homogenous enclaves—and many very vocally detested this turn of events—protection often came in the form of sectarian militias (a catch-all category that can aptly describe official as well as hybrid and nonstate armed groups in Iraq). Even official security institutions were formed out of a patchwork of sectarian agglomerations, with security institutions controlled at the ministerial or unit level by specific factions.[6]

Iraq's rigidly sectarian system seems to contradict the preferences of Iraq's pluralistic, diverse population. The system certainly operates at odds with the interests of Iraqis, who desperately need security, effective governance, and coherent state institutions in order to address a panoply of ongoing crises. How to make sense of this apparent divergence?

In the course of twenty years of reporting and research in Iraq, and more recently, through Century International's Shia Politics Working Group, I've seen irrefutable evidence that ethno-sectarian labels reveal almost nothing about values, governing programs, or preference—and that these labels, in Iraq, have proven especially sticky. (Our study of Shia Islamist politics documented the fuzzy malleability of both terms; the exercise would surely yield similar results with different specifics in a treatment of Kurdish politics or Sunni politics in Iraq.)

The persistence of sectarianism as an organizing principle for armed groups and political factions (usually one and the same) is all the more mysterious given the visible resistance to a sectarian political system from many quarters of Iraq. Many Iraqis, perhaps a plurality, perhaps a majority, have revealed a preference for a non-sectarian political system, through elections, protest movements, and high-risk affiliations with national causes like the war against the Islamic State. The sectarian system and its constituent parties grow ever more solid each time they successfully repel a challenge; I call these cycles "sectarian relapses," in which the ethno-sectarian system and its identity-first principles triumph over mass popular demands for governance based on rules and not on identity.

Elections and Protests Challenge Sectarianism

Iraqis have organized many challenges big and small to the sectarian system since 2003, most notably in elections, protest, and commitment to national struggles.

Prominent electoral challenges to the sectarian system have been part of Iraq's political scene since the first elections in 2005. Nationalist, trans-sectarian or anti-sectarian political parties contested the elections beginning in 2005. The American occupation authority positioned Iyad Allawi as its preferred ruler for Iraq: an exile and former Ba'athist but demonstrably a nationalist with a pluralistic, trans-sectarian base. Allawi served less than one year as prime minister, from June 2004 through May 2005, but finished in third place in the 2005 elections.

By 2010, Allawi's nationalist coalition won parliamentary elections, but when it came time to form a government, he was outmaneuvered by Nouri al-Maliki—a pattern of sectarian relapse through backroom negotiations that has been repeated in more recent Iraqi history. While Allawi's Iraqi National Accord has achieved the most success at the ballot box of any trans- or anti-sectarian political faction, many other leaders and factions have defined themselves in opposition to the sectarian system, including Adnan Pachachi, who eventually joined Allawi's list; the Iraqi Communist Party; and the protest parties that have campaigned under the banner of the Tishreen movement, following the anti-system October 2019 protests.

While it would overstate the case to describe Muqtada al-Sadr as an anti-sectarian leader, he and his movement have, since 2003, fashioned themselves as a homegrown, nationalist alternative to overly sectarian returning exiles. Until 2022, the Sadrists partook in the sectarian spoils and patronage system while simultaneously critiquing that system. Sadrist parliamentary election campaigns in 2018 and 2021 made a decidedly outsider critique of the sectarian system and ultimately precipitated the 2022 challenge to identity-first politics.

Protests have more radically challenged the sectarian system, gaining steam after the American troop withdrawal in 2011. Protest camps in Anbar governorate in 2012–13 included anti-sectarian critics, but became subsumed by Sunni sectarians. During the period of the Islamic State's ascendancy, anti-government protests were muted and sporadic.

Protests broke out every year from 2015 to 2018. Some cases, like the Sadrist takeover of parliament, tapped into popular anger but were part of an elite power struggle. Most of the protests, however, channeled popular rage at failed governance—most notably the protests in Basra in the summer of 2018 over lack of services and eventually, the poisoning of the city's water supply.

The largest protests began in October 2019 and ultimately led to the resignation of Prime Minister Adil Abdul-Mahdi. Those protests explicitly called for a new governing compact in Iraq, and featured reform movements from the north to the south. Notably, protests were absent from Sunni-majority areas, which were still reeling from the Islamic State war and possibly hesitant because of the history of insurgents operating under the cover of protest tents in Ramadi in 2012.[7] The protest movements defined themselves in nationalist and reformist terms. Protest movement membership reflected regional demographics, so movements were predominantly Shia Arab in the south; Kurdish in Kurdistan; and mixed in the Baghdad area.

External Threats Rally Solidarity

External threats have mobilized solidarity across communal lines, beginning with the U.S.-led invasion in 2003. Many Iraqis who disliked Saddam's rule still opposed the foreign war that brought regime change. Armed resistance to the American occupation sometimes had a nationalist flair, as when Sadr's Shia militia extended solidarity to Sunni resistance groups fighting the Americans in Fallujah in 2004.

Several Iraqi prime ministers had what I call "national moments," when they harnessed the widespread popular desire for state-building and service provision on a national, rather than communal, basis—essentially, for an Iraq that functioned like a modern state. Maliki initially consolidated power as a nationalist, taking power in 2006 and working with Sunni militias and the U.S. military to fight al-Qaeda (he turned against both in later years). And Maliki demonstrated a willingness to ignore sectarian bonds when he went to war against Sadr's Mahdi Army in 2008. However, Maliki's national moment proved chimeric; once secure in power, he and his closest advisers pursued policies with sharp sectarian overtones.

Iraq broadly experienced a deeply felt national moment in response to the rise of the Islamic State. Shocked by the group's extreme brutality, and reeling from the simultaneous collapse of so many Iraqi institutions (the military, the peshmerga, the police, the prime minister's office), Iraqis mobilized against an existential threat to all. Shia volunteers from the south fought and died far from home, in Anbar and Nineveh governorates, to liberate Sunnis and others from Islamic State rule. Fighting formations included all of Iraq's communities. Federal police, Ministry of Defense and Counter Terrorism Service troops avoided communal identifiers, but most of the other militias and paramilitaries in the fight grouped by identity. Most Popular Mobilization Unit (PMU) forces were Shia, although there were notable Sunni, Christian, and other PMU groups. All the forces that fought the Islamic State deployed where they were needed, regardless of communal identity.[8]

This grand multi-sectarian coalition raised the prospect that the Iraqi state could organize in a similar manner, serving a national interest that would bring sorely needed dividends to regular people, in the form of security, jobs, and predictability. But the national moment of the counter-Islamic State campaign never translated into a national revival of state institutions. Even at the peak moment of sympathy for nationalist ideas, when the coalition against the Islamic State was liberating Mosul, many Iraqis voiced a fear that nationalism would bring chauvinism—a recurring reason to mistrust a strong national government, cited by members of historically persecuted communities in Iraq.[9] Hints of the nationalist-chauvinist pairing were evident in federal Iraq's quick pushback against the September 2017 Kurdish independence referendum. Shia Arab factions had partnered closely with Kurds in exile and, since 2003, in Iraqi government. And in 2017, Iraq relied on the Kurdistan Regional Government (KRG) to host millions of Sunni Arabs displaced from Islamic State areas. Nonetheless, Haider al-Abadi's government struck hard against the idea of Kurdish independence, deploying troops to contested areas like Kirkuk, and taking away the de facto autonomy that the KRG had previously enjoyed to set its own border and international trade policies.

Elections, protests, solidarity in the face of external threats: all have challenged power and threatened the status quo. They might yet develop enough strength to change Iraq's political system. Until now, however, the guarantors of the sectarian power-sharing system have resorted to any means to smother dissent, including systematic abuse of state resources to persecute critics; kidnapping; and murder. The sustained and violent reaction of Iraqi factions invested in the system suggests it views anti-system and anti-sectarian movements as an existential threat; but the system's maximalist response to calls for reform has, for now, kept that system in place.

Enforcing Sectarianism: The Shia House

In the most consequential and recent enforcement of a sectarian order, a coalition of Shia factions in 2022 successfully insisted that each major ethno-sectarian grouping (Shia, Sunni, and Kurd) had to select its own leaders first, before the identity groups could negotiate with each other to form a government. This reversion to a post-2003 sectarian norm was in no way inevitable; leaders resorted to a sectarian order as the surest path to power for their factions.

Government formation in Iraq has been messy in every cycle since 2005, but the 2021–22 episode was exceptional, because of the viable proposal to end the consensus system and the very plausible risk of widespread violence. The 2021–22 political crisis pitted a trans-sectarian nationalist alliance (the Tripartite Alliance) against a revanchist and reactionary coalition of Shia factions (the Coordination Framework) that insisted that the Shia House—the collective of all Shia factions—come to a unified position before any Shia faction could make an alliance beyond the sect.

The Coordination Framework's success in this contest was a particular surprise because the massive protests of 2019 had shown that many Iraqis wanted change, and it seemed that the longing for a non-sectarian type of governance might finally triumph. But the Shia House factions beat back the threat, relying on three winning tactics: The first tactic was the use of violence to cow rivals. The second was to draw on the structural advantages they had accrued through corruption within two decades of unity governments. The third tactic was to appeal to Iraqis with the claim that the Shia House protected them from forces who would do them harm on the basis of their communal identity.

The story starts with the October 2021 elections. Muqtada al-Sadr won the most seats of any Shia faction. The rival Shia alliance unified all the factions that opposed Sadr, including many strong militias, former premier Nouri al-Maliki's State of Law alliance, and the Fatah Coalition. The United States preferred a government formed by Sadr; Iran preferred a government formed by Sadr's rivals. Sadr formed the Tripartite Alliance, a coalition with the Kurdish and Sunni leaders who had won the most votes in their communities: Masoud Barzani's Kurdistan Democratic Party (KDP) and speaker of parliament Mohammed al-Halbusi's Taqaddum Party.[10] The Tripartite Alliance wanted to form a majority government, which would exclude the State of Law and Fatah; if they succeeded, it would be the first time since Saddam that an Iraqi government would leave any major factions in opposition. The Shia anti-Sadr forces formalized their alliance and called themselves the Coordination Framework.[11]

The brewing face-off between the Tripartite Alliance and the Coordination Framework was a historic moment for modern Iraq. Despite his own checkered and occasionally overtly sectarian history, Sadr was now calling for an end to the era of unity governments that included every party—electoral winners and losers alike. As recently as 2020, Sadr had called for the Shia House to urgently get in order, at a time when his influence was ascendant, and he perhaps thought he could make himself the preeminent Shia leader. In the wake of the October 2021 parliamentary elections, however, Sadr proposed a majority government; those excluded from the government would form an opposition, as in most parliamentary systems. Sadr had changed strategy, and had assembled what briefly appeared to be a potent, potentially system-killing coalition, uniting the leading Shia, Sunni, and Kurdish parliamentary blocs. His Tripartite

Alliance threatened, at its roots, the sectarian arrangement that had ruled Iraq uninterrupted since the end of the formal U.S. occupation. "Fundamental changes in the country's power-sharing formula are being proposed that would sweep away the big-tent consensus arrangement that has governed Iraqi politics since regime change in 2003," Iraqi analyst Raad Alkadiri wrote when Sadr's negotiating position seemed at its zenith.[12]

The Coordination Framework parties, now threatened with a loss of revenue and legal cover, described a majority government in apocalyptic terms, as akin to a dictatorship. Although their main interest was—plainly—promoting the Shia House, they also framed their opposition to the Tripartite Alliance by appealing to the sectarian insecurities of every other group in Iraq. The Coordination Framework took the idea that Shia, Sunni, and Kurdish parties needed to stick together, and made it an iron principle. And the Coordination Framework supported this principle with maximalist threats and disruption.

Almost immediately after the October election results were tallied, the losing Shia factions in the Coordination Framework escalated their actions and rhetoric against Sadr and his Tripartite Alliance, and demanded that negotiations to form a government follow a sectarian path. Important leaders representing major political blocs, significant militias, or both joined the Shia House call, including Maliki, the former prime minister; Hadi al-Amiri, head of the Badr Organization; Ammar al-Hakim, the cleric heading the Hikma Movement who had previously positioned himself as a conciliator; Falih Alfayyadh; and Qais Khazali, from Asa'ib Ahl al-Haq.

The Coordination Framework's response was swift and violent, beginning with an apparent assassination attempt on Prime Minister Mustafa Kadhimi (an ally of Sadr) in November 2021.[13] Pro-Coordination Framework demonstrators massed near the Green Zone beginning in October 2021, even before the election results were certified. Rhetorically, the Coordination Framework began making a "sect-first" case that the Tripartite Alliance was upsetting an order of operations that protected communal rights (no matter that, in the previous decades, the Iraqi status quo had neither protected identity groups from violence nor effectively brought them services). Also in October, as the rival alliances took shape, Maliki, known for his sectarian policies and rhetoric, returned to a position of powerbroker as leader of the Coordination Framework. He referred to the Sadrist coalition's attempt to form a majority government as "regime change." Other members of the coalition dismissed the electoral results as outright fraud.

The Tripartite Alliance nevertheless succeeded in reelecting Halbusi as parliament speaker on January 9, 2022.[14] But the Coordination Framework was able to stop the next step necessary for the formation of a new government—the election (by parliament) of Iraq's largely ceremonial head of state, the president, which requires a supermajority.

The showdown continued unfolding over the better part of 2022. The Coordination Framework factions backed their position with the credible threat of violence, up to and including civil war. Shia faction leaders issued an endless stream of sectarian threats. Alfayyadh spoke of a conspiracy "to tear apart the Shia House." Maliki, Khazali, and others argued that Sadr's trans-sectarian coalition was a foreign plot to disenfranchise the Shia majority. Hakim's sectarian rhetoric was particularly significant, since he had previously styled himself as less sectarian than Maliki, Khazali, and the militia leaders. "The Shia nationalism, whose banner we have raised, and defended ardently, means first preventing division in our own house, preparing the way for opening to other dear demographic groups," Hakim said in a speech in February 2022.[15]

Month after month passed and all attempts to form a new government failed. Parliament sessions deadlocked, stalled, or failed to muster quorum. Threats escalated, with important politicians and militia leaders speculating in public about a violent showdown between Sadr and the Coalition Framework.

Sadr (who did not hold a formal office) announced that he would completely withdraw from electoral politics, and ordered all members of his parliamentary delegation to resign, in an inexplicable forfeit of his greatest political advantage. On June 12, the Sadrist members of parliament formally submitted their resignation.[16] Politicians with whom I spoke in Baghdad speculated that Sadr mistakenly believed that his Sunni and Kurdish allies would follow suit and resign as well, forcing a new election, but in fact what transpired was a windfall for the Coordination Framework and its sectarian-majoritarian Shia House strategy.[17]

Under Iraq's rules, the seats were filled by the next-best-performing candidates from the October 2021 election, which suddenly gave the Coordination Framework a supermajority. The Kurdish and Sunni partners in the Tripartite Alliance reoriented, abandoned their lofty nationalist rhetoric, and cut deals with the Coordination Framework.

By August, both sides of the Shia dispute were openly preparing for civil conflict. Sadr called for new elections. Militias from the Coordination Framework deployed fighters in Baghdad, including in the Green Zone. Sadrists mobilized as well. On August 29 and 30, Sadrists stormed government buildings in the Green Zone, sparking violent clashes with Coordination Framework fighters.[18] Mediation by outside figures, including senior Shia clerics, persuaded Sadr to call on his supporters to withdraw.

In the absence of Sadr and his allies, parliament—now dominated by the Coordination Framework—elected Abdul Latif Rashid, of the Patriotic Union of Kurdistan party, as president in October 2022.[19] Rashid then named Mohammed Shia al-Sudani, the Coordination Framework's favored candidate, as prime minister, and he formed his new government at the end of October.

Explaining the Coordination Framework's Success

The Coordination Framework's formula to fend off the threat of the Tripartite Alliance was clear enough: it capitalized on violence, structural advantages, and fear. Yet its success still came as some surprise to those who thought the Tishreen movement might have heralded a new political era for Iraq.

The government-formation crisis illustrates sectarian persistence and the patterns of Iraq's sectarian relapses, in which the sectarian system triumphs over a popular push for a less sectarian system. Sectarianism had never receded as a source of power and a means of organizing constituencies. For all its complexity, sectarianism has also remained a powerful driver of conflict and insecurity—not least in response to the deadly ur-sectarianism of the Islamic State and its predecessors.

The direct struggle within the Shia political spectrum in 2021–22 provided an almost too-pat coda to a multi-year study of the transformation of Shia Islamist politics in Iraq; but the power struggle was a natural outcome of a sectarian system that is anything but an organic expression of the political will of Iraq's body politic. The sectarian system has to enforce itself over Iraq's repeated and increasingly powerful efforts to shift toward a more national form of government. I believe this analysis would produce similar results if applied to other episodes of sectarian relapse involving Shia factions, and probably episodes involving Kurdish, Sunni, and other identity group factions.

Shia factions invoked the Shia House concept soon after Saddam's fall. Shia politicians worried about efforts to undermine democratic elections and majority rule, and propagated the idea that Shia factions, regardless of programmatic differences, should unify during a transition period to ensure that the Shia majority was able to secure its share of government power, and to secure the restoration of the previously trammeled right to worship freely.

In the ensuing decades, Shia factions have expediently cited an imperative to revert to negotiations within the Shia House during power struggles with Shia rivals. Sadr's maneuvering in 2020–21 suggests that for Iraq's competing political leaders, political sectarianism and anti-sectarianism are both secondary to the pursuit of power.[20]

The Coordination Framework's sectarian rhetoric carried the day because it argued that a political coalition that transcended a Shia base posed a sectarian danger to the Shia. The Coordination Framework "holds an uncompromising sectarian view of politics in which demographic majority is identical to political majority," wrote former Iraqi ambassador to the United States, Rend al-Rahim in April 2022, as the crisis was peaking. "They arouse sectarian passions by sowing fears that a divided Shia front will strip the community of what they deem are its hard-earned gains. They have used this narrative to fan fears of Shia disenfranchisement."[21] And in the end, an outright sectarian political ordering prevailed yet again.

However, the outcome of the 2021–22 crisis broke with post-2003 tradition in two important ways. First, in the 2021–22 political conflict, the sectarianism that had operated implicitly now emerged into the open. Second, the majoritarian sectarians of the Coordination Framework formed Iraq's first majority government since 2003. Previously, all governments had operated on a consensus basis, including representatives of every single faction. Now, for the first time, Iraq's government excluded the Sadrists, a major faction that had finished first in the 2021 elections and had amassed the largest bloc in parliament before Sadr ordered his followers to resign.

These new precedents augur both good and ill for Iraq. The creation of a majority government, rather than national unity government, opens the path for future majority governments that aspire to govern Iraq . The precedent of naming a prime minister over the direct objection of a major, popular political movement, means that in future cycles other coalitions that can muster the numbers in parliament can force through a prime minister who lacks consensus support. After the next elections, for instance, a trans-sectarian grouping like the Tripartite Alliance can argue that Iraq now accepts the principle of a majority government instead of a consensus government, because of the precedent the Coordination Framework established by naming Sudani as a prime minister.

This development is not without downside risks: a strong government, of course, can use its power to engage in corruption and misrule even worse than what Iraq already experiences. Less ambiguously, however, the sectarian inflection of the Shia House tactics makes it even harder for non-identity political factions or alliances to take root in the political system, no matter how widespread the desire among Iraqis for better rule.

The Persistence of Sectarianism

Brilliant analyses have enriched our understanding of sectarianism and made the lazy determinism of the pre-2003 era unthinkable—at least for analysts and scholars. Fanar Haddad has usefully forced a reckoning over the definition of sectarianism, and has proposed more nuanced terms for Iraqi leaders who deploy sect as just one among many axes of self-definition and political mobilization. Zahra Ali has carefully documented the non-sectarian manner in which Iraqis see themselves and their political system, addressing multiple layers of class, and other hierarchies. But the gap between good faith theorists and public rhetoric is striking. Well-meaning thinkers might properly eschew the simplistic reductionism of sect and explain contemporary Iraqi politics with concepts like Haddad's "sect-centricity," Ali's "politics of life" and death, and Maya Mikdashi's "sextarianism."[22]

But many Iraqi political actors, fighters, and citizens who shape their society habitually ascribe their loyalties, motives, or threats to sect. For all the laziness of the formulation, most Iraqis still use the shorthand of Shia, Sunni, and Kurd to refer to the major political groupings and areas of the country—even as they well know the mosaic of families, communities, governorates, and politics at all levels cannot be neatly distilled by these three imprecise and mismatched categories. Extremist takfiri movements like the Islamic State won significant support among Sunnis (in Iraq and worldwide) on a platform galvanized by genocidal campaigns against Shia Muslims, Christians, and Yezidis. Kurdish leaders sabotaged their own hard-won autonomy with a doomed, and polarizing independence referendum in 2017, despite hosting more than a million Arabs in the KRG region and purporting to represent millions more Kurds who live in federal (Arab-majority) Iraq. Some Shia factional leaders traffic in blatantly sectarian discourse and describe Iraqi politics in zero-sum terms as a contest for either Shia or Sunni supremacy, and many Shia fighters in both formal and less formal forces describe their motivation to fight in sectarian rather than national terms.

Observers of Iraq and the wider Middle East often see sectarianism as the product of primordial, atavistic conflicts between the country's diverse ethnic and religious groups, or as the product of external manipulation. But critical scholars and analysts have emphasized the extent to which Iraq's contemporary sectarian politics emerged from relatively recent historical developments.[23]

Faleh al-Jabar has argued that the suppression of the largely Shia but anti-sectarian Iraqi Communist Party under the Ba'ath, the exclusion of Shia from state patronage networks under Saddam, and the increasing targeting of Shia during the Iran–Iraq War gave that sect a fundamentally new political cohesiveness and sectarian orientation by the end of the 20th century.[24] Toby Dodge suggests that Iraqi politics writ large did not come to revolve around sect until after 2003, when "sectarian entrepreneurs" emerged to fill gaps opened by the absence of state services.[25] According to Jabar, the post-2003 apportionment and distribution of state resources along sectarian, clientelist lines generated widespread popular opposition to sectarian politics by the mid-2010s.[26] But despite this popular opposition, Toby Dodge and Renad Mansour argue, sectarian patronage networks have become deeply entrenched and continue to drive Iraqi politics, even as politicians now refrain from overtly sectarian rhetoric.[27]

In 2019, Haddad wrote that "excessive focus on 'sectarianism' and the politics of the Sunni–Shia divide serves to unduly overshadow the far more relevant divide between elites and people."[28] Just a few years later, after a particularly acute episode of sectarian relapse, Haddad's diagnosis remains as true as ever—the elites feast while the people starve—but also rings incomplete. The sectarian system, once again, has decimated the enemies that would reform it.

If Iraqis dislike the sectarian system, and if it serves them poorly, how has it managed to crowd out or squelch alternatives?

Iraqi factions seem to pursue power by any available strategy, alternating between sectarianism and nationalism based on short-term calculations. The same goes for foreign governments that have influenced political negotiations in Iraq. In the Shia House episode of 2021–22, for instance, Iran backed the Coordination Framework, and Iranian officials encouraged an outcome that would include all the Shia factions.[29] However, after the Sadrist withdrawal, the Iranians supported a majority government, albeit one controlled by Iran's closest allies. The United States, despite a policy that theoretically promotes national institutions and democratic political norms, has historically supported consensus governments—and has now evinced a willingness to work with the Sudani government. It isn't possible to understand the interventions of the United States and Iran as purely nationalist or purely sectarian; it is easier to understand the intervening powers as pursuing short-term security and economic interests with whichever available partner is most immediately amenable.

Quite simply, the militant Shia factions that triumphed after the 2021 Iraqi elections used ethno-sectarianism because it worked. It is possible to argue that some Shia factions are more sectarian than others. On the other hand, it's impossible to prove what the factional leaders actually believe—but it is possible to trace their rhetoric, their negotiating positions, and finally, the outcomes of negotiations (whether at the ballot box, in coalition talks, or in armed conflict). Every major faction, from every identity group, has, at one point or another since 2003, employed sectarian rhetoric. And these sectarian leaders have successfully enforced a sectarian code of politics, as well as a sectarian mode of organizing governments, despite a growing divergence from sectarian politics among the Iraqi electorate.

The leaders of the Shia House gambled and won, on the purported basis that they represent the unified interest of the Shia sect, and by arguing that they were enabling other identity groups to also protect their interests. But, in fact, the Shia House does not represent all Shia factions, and excludes the single most popular and powerful Shia faction, led by Muqtada al-Sadr. More pointedly, the Shia factions manifestly do not represent the interests of Shia Iraqis, many of whom don't define themselves by sect and, in any case, aspire to see Iraq governed differently and more effectively—on the basis of popular demands for services, state capacity, and national institution-building.

In the post-Saddam era, sectarian factions in Iraq have entrenched themselves in power but have delivered none of the benefits they have promised their constituents. And increasingly, Iraqis are organizing not along ethno-sectarian but political and ideological lines. This next phase will pose a serious and welcome test for sectarianism in Iraq.

Notes

Chapter 1

1. Frederic Volpi and Ewan Stein, "Islamism and the State after the Arab Uprisings: Between People Power and State Power," *Democratization,* 22, no. 2 (2015): 276–93; Shadi Hamid and William McCants, eds., *Rethinking Political Islam* (New York: Oxford University Press, 2017); Jillian Schwedler, "Conclusion: New Directions in the Study of Islamist Politics," in *Islamists and The Politics of The Arab Uprisings: Governance, Pluralisation and Contention,* ed. Hendrik Kraetzschmar and Paola Rivetti (Edinburgh: Edinburgh University Press, 2018), 359–74.

2. For example, see, "New Analysis of Shia Politics," POMEPS Studies 28, *Project on Middle East Political Science,* December 2017, https://pomeps.org/wp-content/uploads/2017/12/POMEPS_Studies_28_NewAnalysis_Web.pdf

3. See for example Sharon Otterman, "Iraq: Iraq's Governing Council," *Council on Foreign Relations,* February 2, 2005. https://www.cfr.org/backgrounder/iraq-iraqs-governing-council.

4. On the difficulties of defining Islamism see, Jillian Schwedler, "Why 'Islamism' Does Not Help Us Understand the Middle East," POMEPS Studies 17, Project on Middle East Political Science, March 2016, https://pomeps.org/wp-content/uploads/2016/03/POMEPS_Studies_17_Methods_Web.pdf; Joas Wagemaker, "Making Definitional Sense of Islamism," *Orient,* volume II (2021): 7–13.

5. Faleh Abdul Jabar, *The Shi'ite Movement in Iraq* (London: Saqi, 2003).

6. Ibid., 41–42.

7. Ibid., 41.

8. For an overview of sectarian relations in Saudi Arabia and Bahrain (and a counter-example of sorts from Kuwait) see Laurence Louer, "The State and Sectarian Identities in the Persian Gulf Monarchies: Bahrain, Saudi Arabia and Kuwait in Comparative Perspective," in *Sectarian Politics in The Persian Gulf,* ed. Lawrence Potter (London: Hurst, 2013), 117.

9. Abdul-Halim al-Ruhaimi, "Da'wa Islamic Party: Origins, Actors and Ideology," in *Ayatollahs, Sufis and Ideologues: State, Religion and Social Movements in Iraq,* ed. Faleh A. Jabar (London: Saqi, 2002), 149–61. Likewise, it has been argued that the Supreme Council for the Islamic Revolution in Iraq was far more universal in its discourse prior to the 1990s. See Joseph E. Kotinsly, "Brave New World Order: The Supreme Council for Islamic Revolution in Iraq and The Rise of Iraqi Shi'i Identity Politics," *Journal of the Middle East and Africa* 13, no.1 (2022): 49–65.

10. Jabar, *The Shi'ite Movement in Iraq,* 66.

11. Amatzia Baram, *Saddam Husayn and Islam, 1968–2003: Ba'thi Iraq From Secularism to Faith* (Baltimore: Johns Hopkins University Press, 2014), chapter 3.

12. On the disturbances of 1979, see Jabar, *The Shi'ite Movement in Iraq,* 228–31. On the disturbances of 1977, see Jabar, *The Shi'ite Movement in Iraq,* 208–15; Marion F. Sluglett and Peter Sluglett, *Iraq Since 1958: From Revolution to Dictatorship* (London: I.B. Tauris, 2001), 198–99.

13. Hanna Batatu, *The Old Social Classes and the Revolutionary Movements of Iraq: A Study of Iraq's Old Landed and Commercial Classes and of Its Communists,*

Ba'thists and Free Officers, (Princeton: Princeton University Press), 327–28; Peter Sluglett, *Britain in Iraq: Contriving King and Country, 1914–1932,* (New York: Columbia University Press, 2007), 103–5.

14. For details see Fanar Haddad, *Understanding 'Sectarianism': Sunni–Shia Relations in the Modern Arab World,* (London: Hurst, 2020), 271–74.

15. Jabar has a more detailed explanation encompassing five major drivers of Shia sect-centricity (or Shia agitation, as he terms it): underrepresentation, economic grievances, cultural encroachment, citizenship rights, and secularization. With the exception of the last one, these drivers fit into the broader categories of victimhood and entitlement. See Jabar, *The Shi'ite Movement in Iraq,* 67–71.

16. That resonance was evident in the elections of 2005, in which the combined Islamist-dominated Shia list (the United Iraqi Alliance) received 47 percent of the vote. For details regarding the elections of 2005, see the relevant pages of the Iraqi Independent High Electoral Commission, https://ihec.iq/.

17. This much was candidly admitted by former Sadrist parliamentarian and former deputy prime minister Baha' al-A'raji in 2016: "When we came to Iraq [in 2003], we were leaderships without a base... [we] would speak in a sectarian way in order to attract [followers] and create a base." See "Former Iraqi Deputy Prime Minister Mr. Bahaa Al-Araji - Exclusive Interview - Episode 4" (in Arabic), uploaded to the YouTube channel Alsumeria on July 8, 2016, http://www.youtube.com/watch?v=Gz6119ybGLU.

18. The term "the long 2003" is taken from Nida Alahmad, "The Iraqi State: Methodological and Theoretical Considerations," *LSE Middle East Centre Blog,* November 9, 2019, https://blogs.lse.ac.uk/mec/2019/11/14/the-iraqi-state-methodological-and-theoretical-considerations/. The period might be considered to end in 2008, or extend to 2010.

19. For the elections of 2005, see the relevant pages of the Iraqi Independent High Electoral Commission, https://ihec.iq/; Adam Carr's election archive, http://psephos.adam-carr.net/countries/i/iraq/iraqmapindex.shtml; and Toby Dodge, *Iraq: From War to a New Authoritarianism* (London: The International Institute for Strategic Studies, 2012), 44–48.

20. For the elections of 2010, see the relevant pages of the Iraqi Independent High Electoral Commission's website (ibid.); Carr's election archive (ibid.); Kenneth Katzman, "Iraq: Politics, Elections and Benchmarks," Congressional Research Service, March 1, 2011, 9–19, 25, https://www.everycrsreport.com/files/20110301_RS21968_755bf620139afe0896cb6b2d4d5a6fd6bc7d65a8.pdf; and "Iraq's Uncertain Future: Elections and Beyond," International Crisis Group, Middle East Report no. 94, 2010, https://www.crisisgroup.org/middle-east-north-africa/gulf-and-arabian-peninsula/iraq/iraq-s-uncertain-future-elections-and-beyond.

21. For the elections of 2014, see the relevant pages of the Iraqi Independent High Electoral Commission's website (ibid.); and Adam Carr's election archive (ibid.).

22. For the elections of 2018, see the relevant pages of the Iraqi Independent High Electoral Commission's website (ibid.); Adam Carr's election archive (ibid.); Renad Mansour and Christine van den Toorn, "The 2018 Iraqi Federal Elections: A Population in Transition?," LSE Middle East Centre, July 2018. http://eprints.lse. ac.uk/89698/7/MEC_Iraqi-elections_Report_2018.pdf.

23. For the 2021 elections, see the relevant pages of the Iraqi Independent High Electoral Commission's website, https://ihec.iq/wp-content/uploads/2022/01/قوائم-اسماء-المرشحين.pdf. Technically, the top performers were the "independents," who collectively received about 19 percent of the vote. However, their failure to unite into a single coalition, to say nothing of the questionable independence of many of the independents, means that they cannot be treated as a singular entity.

24. For more on these themes, see Fanar Haddad, "The Waning Relevance of the Sunni-Shia Divide," The Century Foundation, April 10, 2019, https://tcf.org/content/report/waning-relevance-sunni-shia-divide/.

25. For an analysis of the declaration, see Fanar Haddad, *Sectarianism in Iraq: Antagonistic Visions of Unity*, (London: Hurst, 2011), 148–50. For an English translation of the declaration, see "Declaration of the Shia of Iraq," al-bab.com, https://al-bab.com/documents-section/declaration-shia-iraq.

26. An extract of the interview, see Twitter user @Ahmed_I_R_A_Q, status, January 20, 2022, https://twitter.com/Ahmed_I_R_A_Q/status/148418413 5887372291. The reference to Muhammad Baqir al-Hakim (the head of what was then called the Supreme Council for the Islamic Revolution in Iraq) indicates that the interview was held sometime between regime change and Hakim's assassination on August 23, 2003.

27. "Did Islamists Win the Elections? Faeq Sheikh Ali Answers and Warns the Iraqi People of a New Big Game" (in Arabic), uploaded to the YouTube channel Utv on October 27, 2021, https://www.youtube.com/watch?v=hDriQYz38tU.

28. Commenting on the elections of 2005, a report by the International Crisis Group from 2006 states: "Even secular Shiites appear to have voted for the [Shia Islamist dominated] UIA rather than for the available alternatives.... In the words of a Western diplomat, they may well have voted 'against the hijacking of a historical opportunity for the Shiites.'" International Crisis Group, "The Next Iraqi War? Sectarianism and Civil Conflict," Middle East Report no. 52, February 27, 2006, 29, https://www.crisisgroup.org/middle-east-north-africa/gulf-and-arabian-peninsula/iraq/next-iraqi-war-sectarianism-and-civil-conflict. For more on the varying sect-coded perceptions towards the transformations of 2003 see Raad Alkadiri and Chris Toensing, "The Iraqi Governing Council's Sectarian Hue," The Middle East Research and Information Project, August 20, 2003, http://www.merip.org/mero/mero082003.

29. Al Ahad TV (@ahadtv), Twitter status, June 13, 2022. https://twitter.com/ahadtv/status/1536410842660495366?s=20&t=Tqw04f_Zw6ToOXAdG8u-Aw.

30. Friday sermon dated November 19, 2021, uploaded in a private video to YouTube on November 20, 2021.

31. For example, in the run-up to the invasion of Iraq, opposition factions agreed on the necessity of a democratic and pluralistic post-Saddam Iraq. See, "Text of the Closing Statement of the Iraqi Opposition Conference in London" (in Arabic), December 17, 2002, https://www.aljazeera.net/news/arabic/2002/12/17/ نص-البيان-الختامي-لمؤتمر-المعارضة.

32. When the author posed this question to an Islamist leader who requested anonymity, his response was that "we [Islamists] are religious and they [non-Islamists] are not." Besides that, he was unable to identify any legislative, ideational, or political difference between them. Islamist leader, interview, Baghdad, August 2021. For more on this theme see, Harith Hasan, "From Radical to Rentier Islamism: The Case of Iraq's Da'wa Party," Diwan: Carnegie Middle East Center, April 2016, https://carnegie-mec.org/2019/04/16/from-radical-to-rentier-islamism-case-of-iraq-s-dawa-party-pub-78887.

33. Shia-centric state-building refers to a broad position that, at its most basic, seeks to ensure that the central levers of the state are in Shia-centric hands and that Iraqi Shias remain the senior partner in Iraq's multi-communal framework. See Fanar Haddad, "Shia-Centric State Building and Sunni Rejection in Post-2003 Iraq," Carnegie Endowment for International Peace, January 7, 2016, https://carnegieendowment.org/2016/01/07/shia-centric-state-building-and-sunni-rejection-in-post-2003-iraq-pub-62408.

34. Faleh A. Jabar, "The Iraqi Protest Movement: From Identity Politics to Issue Politics," LSE Middle East Centre Paper Series no. 25, 2018, http://eprints.lse.ac.uk/88294/1/Faleh_Iraqi%20Protest%20Movement_Published_English.pdf; and Renad Mansour, "Protests Reveal Iraq's New Fault Line: The People vs. the Ruling Class," World Politics Review, July 20, 2018, https://www.worldpoliticsreview.com/articles/25161/protests-reveal-iraq-s-new-fault-line-the-people-vs-the-ruling-class.

35. Marsin Alshamary, "The Protestor Paradox: Why Do Anti-Islamist Activists Look toward Clerical Leadership?" Brookings Institute, April 2022, https://www.brookings.edu/wp-content/uploads/2022/04/FP_20220425_protestor_paradox_alshamary_v2.pdf. The report incisively observes that, in the context of contemporary Iraq, secularism is not so much about the separation of religion and state as it is about the separation of religion and politics. In other words, the references to secularism are calls for so called Islamists to be kept away from the levers of power.

36. Friday sermon, uploaded in a private video to YouTube on October 16, 2019.

37. Marsin Alshamary, "Iraqi Protestors Are Mostly Shiite. And This Identity Is Shaping How They Protest," The Washington Post, December 14, 2019, https://www.washingtonpost.com/politics/2019/12/14/iraqi-protesters-are-mostly-shiite-this-identity-is-shaping-how-they-protest/; Fanar Haddad, "Hip Hop, Poetry and Shia Iconography: How Tahrir Square Gave Birth to a New Iraq," Middle East Eye, December 09, 2019, https://www.middleeasteye.net/opinion/iraq-new-political-awareness-and-culture-have-been-formed.

38. Harith Hasan, "Iraqi Factions and the Question of Social Identity" (in Arabic), *An-Nahar al-Arabi,* February 5, 2022, https://www.annaharar.com/arabic/makalat/opinions/04022022012702978.

Chapter 2

1. Yasser Eljuboori (@YasserEljuboori), Twitter status update, September 25, 2019, https://twitter.com/YasserEljuboori/status/1176874596328497152.

2. Qassim Abdul-Zahra, "Iraqi Protestors Defy Curfew as Violence Leaves 33 Dead," Associated Press, October 3, 2019, https://apnews.com/article/shootings-ap-top-news-baghdad-middle-east-international-news-cff518843b1b4a5c-886bc431cc2fcdcb.

3. "We are faced with a choice between the state and the anti-state," he said. "Statement by Iraqi Prime Minister Adil Abdul-Mahdi" (in Arabic), uploaded to YouTube by Al-Ghad TV on October 4, 2019, https://www.youtube.com/watch?v=um72DWbyH0M.

4. "Iraqi Security and Humanitarian Monitor," Enabling Peace in Iraq Center, October 3, 2019, https://enablingpeace.org/ishm224/.

5. Renad Mansour, "The 'Hybrid Armed Actors' Paradox: A Necessary Compromise?," *War on the Rock,* January 21, 2021, https://warontherocks.com/2021/01/the-hybrid-armed-actors-paradox-a-necessary-compromise/. For a more detailed look at the concept of hybridity, see, "Hybrid Actors: Armed Groups and State Fragmentation in the Middle East," The Century Foundation, November 12, 2019, https://tcf.org/content/report/hybrid-actors/; and Renad Mansour and Thanassis Cambanis, "Look at the State, Not the Hybrid Actors," *Century International,* May 5, 2022, https://tcf.org/content/commentary/look-state-not-hybrid-actors/.

6. Michal Krzyzanowski, "Discursive Shifts in Ethno-Nationalist Politics: On Politicisation and Mediatisation of the 'Refugee Crisis' in Poland," University of Liverpool, 2020, https://core.ac.uk/download/pdf/131171083.pdf.

7. "*Kitab al-la-dawla* by Faleh Abdul Jabar: Prospects for the Iraqi Situation" (in Arabic), *Al-Araby Al-Jadeed,* December 26, 2019, https://www.alaraby.co.uk/"كتاب-اللادولة»-لفالح-عبد-الجبار-مآلات-الحالة-العراقية.

8. "The Current Protest in Iraq Are a Foundation Stone That Will Steer Iraqi Awareness toward Reclaiming Its Identity" (in Arabic), Swissinfo.ch, July 25, 2018, https://www.swissinfo.ch/ara/44276382/--التظاهرات-الحالية--سويسرا-في-مقيمون-عراقيون هي-ح-ج-ر-الأساس-الذي-سي-نق-ل-الو-عي-العراقي-باتجاه-استرجاع-هويته.

9. "Iraq in the Midst of the October Uprising" (in Arabic), Al Jazeera, October 8, 2019, https://www.aljazeera.net/blogs/2019/10/8/تشرين-انتفاضة-مهب-في-العراق.

10. "Young Iraq, Defenseless in the Face of the Anti-state" (in Arabic), *As-Safir,* October 22, 2019, https://assafirarabi.com/ar/27622/2019/10/22/اللادولة-وجه-في-أعزل-الشاب-العراق/.

11. "Iraq and the Choices of the Political Class: The State or the Anti-State" (in Arabic), Alhurra, January 28, 2020, https://www.alhurra.com/different-angle/2020/01/28/العراق-وخيارات-الطبقة-السياسية-اللادولة-اللادولة.

12. "Iraq: Struggle between the State and the Anti-state" (in Arabic), March 23, 2020, *Noon Post,* https://www.noonpost.com/content/36406.

13. "Iraq: Sovereignty of the Anti-state" (in Arabic), March 16, 2020, *Al-Araby Al-Jadeed,* https://www.alaraby.co.uk/العراق-سيادة-اللادولة.

14. "Iraq: Confrontation between the State and the Anti-state" (in Arabic), Al Jazeera, July 1, 2020, https://mubasher.aljazeera.net/blogs/2020/7/1/العراق-مواجهة-الدولة-واللا-دولة.

15. "Iraq: State of the Anti-state" (in Arabic), *Al-Arab,* August 25, 2020, https://alarab.co.uk/العراق-دولة-اللادولة.

16. Steven Nabil (@thestevennabil), Twitter status update, August 22, 2020, https://twitter.com/thestevennabil/status/1297297309810614272?s=20.

17. Osama Al-Nujaifi (@Osama_Alnujaifi), Twitter status update, August 23, 2020, https://twitter.com/Osama_Alnujaifi/status/1297638068980199428?s=20.

18. "Kadhimi: We Must Choose between the State and the Anti-state" (in Arabic), uploaded to YouTube by Samarra TV—News on August 30, 2020, https://www.youtube.com/watch?v=iSNXtarAK0c.

19. "Party Slogans in the Elections: In Search of the Lost State and Merging the Hashd with the Army" (in Arabic), *Sawt al-Iraq,* September 12, 2021, https://www.sotaliraq.com/2021/09/12/شعارات-الأحزاب-في-الانتخابات-البحث-عن/.

20. Munqith Dagher and Karl Kaltenthaler, "The Iraqi Opinion Thermometer," Center for Strategic and International Studies, May 2021, https://csis-website-prod.s3.amazonaws.com/s3fs-public/publication/210622_Dagher_Kaltenthaler_OpinionThermometer.pdf?8WoKdbu2WkpZBdUs_lXVZt253ptr3Rek.

21. "The Secretary General for Asa'ib Ahl al-Haq: The Choice of the Next Prime Minister Will Not Be Personalized," uploaded to YouTube by Dijla TV on October 2, 2021, https://www.youtube.com/watch?v=MI8w_M1qtKk.

22. Alaa Hataab (@alaahataab), Twitter status update, April 25, 2021, https://twitter.com/alaahataab/status/1386302096056651780.

23. Dagher and Kaltenthaler, "The Iraqi Opinion Thermometer."

24. Munqith Dagher, "Iraqi Public Opinion on the 2018 Parliamentary Elections," Center for Strategic and International Studies, March 28, 2018, https://csis-website-prod.s3.amazonaws.com/s3fs-public/event/180402_Iraq_Elections_Slides.pdf.

25. Juan Cole, "The Rise of Religious and Ethnic Mass Politics in Iraq," in *Religion and Nationalism in Iraq: A Comparative Perspective,* ed. David Little and David Swearer (Cambridge: Harvard University Press, 2006), 48–49.

26. Abbas Kadhim, *Reclaiming Iraq: The 1920 Revolution and the Founding of the Modern State* (Austin, TX: University of Texas Press, 2012), 149.

27. Ibid., 63–64.

28. Nakash, *The Shi'is of Iraq* (Princeton, NJ: Princeton University Press, 2018), 114.

29. Cole, "The Rise of Religious and Ethnic Mass Politics in Iraq," 50.

30. Nakash, *The Shi'is of Iraq,* 114–115.

31. Reidar Visser and Gareth Stansfield, eds., *An Iraq of Its Regions: Cornerstones of a Federal Democracy?* (New York: Columbia University Press, 2007), 30.

32. Fanar Haddad and Sajjad Rizvi, "Fitting Baghdad In," in *An Iraq of Its Regions: Cornerstones of a Federal Democracy?,* ed. Reidar Visser and Gareth Stansfield (New York: Columbia University Press, 2007), 53.

33. Ibid., 55.

34. Phebe Marr, "Kurds and Arabs, Sunnis and Shiites: Can an Iraqi Identity be Salvaged?," in Little and Swearer, *Religion and Nationalism in Iraq,* 68.

35. Haddad and Rizvi "Fitting Baghdad In," 69.

36. Joyce Wiley, *The Islamic Movement of Iraqi Shi'as,* (Boulder, CO: Lynne Rienner Publishers, 1991), 148.

37. Ibid., 144–45

38. Ibid., 144.

39. Semi-structured interviews with Dawa Party members between the ages of thirty and forty-five were conducted by the author between December 2021 and January 2022, including a remote focus group discussion with seven members on January 13, 2022. Interviewees made anonymity a condition of their participation, which I honored in order to encourage them to speak freely. Details about the time and location of individual interviews cited below have been removed to protect that anonymity.

40. Ibid.

41. Ibid.

42. Ibid.

43. Ibid.

44. Ibid.

45. Ibid.

Chapter 3

1. Samuel Helfont, *Compulsion in Religion,* vol. 1 (Oxford: Oxford University Press, 2018); and Abbas Kadhim, "The Hawza Under Siege," Boston University, 2013.

2. For a discussion of the religious endowment and its relation to Shia theology, see Haider Ala Hamoudi, "Engagements and Entanglements: The Contemporary Waqf and the Fragility of Shi'i Quietism," *The Journal of Law and Religion* 35, no. 2 (2020): 215–49.

3. Abbas Kadhim, "Forging A Third Way: Sistani's Marja'iyya between Quietism and Wilayat Al-Faqih," in *Iraq, Democracy and the Future of the Muslim World,* ed. Ali Paya and John Esposito (New York: Routledge, 2010), 69–73.

4. Mustafa al-Kadhimi, "Sistani Calls for 'Civil State' in Iraq," *Al-Monitor,* January 16, 2013, https://www.al-monitor.com/originals/2013/01/iraq-sistani-calls-civil-state.html.

5. Ismail Fajrie Alatas, *What Is Religious Authority?* (Princeton: Princeton University Press, 2021).

6. Marsin Alshamary, "Prophets and Priests: Religious Leaders and Protest in Iraq" (PhD Dissertation, MIT, 2020).

7. Juan R. I. Cole, Juan, "The Decline of Grand Ayatollah Sistani's Influence in 2006-2007," *Die Friedens-Warte* 82 no. 2–3 (2007): 67–83.

8. Activist from Baghdad, Iraq, interview with the author, October 2021.

9. Activist from Najaf, Iraq, interview with the author, November 2021.

10. For a review of relations between liberal activists and clerics, see Marsin Alshamary, "The Protestor Paradox: Who do anti-Islamist Activists Look Toward Clerical Leadership?," The Brookings Institution, 2022, https://www.brookings.edu/wp-content/uploads/2022/04/FP_20220425_protestor_paradox_alshamary_v2.pdf.

11. Marsin Alshamary, "Religious Peacebuilding in Iraq: Prospects and Challenges from the Hawza," *Journal of Intervention and Statebuilding* 15, no. 4 (2021): 494–509.

12. Ali Al-Mawlawi, 2022, "Discursive Politics and the Portrayal of Shia Islamists vis-à-vis the Iraqi State," forthcoming in this series.

13. Grand Ayatollah Ali Al-Sistani, "The Statement of His Eminence's Office Issued Concerning the Upcoming Parliamentary Elections in Iraq" (in Arabic), Najaf: The Office of the Grand Ayatollah Ali Al-Husseini Al-Sistani, September 29, 2021, https://www.sistani.org/arabic/statement/26536/.

14. Kadhim, "Forging a Third Way."

15. E. H. Braam, "All Roads Lead to Najaf: Grand Ayatollah Al-Sistani's Quiet Impact on Iraq's 2010 Ballot and Its Aftermath," *Journal of International & Global Studies* 2, no. 1 (2010): 1; and

Babak Rahimi, *Ayatollah Sistani and the Democratization of Post-Ba'athist Iraq* (United States Institute of Peace, 2007).

16. Grand Ayatollah Ali Al-Sistani, "A Question Regarding the Iraqi Elections" (in Arabic), Najaf: The Office of the Grand Ayatollah Ali Al-Husseini Al-Sistani, 2005, https://www.sistani.org/arabic/archive/288/.

17. Rahimi, *Ayatollah Sistani.*

18. Braam, "All Roads Lead to Najaf."

19. Independent High Electoral Commission, "2021 Iraqi Council of Representatives Elections—Final Results by Electoral District," https://ihec.iq.

20. Grand Ayatollah Ali Al-Sistani, "His Eminence (May His Shadow Persist) Permits His Followers in Iran to Help Those Affected by the Recent Earthquake," Najaf: The Office of the Grand Ayatollah Ali Al-Husseini Al-Sistani, 2018, https://www.sistani.org/arabic/archive/25692/.

21. Interview with the author, Baghdad, Iraq, June 2019. On "madani," see Alshamary, "The Protestor Paradox.

22. Author interview with advanced seminary student in Najaf, Iraq, January 2019.

23. Arab Barometer Wave III, V, and VI (Iraq).

24. Hakim, interview.

25. Anonymous cleric, interview with the author, Baghdad, Iraq, September 2021.

26. Activist from Basra, interview with the author, September 2020.

27. Hamzeh Hadad, "Path to Government Formation in Iraq," Konrad Adenaeur Foundation, 2022, https://www.kas.de/documents/266761/0/Hamzeh+Hadad+-+Path+to+Government+Formation+in+Iraq+2022.pdf/54d58e79-343a-8460-6c1d-a02c34f986b1?version=1.0&t=1641904073323.

28. Abbas Kadhim, "A Major Crack In Iraqi Shia Politics," *The Huffington Post,* July 24, 2017, https://www.huffpost.com/entry/a-major-crack-in-iraqi-shia-politics_b_59766ab6e4b01cf1c4bb72bd.

29. By contrast, Ammar al-Hakim is one of many prominent members of the Hakim family. The legacy of the family is undoubtedly held by the recently deceased Grand Ayatollah Mohammad Saeed al-Hakim.

30. Jonathan Guyer, "Why Iraq Could Be Approaching Another Civil War, Explained by an Expert," *Vox,* September 1, 2022, https://www.vox.com/policy-and-politics/2022/9/1/23331369/iraq-civil-war-muqtada-al-sadr.

31. Ben Robin-D'Cruz, "The Sadrist Electoral Machine in Basra," Century International, October 11, 2022, https://tcf.org/content/report/the-sadrist-electoral-machine-in-basra/.

32. Anonymous member of Ishraqat Kanoon, interview with the author, November 2021.

33. Anonymous activists in Karbala and Najaf, interviews with the author, November 2021.

34. Loveday Morris, "A Letter from Sistani Turned the Tide against Iraq's Leader," *Washington Post,* August 12, 2014, https://www.washingtonpost.com/world/middle_east/a-letter-from-sistani-turned-the-tide-against-iraqs-leader/2014/08/13/3b3426cf-60ee-4856-ad26-d01a9c6cc9c3_story.html.

35. See "Iraqi President Visits Shiite Cleric Al Sistani Adds Presser," published to AP Archive YouTube channel, July 21, 2015, https://www.youtube.com/watch?v=g-8-6jq5WNA; "Iraqi President Visits Grand Ayatollah Al-Sistani in the Holy City of Najaf," published to AP Archive YouTube channel, August 3, 2015, https://www.youtube.com/watch?v=SG9NjyiGPfc; Grand Ayatollah Ali al-Sistani, "His Eminence Sayyid Sistani receives a visit from Iranian President Dr. Hasan Rouhani" (in Arabic), Najaf: The Office of the Grand Ayatollah Ali al-Husseini Al-Sistani, March 13, 2019, https://www.sistani.org/english/archive/26259/; "Iraq's Top Shiite Cleric Backs Early Parliamentary Elections," September 13, 2020, https://

apnews.com/article/virus-outbreak-middle-east-ali-al-sistani-elections-iraq-b03 bfca1e93d0e2efd5986fe022b5137; and Grand Ayatollah Ali al-Sistani, "A Statement Issued by the Office of the Supreme Religious Authority of World's Shia Muslims, Grand Ayatollah Sistani, Regarding His Meeting with the Grand Pontiff, the Pope," Najaf: The Office of the Grand Ayatollah Ali al-Husseini al-Sistani, March 6, 2021, https://www.sistani.org/english/statement/26508/.

36. Grand Ayatollah Sistani's Office, "A Statement from a Source in the Office of His Eminence with Regard to New Government Formation in Iraq," November 2, 2021, https://www.sistani.org/arabic/archive/26538/.

37. "Pope Francis Meets Iraq's Shia Leader al-Sistani," Al Jazeera, March 6, 2021, https://www.aljazeera.com/news/2021/3/6/pope-francis-meets-iraqs-shia-leader-al-sistani#:~:text=Pope%20Francis%20has%20met%20with,Iraq's%20long%2Dbeleaguered%20Christian%20minority.

Chapter 4

1. "Masum Praises the Role of Sayed Sistani and Confirms His Advice in Writing the Constitution" (in Arabic), *Shafaqna*, January 3, 2019, https://iraq.shafaqna.com/AR/136294/معصوم-يشيد-بدور-السيد-السيستاني-ويؤكد/.

2. "Iraqis Protest over Power Outages and Poor Services," Al Jazeera, August 3, 2015, https://www.aljazeera.com/news/2015/8/3/iraqis-protest-over-power-outages-and-poor-services.

3. "The Supreme Religious Authority Calls on the Iraqi Government to Do Its Utmost to Fulfill the Legitimate Demands of Citizens through Appropriate Methods, Warning against Underestimating Them and Not Being Indifferent to Their Consequences" (in Arabic), the official website of the Al-Abbas Holy Shrine, July 31, 2015, https://alkafeel.net/inspiredfriday/index.php?id=223&ser=2&lang=ar.

4. "What Is Required of the Prime Minister Is to Be More Daring and Courageous in His Reform Steps and Not to Be Content with Secondary Steps and to Strike with an Iron Fist Anyone Who Tampers with the People's Wealth" (in Arabic), the official website of the Al-Abbas Holy Shrine, August 7, 2015, https://alkafeel.net/inspiredfriday/index.php?id=224&ser=2&lang=ar.

5. Ahmed Rasheed, "Iraq's Abadi Proposes Clear-Out of Top Government Posts," *Reuters,* August 9, 2015, https://www.reuters.com/article/uk-mideast-crisis-iraq-reform-idUKKCN0QE05K20150809.

6. "The Supreme Religious Authority Calls for the Adoption of the Principle of Competence and Integrity in Assuming Official Positions and Positions Instead of Partisan Quotas" (in Arabic), the official website of the Al-Abbas Holy Shrine, November 6, 2015, https://alkafeel.net/inspiredfriday/index.php?id=237&ser=2&lang=ar.

7. Kirk H. Sowell, "Abadi's Failed Reforms," Carnegie Endowment, November 17, 2015, https://carnegieendowment.org/sada/62004.

8. "The Supreme Religious Authority: The Battle of Reforms That We Are Waging These Days Is a Crucial Battle That Determines Our Future and the Future of Our Country, and We, as a People and Government, Have No Choice but to Win It," (in Arabic), the official website of the Al-Abbas Holy Shrine, August 21, 2015, https://alkafeel.net/inspiredfriday/index.php?id=226&ser=2&lang=ar.

9. "The Supreme Religious Authority Stresses the Need to Support the Iraqi Army and Continue to Build It on National Foundations, and Expresses Regret at the Failure to Achieve Reforms" (in Arabic), the official website of the Al-Abbas Holy Shrine, January 8, 2016, https://alkafeel.net/inspiredfriday/index.php?id=246&ser=2&lang=ar.

10. "The Supreme Religious Authority Calls on Officials and Political Forces to Be Aware of the Size of the Responsibility Placed on Their Shoulders and That the Iraqi People Deserve to Harness All Their Capabilities to Serve Them" (in Arabic), the official website of the Al-Abbas Holy Shrine, January 22, 2016, https://alkafeel.net/inspiredfriday/index.php?id=248&ser=2&lang=ar.

11. "The Supreme Religious Authority Decides to Make the Political Sermon According to the Requirements of Events and Developments in Iraqi Affairs, and Not on a Weekly Basis" (in Arabic), the official website of the Al-Abbas Holy Shrine, February 5, 2016, https://alkafeel.net/inspiredfriday/index.php?id=250&ser=2&lang=ar.

12. Kareem Raheem and Stephen Kalin, "Iraq's Sadr Begins Sit-in inside Green Zone to Push for Reforms," Reuters, March 27, 2016, https://www.reuters.com/article/uk-mideast-crisis-iraq-sadr-idUKKCN0WT0I8.

13. Nizar Hatem, "The Iraqi Crisis Breaks the Silence of Al-Sistani: Beware of Going Too Far" (in Arabic), Al-Qabas, May 5, 2016, https://www.alqabas.com/article/23850-حذ-السيستاني-صمت-تكسر-العراقية-الأزمة.

14. "SRSG Kubiš Meets with His Eminence Grand Ayatollah Ali Al-Sistani in Najaf—30 May 2016," uploaded to the YouTube channel by UN Iraq (@UN_Iraq) on May 30, 2016, https://www.youtube.com/watch?v=xa44MVZMf_Y.

15. "The Secretary General of the Holy Shrine of Imam Ali Receives the Iraqi Prime Minister and His Accompanying Delegation" (in Arabic), the Holy Alawi Shrine, https://www.imamali.net/index.php?id=316&sid=5419.

16. "The Text of the Second Sermon Delivered by the Representative of the Supreme Religious Authority, His Eminence Sheikh Abd al-Mahdi al-Karbalai on Friday (19 Muharram 1438 AH)" (in Arabic), the official website of the Office of His Eminence al-Sayyid Ali al-Husseini al-Sistani, https://www.sistani.org/arabic/archive/25485/.

17. "The Supreme Religious Authority Clarifies Its Position on the Referendum on the Secession of Northern Iraq (Kurdistan)" (in Arabic), the official website of the Al-Abbas Holy Shrine, September 29, 2017, https://alkafeel.net/inspiredfriday/index.php?id=343&ser=2&lang=ar.

18. "The Supreme Religious Authority Considers What Happened in Kirkuk Not a Victory for One Party over Another, but Rather a Victory for All Iraqis" (in

Arabic), the official website of the Al-Abbas Holy Shrine, October 20, 2017, https://alkafeel.net/inspiredfriday/index.php?id=349&ser=2&lang=ar.

19. "Victory Sermon from Holy Karbala" (in Arabic), the official website of the Office of His Eminence al-Sayyid Ali al-Husseini al-Sistani, https://www.sistani.org/arabic/statement/25875//.

20. "Statement of the Office of His Eminence on the Parliamentary Elections in Iraq in 2018" (in Arabic), the official website of the Office of His Eminence al-Sayyid Ali al-Husseini al-Sistani, https://www.sistani.org/arabic/statement/26025/.

21. "The Supreme Religious Authority: The Current Government Must Strive to Achieve What Can Be Urgently Achieved of the Citizens' Demands, and That the Next Government Should Be Formed on the Right Basis of Effective and Impartial Competencies" (in Arabic), the official website of the Al-Abbas Holy Shrine, July 27, 2018, https://alkafeel.net/inspiredfriday/index.php?id=396&ser=2&lang=ar.

22. "Supreme Marja'iyya: We Do Not Support Those Who Were in Power in Previous Years for the Position of Prime Minister" (in Arabic), the official website of the Office of His Eminence al-Sayyid Ali al-Husseini al-Sistani, https://www.sistani.org/arabic/statement/26114/.

23. "Dialogue with the Director of the Office of His Eminence in Lebanon about the Role of Religious Authority in the Religious and Political Scene" (in Arabic), the official website of the Office of His Eminence al-Sayyid Ali al-Husseini al-Sistani, https://www.sistani.org/arabic/archive/26342/.

24. Former member of parliament involved in the negotiations, comments to the author, Baghdad, January 2023.

25. For example, the Iranian president and the Lebanese speaker of parliament, see "His Eminence's Reception of the Iranian President, Dr. Hassan al-Rouhani (13/3/2019)" (in Arabic), the official website of the Office of His Eminence al-Sayyid Ali al-Husseini al-Sistani, https://www.sistani.org/arabic/archive/26257/; and "His Eminence's Reception of Mr. Nabih Berri, Speaker of the Lebanese Parliament (1/4/2019)" (in Arabic), the official website of the Office of His Eminence al-Sayyid Ali al-Husseini al-Sistani, https://www.sistani.org/arabic/archive/26263/.

26. "His Eminence's Reception of the Representative of the Secretary-General of the United Nations in Iraq (29/11/2018)" (in Arabic), the official website of the Office of His Eminence al-Sayyid Ali al-Husseini al-Sistani, https://www.sistani.org/arabic/archive/26116/.

27. "His Eminence's Meeting with the Special Representative of the Secretary-General of the United Nations in Iraq (6/2/2019)" (in Arabic), the official website of the Office of His Eminence al-Sayyid Ali al-Husseini al-Sistani, https://www.sistani.org/arabic/archive/26231/.

28. "The Text of the Second Sermon Delivered by the Representative of the Supreme Religious Authority, His Eminence Sayed Ahmad Al-Safi, on Friday (10 Shawwal 1440 AH) Corresponding to (14/6/2019)" (in Arabic), the official website of the Office of His Eminence al-Sayyid Ali al-Husseini al-Sistani, https://www.sistani.org/arabic/archive/26306/.

29. "Al-Karbalai: The Religious Authority Advised, but What the Country Has Reached Was the Result of Widespread Financial and Administrative Corruption in the Various State Facilities and Institutions" (in Arabic), Imam Hussain Holy Shrine, https://imamhussain.org/arabic/21158.

30. "The Text of the Second Sermon Delivered by the Representative of the Supreme Religious Authority, His Eminence Sayed Ahmed al-Safi on Friday (5 Safar 1441 AH) Corresponding to (4/10/2019)" (in Arabic), the official website of the Office of His Eminence al-Sayyid Ali al-Husseini al-Sistani, https://www.sistani.org/arabic/archive/26344/.

31. "The Text of the Second Sermon Delivered by the Representative of the Supreme Religious Authority, His Eminence Sheikh Abd al-Mahdi al-Karbalai, on Friday (12 Safar 1441 AH) Corresponding to (10/11/2019)" (in Arabic), the official website of the Office of His Eminence al-Sayyid Ali al-Husseini al-Sistani, https://www.sistani.org/arabic/archive/26350/.

32. See the Friday prayer speeches between 25 October 2019 and 22 November 2019.

33. Reflected in his own comments, see for example readouts from the November 2019 meeting with the UNAMI head Hennis-Plasschaert and the March 2021 meeting with Pope Francis.

34. "His Eminence's Reception of the Head of the United Nations Mission in Iraq (11/11/2019)" (in Arabic), the official website of the Office of His Eminence al-Sayyid Ali al-Husseini al-Sistani, https://www.sistani.org/arabic/archive/26358/.

35. "The Text of the Second Sermon Delivered by the Representative of the Supreme Religious Authority, His Eminence Sayed Ahmad Al-Safi, on Friday (17 Rabi' al-Awwal 1441 AH) Corresponding to (15/11/2019)" (in Arabic), the official website of the Office of His Eminence al-Sayyid Ali al-Husseini al-Sistani, https://www.sistani.org/arabic/archive/26359/.

36. "The Text of the Second Sermon Delivered by the Representative of the Supreme Religious Authority, His Eminence Sayed Ahmad Al-Safi on Friday (2 Rabi' al-Akhir 1441 AH) Corresponding to (29/11/2019)" (in Arabic), the official website of the Office of His Eminence al-Sayyid Ali al-Husseini al-Sistani, https://www.sistani.org/arabic/archive/26361/.

37. Sistani's statements are here: "A Statement by an Official Source in the Office of His Eminence Sayyid (May His Shadow Be Long) About the Attack on the Iraqi Forces in the City of Al-Qaim (30/12/2019)" (in Arabic), the official website of the Office of His Eminence al-Sayyid Ali al-Husseini al-Sistani, https://www.sistani.org/arabic/archive/26373/; "The Text of the Second Sermon Delivered by the Representative of the Supreme Religious Authority, His Eminence Shaykh Abd Al-Mahdi Al-Karbalai, on Friday (7 Jumada al-Awwal 1441 AH) Corresponding to (3/1/2020)" (in Arabic), the official website of the Office of His Eminence al-Sayyid Ali al-Husseini al-Sistani, https://www.sistani.org/arabic/archive/26374/; and "The Text of the Second Sermon Delivered by the Representative of the Supreme Religious Authority, His Eminence Sayed Ahmad Al-Safi, on Friday (14 Jumada

al-Awwal 1441 AH) Corresponding to (10/1/2020)" (in Arabic), the official website of the Office of His Eminence al-Sayyid Ali al-Husseini al-Sistani, https://www.sistani.org/arabic/archive/26375/.

38. "Sayed Sistani Offers Condolences to Sayed Khamenei for the Martyrdom of Major General Qassem Soleimani" (in Arabic), Shafaqna, January 5, 2021, https://ar.shafaqna.com/AR/204294/السيد-السيستاني-يعزي-بشهادة-اللواء-قا/. His son Muhammad Ridha also participated in the funeral processions of Soleimani and Muhandis in Najaf.

39. "A Statement by an Official Source in the Office of His Eminence (16/1/2020)" (in Arabic), the official website of the Office of His Eminence al-Sayyid Ali al-Husseini al-Sistani, https://www.sistani.org/arabic/archive/26376/.

40. "The Text of the Second Sermon Delivered by the Representative of the Supreme Religious Authority, His Eminence Sheikh Abdul-Mahdi al-Karbalai, on Friday (5 Jumada al-Akhira 1441 AH) Corresponding to (31/1/2020)" (in Arabic), the official website of the Office of His Eminence al-Sayyid Ali al-Husseini al-Sistani, https://www.sistani.org/arabic/archive/26381/.

41. "The Text of the Second Sermon Delivered by the Representative of the Supreme Religious Authority, His Eminence Sayed Ahmad Al-Safi, on Friday (12 Jumada al-Akhira 1441 AH) Corresponding to (7/2/2020)" (in Arabic), the official website of the Office of His Eminence al-Sayyid Ali al-Husseini al-Sistani, https://www.sistani.org/arabic/archive/26383/.

42. "The Representative of the Supreme Religious Authority Reveals the Reasons for Not Returning the Friday Sermon and Blames the Politicians" (in Arabic), uploaded to the YouTube channel of Al Rabiaa TV (@alrabiaatv) on April 9, 2022, https://www.youtube.com/watch?v=xRGdhuQwVw0.

43. "The Supreme Religious Authority: Medical Instructions Must Be Followed and Applied, and Dealing with the Corona Virus Should Be Done with Caution and Not with Panic and Fear" (in Arabic), the official website of the Al-Abbas Holy Shrine, February 28, 2020, https://alkafeel.net/inspiredfriday/index.php?id=484&ser=2&lang=ar.

44. "The Call of His Eminence's Office to Take Care of Preventive Measures after the Increase in the Number of Infections with the Corona Epidemic in Iraq (6/6/2020)" (in Arabic), the official website of the Office of His Eminence al-Sayyid Ali al-Husseini al-Sistani, https://www.sistani.org/arabic/archive/26450/.

45. "The Representative of the Supreme Religious Authority Reveals the Reasons for Not Returning the Friday Sermon and Blames the Politicians" (in Arabic), uploaded to the YouTube channel of Al Rabiaa TV (@alrabiaatv) on April 9, 2022, https://www.youtube.com/watch?v=xRGdhuQwVw0.

46. "His Eminence's Reception of the Special Representative of the Secretary-General of the United Nations (13/9/2020)" (in Arabic), the official website of the Office of His Eminence al-Sayyid Ali al-Husseini al-Sistani, https://www.sistani.org/arabic/archive/26461/.

47. Sajad Jiyad, "The Vatican Comes to Najaf, Meeting Power and Piety," *1001 Iraqi Thoughts,* March 6, 2021, https://1001iraqithoughts.com/2021/03/06/the-vatican-comes-to-najaf-meeting-power-and-piety/.

48. "A Statement Issued by His Eminence's Office about His Meeting with the Pope of the Vatican" (in Arabic), the official website of the Office of His Eminence al-Sayyid Ali al-Husseini al-Sistani, https://www.sistani.org/arabic/statement/26506/.

49. "Pope Stresses Fraternity in Meeting with Iraq's Grand Ayatollah," *Vatican News,* March 6, 2021, https://www.vaticannews.va/en/pope/news/2021-03/pope-francis-stresses-importance-of-cooperation-fraternity-in-m.html.

50. Jason Horowitz and Jane Arraf, "Pope Francis Meets Iraq's Top Ayatollah as Both Urge Peace," *New York Times,* March 6, 2021, https://www.nytimes.com/2021/03/06/world/europe/pope-francis-iraq-ayatollah-sistani.html.

51. "Pope: Charity, Love and Fraternity Are the Way Forward," *Vatican News,* March 8, 2021, https://www.vaticannews.va/en/pope/news/2021-03/pope-francis-inflight-presser-iraq-journalists0.html.

52. "Statement of His Eminence's Office on the Upcoming Parliamentary Elections in Iraq" (in Arabic), the official website of the Office of His Eminence al-Sayyid Ali al-Husseini al-Sistani, https://www.sistani.org/arabic/statement/26536/.

53. "A Statement by an Official Source in the Office of His Eminence Regarding the Formation of the New Government in Iraq (2/11/2021)" (in Arabic), the official website of the Office of His Eminence al-Sayyid Ali al-Husseini al-Sistani, https://www.sistani.org/arabic/archive/26538/.

54. John Davison, "Iraqi Cleric Sadr Calls off Protests after Worst Baghdad Violence in Years," Reuters, August 30, 2022, https://www.reuters.com/world/middle-east/iraq-security-forces-say-four-rockets-land-baghdads-green-zone-2022-08-30/.

55. John Davison, Parisa Hafezi, and Laila Bassam, "How a 92-Year-Old Cleric Silently Halted Iraq's Slide Back into War," *Reuters,* September 3, 2022, https://www.reuters.com/world/middle-east/how-92-year-old-cleric-silently-halted-iraqs-slide-back-into-war-2022-09-03/.

56. Based on the words of Imam Ali, "There is no opinion for those who are not obeyed."

57. "Statement of His Eminence's Office on the Occasion of Receiving the Under-Secretary-General of the United Nations" (in Arabic), the official website of the Office of His Eminence al-Sayyid Ali al-Husseini al-Sistani, https://www.sistani.org/arabic/statement/26646/.

58. "Statement of His Eminence's Office on the Occasion of His Reception of the Head of the United Nations Investigation Team to Promote Accountability for ISIS Crimes" (in Arabic), the official website of the Office of His Eminence al-Sayyid Ali al-Husseini al-Sistani, https://www.sistani.org/arabic/statement/26650/.

59. "The Statement Issued by His Eminence's Office on the Earthquake That Hit Turkish and Syrian Territories" (in Arabic), the official website of the Office of

His Eminence al-Sayyid Ali al-Husseini al-Sistani, https://www.sistani.org/arabic/statement/26712/.

60. "A Letter from the Office of His Eminence to the Secretary-General of the United Nations Regarding the Assault on a Copy of the Holy Qur'an with a License from the Swedish Police" (in Arabic), the official website of the Office of His Eminence al-Sayyid Ali al-Husseini al-Sistani, https://www.sistani.org/arabic/statement/26747/.

61. Some writers, such as Abd al-Hadi al-Hakim, who is close to Sistani, have frequently used the term *iradat al-umma* (will of the people), though Sistani himself is not known to use it.

62. "Questions of the Polish Newspaper *Gazeta Wyborcza*" (in Arabic), the official website of the Office of His Eminence al-Sayyid Ali al-Husseini al-Sistani, https://www.sistani.org/arabic/archive/239/.

Chapter 5

1. "Shia Islamist rivals" refers to those political parties in the Shia Coordination Framework, but not other parties, such as Tasmeem, or independents, who could be construed a Shia Islamist actors.

2. Marc Lynch and Jillian Schwedler, "Introduction to the Special Issue on 'Islamist Politics After the Arab Uprisings," *Middle East Law and Governance* 12 (2020): 3-13. François Burgat, "Were the Islamists Wrong-Footed by the Arab Spring?," memo for the POMEPS "Rethinking Islamist Politics" conference, January, 24, 2014.

3. The quoted definition comes from International Crisis Group, "Understanding Islamism," Middle East/North Africa Report No. 37, March 2, 2005, crisisgroup.org/middle-east-north-africa/understanding-islamism.

4. See Fanar Haddad's report in this series, on Shia politics, forthcoming this fall.

5. For instance, in 2016 the Iraqi parliament passed a law banning the manufacture and sale of alcohol "to preserve Iraq's identity as a Muslim country," according to one Shia Islamist member of parliament. However, the law has never been enforced, in part because the Islamists themselves are the main financial beneficiaries of Iraq's liquor trade.

6. Benedict Robin-D'Cruz and Renad Mansour, "Making Sense of the Sadrists: Fragmentation and Unstable Politics," The Foreign Policy Research Institute, 2020, https://www.fpri.org/article/2020/03/making-sense-sadrists-fragmentation-unstable-politics/; Nicholas Krohley, *The Death of the Mehdi Army: The Rise, Fall, and Revival of Iraq's Most Powerful Militia* (London: C. Hurst, 2015); Paul Staniland, *Networks of Rebellion: Explaining Insurgent Cohesion and Collapse* (London: Cornell University Press, 2014); Marisa Cochrane, "The Fragmentation of the Sadrist Movement," Institute for the Study of War, 2009, https://www.understandingwar.org/report/fragmentation-sadrist-movement.

7. For example, the splits involving Ayatollah Muhammad al-Yacoubi, Qais al-Khazali, Akram al-Kaabi, Shibl al-Zaidi, and Sheikh Muhammad Tabatabai, Isma'il Hafiz al-Lami (also known as Abu Dura), among many others.

8. Melani Cammett and Pauline Jones Luong, "Is There an Islamist Political Advantage?," *Annual Review of Political Science* 17 (2014): 187–206; Toygar Sinan Baykan, "Electoral Islamism in the Mediterranean: Explaining the Success (and Failure) of Islamist Parties," *Mediterranean Politics* 25, no. 5 (2020): 690–96; Steven Brooke, *Winning Hearts and Votes: Social Services and the Islamist Political Advantage* (New York: Cornell University Press, 2019); Melani Cammett, *Compassionate Communalism: Welfare and Sectarianism in Lebanon* (New York: Cornell University Press, 2014).

9. Robin-D'Cruz and Mansour, "Making Sense of the Sadrists;"; Benedict Robin-D'Cruz, "The Prophetic Power of Muqtada al-Sadr: Theorizing the Role of Religion in Shii Islamist Politics," unpublished manuscript; see also chapter three in Benedict Robin-D'Cruz, "The Leftist-Sadrist Alliance; Social Movements and Strategic Politics in Iraq" (PhD diss., University of Edinburgh, 2019).

10. "Electoral success" is taken to mean not merely tallying votes, but how electoral politics translates into political power. As will be shown, the Sadrists excel at maximizing the power of each vote, even while their gross vote tally declined from 2018 to 2021.

11. See chapter two in Frank Ledwidge, *Losing Small Wars: British Military Failure in Iraq and Afghanistan* (London: Yale University Press, 2011).

12. Basra-based source, interview with the author, multiple communications between 2020 and 2022.

13. Ibid.

14. Basra-based source, interview with the author, August 2022.

15. Marisa Cochrane, *The Fragmentation of the Sadrist Movement* (Washington, DC: Institute for the Study of War, 2009), 12.

16. Basra-based source, interview with the author via multiple communications between 2020 and 2022; anonymous sources, interviews with the author, last updated August 2022.

17. Basra-based source, interviews with the author via multiple communications, last updated via electronic communication in June 2021.

18. Basra-based source, interviews with the author via multiple communications between 2020 and 2022; supplemented by the author's own monitoring of this protest activity.

19. Basra-based sources, interview with the author via multiple communications between 2020 and 2022; analysis of Sadrists' Basra social media sites and communications from Muqtada al-Sadr announcing appointments to key positions within the movement.

20. For example, see recent commentary by Abbas Kadhim (@DrAbbasKadhim) via Twitter thread, posted on August 29, 2022, https://twitter.com/DrAbbasKadhim/status/1564319677374861312?s=20&t=k_nufZIxi7xG-amQIaPrng.

21. Basra-based source, interview with the author, April 2021.

22. Basra-based source, interview and regular communication with the author, last updated in August 2022.

23. These examples were taken from messaging from the prominent Sadrist Twitter account Salih Mohammad al-Iraqi (@salih_m_iraqi, https://twitter.com/salih_m_iraqi), a proxy account for Sadr himself.

24. A common tactic, deployed particularly by Sadr's proxy Twitter account Salih Mohammad al-Iraqi (ibid.), was to associate the Tishreeni activists with alcohol and drug abuse. Sadr also condemned the mixing of men and women at protests, calling for gender segregation of Sadrist protesters.

25. Benedict Robin-D'Cruz, "The Social Logics of Protest Violence in Iraq: Explaining Divergent Dynamics in the Southeast," London School of Economics, September 2021, http://eprints.lse.ac.uk/111784/2/SocialLogicsofProtestViolence.pdf.

26. Benedict Robin-D'Cruz and Renad Mansour, "Why Muqtada al-Sadr Failed to Reform Iraq," *Foreign Policy*, March 10, 2022, https://foreignpolicy.com/2022/03/10/why-muqtada-al-sadr-failed-to-reform-iraq/.

27. Renad Mansour and Benedict Robin-D'Cruz, "Understanding Iraq's Muqtada al-Sadr: Inside Baghdad's Sadr City," Chatham House, August 8, 2022, https://www.chathamhouse.org/2022/08/understanding-iraqs-muqtada-al-sadr-inside-baghdads-sadr-city.

28. "Iraq's October 2021 Election," Congressional Research Service, October 18, 2021, https://crsreports.congress.gov/product/pdf/IN/IN11769#:~:text=Under%20a%20new%20voting%20law,seats%20reserved%20for%20minority%20groups; Renad Mansour and Victoria Stewart-Jolley, "Explaining Iraq's Election Results," Chatham House, October 22, 2021, https://www.chathamhouse.org/2021/10/explaining-iraqs-election-results.

29. Fatah lost former members of parliament who opted to stand as independents or in new, more localized blocs such as Tasmeem in Basra. It also ran too many candidates from its component parties in each district, spreading its vote base too thinly while its most dominant personalities sucked up more votes than needed, and were unable to distribute their excess votes to other candidates in their coalition (as would have happened under the old closed and open-list systems).

30. Two non-Sadrist Iraqi sources with in-depth knowledge of Karimawi's background and role as an election strategist, remote interviews with the author, September 2022.

31. Iraqi researcher with first-hand knowledge of Karimawi's role, interview with the author, September 2022.

32. Mohanad Adnan, an Iraq-based political analyst who conducted close analysis of the election strategies of various political parties during the October 2021 election, remote interview with the author, September 15, 2022. Adnan also indicated that the fourth tier of the Sadrist strategy was areas where no candidates were run, mainly due to the low chances of winning a seat but also to build

political capital for the post-election alliance formation strategy by not competing against potential coalition partners.

33. Personal communications between the author and several Basra-based sources during the election campaign in 2021, anonymized.

34. Hamdi Malik has noted that this was particularly important in 2021 given that the new electoral system had radically changed where and how voters were to cast ballots, leading to potential confusion and apathy.

35. One example would be independent member of parliament Mustafa Jabbar Sanad, who came third in District One with 8,339 votes. Sanad has connections to the Sadrists through the Al Marayan tribe, and family connections to former prime minister Adil Abdul-Mahdi. Since gaining his seat in parliament, however, Sanad has drawn closer to the Coordination Framework and openly clashed with the Sadrists, illustrating how fluid tactical political allegiances can be.

36. Many of these features can be seen in the Sadrist candidates who ran in Basra in 2021. Examples include Ayad al-Muhamadawi al-Muslikh and Wafaa al-Mayahi, who are both academics at the University of Basra with personal or familial connections to Saraya al-Salam and long histories of Sadrist activism.

37. Adnan, interview.

38. The best example of this was the Sadrists adaptation to the rising popularity of "madani" ("civil") politics between 2015 and 2018, only to reverse course for a religion-focused electoral strategy in 2021.

39. On the Dawa Party, see Harith Hassan, "From Radical to Rentier Islamism: The Case of Iraq's Dawa Party," The Carnegie Middle East Center, April 16, 2019, https://carnegie-mec.org/2019/04/16/from-radical-to-rentier-islamism-case-of-iraq-s-dawa-party-pub-78887. On Hezbollah, see Jason Wimberly, "Wilayat al-Faqih in Hizballah's Web of Concepts: A Perspective on Ideology," Middle Eastern Studies 51, no. 5 (2015): 687–710

40. Many of these features can be seen in the Sadrist candidates who ran in Basra in 2021. Examples include Ayad al-Muhamadawi al-Muslikh and Wafaa al-Mayahi.

41. Based on analysis of figures provided by Kirk Sowell and published in his Inside Iraqi Politics 65, 2018.

42. As explored in my forthcoming paper with Renad Mansour, the Sadrist base remains split in its views on Tishreen, with considerable support for the protest movement among younger members of the movement despite sustained rhetorical attacks on Tishreen by the Sadrist leadership. See Benedict Robin-D'Cruz and Renad Mansour, "The Sadrists and Iraq's Tilt Towards Chaos," Chatham House, forthcoming.

43. Idani could be construed as a natural ally of the Coordination Framework, having been close to both Hikma and Nasr, and was considered a potential prime minister candidate for the Binaa Bloc (Fatah and State of Law) after Adil Abdul-Mahdi resigned as prime minister. However, Idani is politically fluid and has made considerable efforts to build his Sadrist relationships since the October 2021 election left the Sadrists and Tasmeem as the two dominant political forces in Basra.

44. Awad has been involved in several campaigns of this sort, but his most prominent and successful has been working alongside Sheikh Ammar al-Zaidi on behalf of the so-called "30,000", a large group of Basrawis promised jobs under Governor Idani's jobs lottery scheme, who have subsequently been campaigning to have their contracts upgraded to permanent public sector employment.

45. See survey data for Iraq from Arab Barometer, Wave V 2018, questions on political Islam, https://www.arabbarometer.org/survey-data/data-analysis-tool/.

46. The Sadrists' comparative lack of judicial power compared to Nouri al-Maliki has also been a crucial factor explaining how Maliki has been able to unravel the Sadrists' attempt to translate their 2021 electoral success into government formation.

47. This notion of Sadrist activity as sacrificial practice draws on the author's conversations with Elizabeth Tsurkov, who is currently researching the Sadrist trend. Personal communication, September 2022.

Chapter 6

1. The report relies on both primary and secondary sources, including some twenty hours of Arabic-language television interviews and in-person interviews with ten Dawa leaders of different generations. Author interviews with Dawa's members include Sadiq al-Rikabi, Baghdad, September 2015; Mowaffak al-Rubaie, Baghdad, September 2015 and May 2018; Fahad al-Shammari, Najaf, September 2015; Hussein Shubbar, Najaf, September 2015; Adnan al-Zurfi, Najaf, September 2015; Abbas al-Bayati, multiple interviews with the author, Baghdad, 2015–22; Ibrahim al-Jaafari, interview with the author, Baghdad, September 2015.

2. See Hanna Batatu, *The Old Social Classes and the Revolutionary Movements of Iraq* (Princeton, NJ: Princeton University Press, 1978). For an analysis of the economic conditions of rural Shia districts in Iraq see Hanna Batatu, "Iraq's Underground Shia Movements: Characteristics, Causes, and Prospects," *Middle East Journal* 35, no. 4 (1981): 582–84.

3. "Interview with Ibrahim al-Jaafari" (in Arabic), Al Iraqiya, uploaded to the YouTube channel of Ibrahim al-Jaafari (@aljaffaary, unverified) in January to February 2013, in four different segments: segment one, https://www.youtube.com/watch?v=h-EBXBY80aw; segment two, https://www.youtube.com/watch?v=n-RiG3EIKR7A; segment three, https://www.youtube.com/watch?v=AK-ZFUBfGYw; segment four, https://www.youtube.com/watch?v=DXYsBiwSYHY.

4. Rikabi, interview.

5. Rikabi, interview.

6. Al Iraqiya, "Interview with Ibrahim al-Jaafari."

7. Talib Aziz, "The Role of Muhammad Baqir Al-Sadr in Shi'i Political Activism in Iraq from 1958 to 1980," *International Journal of Middle East Studies* 25, no. 2 (1993): 207–22.

8. Dai Yamao, "Transformation of the Islamic Da'wa Party in Iraq: From the Revolutionary Period to the Diaspora Era," *Asian and African Area Studies* 7, no. 2 (2008): 242; and Dai Yamao, "Iraqi Islamist Parties in International Politics: The Impact of Historical and International Politics on Political Conflict in Post-war Iraq," *International Journal of Contemporary Iraqi Studies* 6, no. 1 (2012): 27–52.

9. Bayati, interview.

10. Aziz, "The Role of Muhammad Baqir Al-Sadr," 216.

11. Ibid., 214.

12. Yamao, "Transformation of the Islamic Da'wa Party," 253.

13. Al Iraqiya, "Interview with Ibrahim al-Jaafari."

14. "Interview with Nouri al-Maliki" (in Arabic), Al Iraqiya, uploaded to YouTube in September 2012, in three different segments: segment 1, uploaded to the channel of ICVtube (@ICVtube), https://www.youtube.com/watch?v=Yuikv RpHC-E&t=19s; segment 2, uploaded to the channel Qana'at al-Iraqia al-Akhbaria (@IraqiaNews), https://www.youtube.com/watch?v=LvBrPw30Y4w; and segment 3, uploaded to the channel Qana'at al-Iraqia al-Akhbaria (@IraqiaNews), https://www.youtube.com/watch?v=WXrNqDxjEZs&t=31s.

15. Elvire Corboz, "Between Action and Symbols: The Supreme Assembly for the Islamic Revolution in Iraq and Its Bid for Political Leadership," in *Writing the Modern History of Iraq: Historiographical and Political Challenges,* ed. Peter Sluglett and Jordi Tejel (Singapore: World Scientific Publishing Company, 2012), 339–58.

16. Al Iraqiya, "Interview with Nouri al-Maliki."

17. Rikabi, interview.

18. Corboz, "Between Action and Symbols," 354.

19. Ibid.

20. Yamao, "Transformation of the Islamic Da'wa Party," 250.

21. Al Iraqiya, "Interview with Ibrahim al-Jaafari."

22. Batatu, "Iraq's Underground Shia Movements," 593.

23. Rikabi, interview.

24. Ibid.

25. See the composition of SCIRI's central committee (1982–86) as described in Elvire Corboz, *Guardians of Shi'ism: Sacred Authority and Transnational Family Networks* (Edinburgh: Edinburgh University Press, 2015), 38. See also Corboz, "Between Action and Symbols," 339.

26. Al Iraqiya, "Interview with Ibrahim al-Jaafari."

27. Ibid.

28. Juan Cole, "Shiite Religious Parties Fill in the Vacuum in Southern Iraq," MERIP, April 22, 2003, https://merip.org/2003/04/shiite-religious-parties-fill-vacuum-in-southern-iraq/.

29. For example, Abdul Karim al-Anizi, a veteran of a Dawa splinter faction ideologically closer to Iran, replaced Mowaffak al-Rubaie, a London-based Dawa exile, in the position of national security adviser.

30. "Jaysh al-Mahdi," Institute for the Study of War, https://www.understanding war.org/jaysh-al-mahdi.

31. Al Iraqiya, "Interview with Nouri al-Maliki."

32. Former Iraqi lawmaker, interview with the author by phone, April 2023.

33. Al Iraqiya, "Interview with Nouri al-Maliki."

34. Ibid.

35. Ibid.

36. Ibid.

37. Ali A. Allawi, *The Occupation of Iraq: Winning the War, Losing the Peace* (New Haven, CT: Yale University Press, 2008), 49.

38. "Shiite Politics in Iraq: The Role of the Supreme Islamic Council," International Crisis Group, November 5, 2007, https://www.crisisgroup.org/middle-east-north-africa/gulf-and-arabian-peninsula/iraq/shiite-politics-iraq-role-supreme-council.

39. Rubaie, interview. See full declaration "Declaration of the Shia of Iraq," https://al-bab.com/documents-section/declaration-shia-iraq.

40. Shammari, interview.

41. U.S. State Department diplomat, interview with the author, Amman, September 2022.

42. Al Iraqiya, "Interview with Nouri al-Maliki."

43. New Parker and Raheem Salman, "Notes from the Underground: The Rise of Nouri Al-Maliki and the New Islamists," *World Policy Journal* 30, no. 1 (2013): 63–76.

44. Yamao, "Transformation of the Islamic Da'wa Party," 253.

45. Shammari, interview

46. Bayati, interview.

47. Allawi, *The Occupation of Iraq,* 50.

48. Al Iraqiya, "Interview with Nouri al-Maliki."

49. Ibid.

50. Bayati, interview.

51. Ali al-Dabbagh, member of the Constitution Drafting Committee, interview with the author, Baghdad, September 2022.

52. Maria Fantappie "Politicians and Officers: Political Transition in Post-2003 Iraq," *Third World Quarterly Special Iraq Edition* (forthcoming).

53. Al Iraqiya, "Interview with Nouri al-Maliki."

54. Bayati, interview.

55. Ibid.

56. Maria Fantappie, "Contested Consolidation of Power in Iraq," Carnegie Endowment for International Peace, February 2013, https://www.files.ethz.ch/isn/161331/CMEC_36_contested_consolidation.pdf.

57. Lisa Blaydes, *State of Repression* (Princeton, NJ: Princeton University Press, 2018).

58. See for instance, Retirement Law (27) amended in 2007, accessible at http://wiki.dorar-aliraq.net/iraqilaws/law/20857.html; and Law on Salaries and Grades of Public Sector Employees (2008), http://wiki.dorar-aliraq.net/iraqilaws/law/21054.html.

59. Former Iraqi lawmaker, interview with the author, Baghdad, 2015.

60. Former Iraqi lawmaker, interview with the author, Baghdad, September 2022.

61. Al Iraqiya, "Interview with Ibrahim al-Jaafari."

62. Rikabi, interview.

63. Shammari, interview.

64. Ibid.

65. Member of the Dawa Party, interview with the author, Najaf, 2015.

66. Shammari, interview.

67. Member of Basra governorate council, interview with the author, Basra, September 2015.

68. Rikabi, interview.

69. "Iraq's Prime Minister Nouri al-Maliki Quits," uploaded to the YouTube channel of the *Wall Street Journal* (@wsj), August 15, 2014, https://www.youtube.com/watch?v=-9Pw87vH_oQ.

70. "An Exclusive Interview with Iraqi Prime Minister Dr. Haider al-Abadi" (in Arabic), Al Iraqiya, uploaded to the YouTube channel Qana'at al-Iraqia al-Akhbaria (@IraqiaNews), September 16, 2014, https://www.youtube.com/watch?v=Jq8B9ziMesk&t=2906s.

71. Rubaie, interview, Baghdad,, 2018.

72. Shammari, interview.

73. Bayati, interview.

74. Marsin Alshamary, "Religious Peacebuilding in Iraq: Prospects and Challenges from the Hawza," *Journal of Intervention and Statebuilding* 15, no. 4 (2021): 494–509.

75. Shammari, interview.

76. Interview with the author, Karbala, September 2015.

77. Rubaie, interview, 2015.

78. Al Iraqiya, "An Exclusive Interview with Haider al-Abadi".

79. Shubbar, interview.

80. Interview with the author, Basra, 2019.

81. Maria Fantappie, "Widespread Protests Point to Iraq's Cycle of Social Crisis," *International Crisis Group,* October 10, 2019, https://www.crisisgroup.org/middle-east-north-africa/gulf-and-arabian-peninsula/iraq/widespread-protests-point-iraqs-cycle-social-crisis.

82. Taif Alkhudary et al., "A Summer of Danger for Iraq—With Little Hope for Change," Century International, August 8, 2022, https://tcf.org/content/report/a-summer-of-danger-for-iraq-with-little-hope-for-change/. Maria Fantappie, "Why Iraq's Consocation Has Become a Driver of Chronic Instability," *SAIS Review of*

International Affairs, December 23, 2022, https://saisreview.sais.jhu.edu/iraq-consociation-instability/.

83. Adnan Abu Zeed, "Division Threatens Islamic Dawa after Maliki's Reelection," *Al-Monitor,* August 3, 2019, https://www.al-monitor.com/originals/2019/08/iraq-shiite-dawa-party-nouri-maliki.html.

84. Member of the Dawa Party leadership, interview with the author by phone, April 2023.

85. Bayati, interview.

Chapter 7

1. "Iraq: Teargas Cartridges Killing Protesters," Human Rights Watch, November 8, 2019, https://www.hrw.org/news/2019/11/08/iraq-teargas-cartridges-killing-protesters.

2. Ahmed Abd al-Hussein, "The Dissolution of the Political Process and the End of the 'Foolish' Decade" (in Arabic), *Tuk Tuk* iss. 1 (November 2019): 3.

3. Toby Dodge, "Beyond Structure and Agency: Rethinking Political Identities in Iraq after 2003," *Nations and Nationalism* 26, no. 1 (January 2020): 114.

4. "The Closing Statement of the Iraqi Opposition Conference in London," Al Jazeera, December 17, 2002, https://www.aljazeera.net/news/arabic/2002/12/17/نص-البيان-الختامي-لمؤتمر-المعارضة.

5. Toby Dodge, "Iraq and Muhasasa Ta'ifia; The External Imposition of Sectarian Politics," November 12, 2018, https://fpc.org.uk/iraq-and-muhasasa-taifia-the-external-imposition-of-sectarian-politics/.

6. Ibid.

7. Dodge, "Beyond Structure and Agency," 114.

8. Al Jazeera, "The Closing Statement of the Iraqi Opposition Conference in London."

9. Ibid.

10. Mouyad Fayyad, "The Iraqi Opposition Conference in London Opens in the Midst of Very Tight Security" (in Arabic), *Asharq Al-Awsat,* December 15, 2002.

11. Al Jazeera, "The Closing Statement of the Iraqi Opposition Conference in London."

12. Carrie Manning, "Political Elite and Democratic State-Building Efforts in Bosnia and Iraq," *Democratization* 13, no. 5 (December 2006): 731.

13. Ibid., 729.

14. Taif Alkhudary, "How Iraq's Sectarian System Came To Be… and How It Will Be Undone," Al Jazeera, March 29, 2020, https://www.aljazeera.com/opinions/2020/3/29/how-iraqs-sectarian-system-came-to-be.

15. Denis M. Tull and Andreas Mehler, "The Hidden Costs of Power-Sharing: Reproducing Insurgent Violence in Africa," *African Affairs* 104, no. 416 (July 2005): 375–98.

16. There is no official figure for how many civilians were killed during this period.

17. Toby Dodge, *From War to New Authoritarianism* (Abingdon: Routledge for the International Institute for Strategic Studies, 2012). 54.

18. Renad Mansour, "The Sunni Predicament in Iraq," Carnegie Endowment for National Peace, March 3, 2016, https://carnegieendowment.org/files/CMEC_59_Mansour_Sunni_Final.pdf.

19. Toby Dodge and Renad Mansour, "Politically Sanctioned Corruption and Barriers to Reform in Iraq," Chatham House, 2021, https://www.chathamhouse.org/2021/06/politically-sanctioned-corruption-and-barriers-reform-iraq.

20. Sajad Jiyad, "Corruption Is Strangling Iraq," The Century Foundation, https://tcf.org/content/report/corruption-is-strangling-iraq/. Some estimates have ranged even higher; see Renad Mansour, "The Deadly Greed of Iraq's Elites," *World Today,* September 29, 2022, https://www.chathamhouse.org/publications/the-world-today/2022-10/deadly-greed-iraqs-elite.

21. "Iraq's Oil Revenues During the First Half of 2022 Exceed $60 Bln," Reuters, July 6, 2022, https://www.reuters.com/article/iraq-oil-idUSC6N2W6059; and Ahmad Hassan, "Poverty in Southern Iraq: The 'Protectors of the Doctrine' Are Starving," *Daraj,* July 12, 2020, https://daraj.com/en/51234/.

22. Idris Okuduci, "Oil-Rich Iraq Grapples with Power Outages for 30 Years," *AA,* July 8, 2021, https://www.aa.com.tr/en/middle-east/oil-rich-iraq-grapples-with-power-outages-for-30-years/2297835#.

23. "Unemployment, Youth Total (% of Total Labour Force Ages 15–24) (Modelled ILO Estimate)—Iraq," World Bank, December 2021 (latest available), https://data.worldbank.org/indicator/SL.UEM.1524.ZS?locations=IQ.

24. Ahmed Al Sheikh Majid, "Iran's View toward the Tishreen Protests…Enemies of Iraq's Shia" (in Arabic), *Tuk Tuk* iss. 1 (2019): 2.

25. Ibid.

26. Abu al-Tuk Tuk, "Newspapers are back", *Tuk Tuk* iss. 4 (November 12, 2019): 1.

27. Ghofran Younes, "Crimes That Amount to Genocide. Who Is the Invisible Side That Is Killing Iraq's Youth?" (in Arabic), *Tuk Tuk* iss. 6 (November 19, 2019): 1.

28. Mohammed al-Mahmoudi, "The Turmoil before October 25, the Moment of No Return" (in Arabic), *Tuk Tuk* iss. 6 (November 19, 2019): 7.

29. Abu al-Tuk Tuk, "There Is No Such Thing as Impossible for Iraqi. All of Iraq Is in Tahrir Square Right Now" (in Arabic), *Tuk Tuk* iss. 4 (November 12, 2019): 1.

30. Interview with the author, June 2021.

31. Caroline A Hartzell and Mathew Hoddie, "The Art of the Possible: Power Sharing and Post-Civil War Democracy," *World Politics* 67, no. 1 (2015): 37–71; Taif Alkhudary, "Organised Opposition After Tishreen: The Role of Iraq's Movement Parties in Consolidating Democracy," LSE Middle East Centre Paper Series, forthcoming.

32. Paul Dixon, "Power-Sharing in Deeply Divided Societies: Consociational-ism and Sectarian Authoritarianism," *Studies in Ethnicity and Nationalism* 20, no. 2 (2020): 117–27.

33. "The Road Map to Saving Iraq" (in Arabic), *Tuk Tuk* iss. 1 (November 2019): 1.

34. Interview with the author, June 2021.

35. Interview with the author, June 2021.

36. Majid, "Iran's View toward the Tishreen Protests," 2.

37. Fanar Haddad, "Hip Hop, Poetry and Shia Iconography: How Tahrir Square Gave Birth to a New Iraq," *Middle East Eye,* December 9, 2019, https://www.middle easteye.net/opinion/iraq-new-political-awareness-and-culture-have-been-formed.

38. Protester from Najaf, interview with the author, May 2022. The protester used the word *mawatania,* literally "citizenship," which, in this context, I interpret as meaning civic duty.

39. Member of Emtidad, interview with the author, May 2022.

40. "For the People" (in Arabic), news video posted to Facebook by Emti-dad, December 15, 2021, https://www.facebook.com/emtidadiraq/videos/123801 6896689989/.

41. Member of the National House, interview with the author, June 2021.

42. Several members of the National House, interview with the author, May 2022.

43. Member of the National House, interview with the author, May 2022.

44. Member of Emtidad, interview with the author, May 2022.

45. Several members of the National House, interview with the author, May 2022.

46. Rima Majed, "Lebanon and Iraq in 2019: Revolutionary Uprisings against 'Sectarian Neoliberalism,'" February 1, 2021, https://longreads.tni.org/lebanon-and-iraq-in-2019.

47. Abdullah Salam, "The Curse of Halbousi Is Afflicting Emtidad…Will the Iraqi Protesters Lose Their Parliamentary Bloc?" (in Arabic), *7al,* March 8, 2022, https://7al.net/2022/03/08/لعنة-الحلبوسي-تعصف-بـامتداد-هل-يفقد/abdullah/news/.

48. Protester from Baghdad, interview with the author, May 2022.

49. Rami Latif, "One of the Most Prominent Powers of 'Tishreen': How Did the 'National House' Project Collapse?" (in Arabic), *7al,* 14 April 2022, https://7al.net/2022/04/14/البيت-الوطني/rami-l/news/.

50. Salam, "The curse of Halbousi."

51. "We Were Accused of Corruption . . . Five Emtidad Representatives Announce a Final Decision after Announcing Their Resignation" (in Arabic), *Baghdad Today,* May 23, 2022, https://baghdadtoday.news/189813--.html.

52. Chantal Mouffe, *Agonistics: Thinking the World Politically,* (London: Verso, 2013), 2.

53. Ibid., 2.

54. Ibid., 75.

55. Ibid., 8.

56. Ibid., 116–17.

57. Ibid., 120.

58. Activist from Diyala, interview with the author, May 2022.

59. "The Assassination of Qasim Soleimani and Abu Mahdi al-Muhandis: National and Regional Consequences," a closed workshop with LSE Middle East Centre, January 10, 2020; Zahra Ali, "From Recognition to Redistribution? Protest Movements in the Age of 'New Civil Society,'" *Journal of Intervention and State Building 15*, no. 4 (March 2021): 6.

60. Member of Nasser Alliance, interview with the author, May 2022.

61. "The Coordination Framework Presents Nine-Point Imitative to Break Political Deadlock" (in Arabic), *Nas News*, 4 May 2022, https://www.nasnews.com/view.php?cat=85137; 'Al Sadr Invites Independent MPs to Form the Iraqi Government within 15 Days" (in Arabic), *Al-Ain,* May 4, 2022, https://al-ain.com/article/1651674687.

Chapter 8

1. "Iran-Backed Militia Staged Drone Attack on Iraqi PM - Officials," Reuters, November 8, 2021, https://www.reuters.com/world/middle-east/iran-backed-militia-behind-attack-iraqi-pm-sources-2021-11-08/.

2. Gudrun Ostby, "Inequalities, the Political Environment and Civil Conflict: Evidence from 55 Developing Countries," Horizontal Inequalities and Conflict, ed. F. Stewart (London: Palgrave Macmillan, 2008), 136–59.

3. Clionadh Raleigh, Hyun Jin Choi, and Daniel Wigmore-Shepherd, "Inclusive Conflict? Competitive Clientelism and the Rise of Political Violence," *Review of International Studies* 48, no. 1 (2022): 45.

4. Renad Mansour and Faleh A. Jabar, "The Popular Mobilization Forces and Iraq's Future," Carnegie Middle East Center, April 28, 2017, https://carnegie-mec.org/2017/04/28/popular-mobilization-forces-and-iraq-s-future-pub-68810.

5. "Study about the Disloyal Badr Corps 9," General Security Office, 2002, https://ctc.westpoint.edu/wp-content/uploads/2013/09/Iraqi-Intelligence-Study-about-the-Badr-Corps-Translation.pdf.

6. Faleh A. Jabar, *The Shia Movement in Iraq* (Saqi Books, 2003), 253.

7. Ali Allawi, *The Occupation of Iraq* (New Haven: Yale University Press, 2008), 111.

8. Andrew Rathmell, "Fixing Iraq's Internal Security Forces: Why Is Reform of the Ministry of Interior so Hard?," 2007, Center for Strategic and International Studies, https://issat.dcaf.ch/Learn/Resource-Library/Policy-and-Research-Papers/Fixing-Iraq-s-Internal-Security-Forces-Why-is-reform-of-the-Ministry-of-Interior-so-hard.

9. Kirk Semple, "Attack on Iraqi City Shows Militia's Power," *New York Times,* October 20, 2006, https://www.nytimes.com/2006/10/20/world/middleeast/21iraqcnd.html.

10. Omar Sirri and Renad Mansour, "Surviving on Violence: Iraq's Political Elite," *Mada Masr,* November 10, 2019, https://www.madamasr.com/en/2019/11/10/opinion/u/surviving-on-violence-iraqs-political-elite/.

11. Ranj Alaaldin, "Iraq's Next War," *Foreign Affairs,* September 13, 2018, https://www.foreignaffairs.com/articles/middle-east/2018-09-13/iraqs-next-war.

12. Nadeen Embrahim, "What's behind Iraq's Explosive Political Crisis?," CNN, August 1, 2022, https://edition.cnn.com/2022/08/01/middleeast/iraq-protests-parliament-deadlock-mime-intl/index.html.

Chapter 9

1. Excellent fieldwork by researchers such as Zahra Ali and Omar Sirri details the complex, non-sectarian ways that Iraqis view political power and exclusion. See Zahra Ali, "Theorising Uprisings: Iraq's Thawra Teshreen," *Third World Quarterly,* 2023, https://www.tandfonline.com/doi/abs/10.1080/01436597.2022.2161359; and Omar Sirri, "Destructive Creations: Social-Spatial Transformations in Contemporary Baghdad," LSE Middle East Centre Paper Series 45, February 2021, http://eprints.lse.ac.uk/108866/3/DestructiveCreations.pdf.

2. "Khazali: Selecting the Prime Minister Will Not Be Personalized," Dijla TV, October 2, 2021, cited in Inside Iraqi Politics, Utica Risk Services, no. 228.

3. Zaid Al-Ali, "Flawed by Design: Ethno-Sectarian Power-Sharing and Iraq's Constitutional Development," Chatham House, April 4, 2023, https://www.chathamhouse.org/2023/03/iraq-20-years-insider-reflections-war-and-its-aftermath/flawed-design-ethno-sectarian-power; and Ranj Alaldin, "Sectarianism, Governance, and Iraq's Future," Brookings Doha Center Analysis Paper no. 24, November2018,https://www.brookings.edu/wp-content/uploads/2018/11/Sectarianism-governance-and-Iraqs-future_English.pdf.

4. Beth K. Dougherty, "De-Ba`thification in Iraq: How Not to Pursue Transitional Justice," Middle East Institute, January 30, 2014, https://www.mei.edu/publications/de-bathification-iraq-how-not-pursue-transitional-justice.

5. Harith Hassan Al-Qarawee, "Iraq's Sectarian Crisis: A Legacy of Exclusion," *Sada,* Carnegie Middle East Center, April 23, 2014, https://carnegieendowment.org/sada/55372.

6. Safa al-Sheikh Hussein, "Iraq 20 Years On: Insider Reflections on the War and Its Aftermath," Chatham House, March 20, 2023, https://www.chathamhouse.org/2023/03/iraq-20-years-insider-reflections-war-and-its-aftermath/iraqs-security-sector-twenty-years.

7. Renad Mansour, "The Sunni Predicament," Carnegie Middle East Center, March 2016, https://carnegieendowment.org/files/CMEC_59_Mansour_Sunni_Final.pdf.

8. James Verini, *They Will Have to Die Now: Mosul and the Fall of the Caliphate* (New York: W. W. Norton, 2019).

9. Safa al-Sheikh Hussein, "Iraq 20 Years On."

10. Mustafa Saadoun, "Understanding Iraq's Coordination Framework," *Al-Monitor,* August 13, 2022, https://www.al-monitor.com/originals/2022/08/understanding-iraqs-coordination-framework.

11. Philip Loft, "Iraq in 2022: Forming a Government," House of Commons Library (UK), November 2, 2022, https://researchbriefings.files.parliament.uk/documents/CBP-9605/CBP-9605.pdf.

12. Raad Alkadiri, "Iraq's New Sultans," London School of Economics, February 4, 2022, https://blogs.lse.ac.uk/mec/2022/02/04/iraqs-new-sultans/.

13. "Iraqi Prime Minister Survives Assassination Bid with Drones," Associated Press, November 7, 2021, https://apnews.com/article/middle-east-fires-iraq-baghdad-embassies-4069e75a45ee9b4eaa5e93648fa15211.

14. Sarhang Hamasaeed, "A Year after Elections, Iraq May Finally Be Set to Form a Government," United States Institute of Peace, October 20, 2022, https://www.usip.org/publications/2022/10/year-after-elections-iraq-may-finally-be-set-form-government.

15. "Speech by Ammar al-Hakim," published to the YouTube channel Alforat HD (@alforat_tv_hd) on February 4, 2022, https://www.youtube.com/watch?v=n0Wwr4e_Yzs, and cited in Inside Iraqi Politics, Utica Risk Services, no. 230.

16. "Iraqi MPs from Muqtada al-Sadr's Bloc Resign," Al Jazeera, June 12, 2022, https://www.aljazeera.com/news/2022/6/12/iraqi-mps-from-firebrand-cleric-moqtada-sadrs-bloc-resign; and "Iraqi Cleric Sadr Calls for Wider Protest as Supporters Occupy Parliament," Agence France-Presse, August 1, 2022, https://www.france24.com/en/middle-east/20220731-iraqi-cleric-sadr-calls-for-wider-protest-as-supporters-occupy-parliament.

17. Interviews with the author, Baghdad, Iraq, January and May 2023.

18. "Iraq: Staving Off Instability in the Near and Distant Futures," International Crisis Group, January 31, 2023, https://www.crisisgroup.org/middle-east-north-africa/gulf-and-arabian-peninsula/iraq/iraq-staving-instability-near-and-distant-futures.

19. Loft, "Iraq in 2022."

20. See this 2017 report on Shia politics, which makes a detailed case that Shia leaders compete for resources with little sectarian solidarity: Erwin van Veen, Nick Grinstead, and Floor El Kamouni-Janssen, "A House Divided: Political Relations and Coalition-Building between Iraq's Shi'a," The Clingendael Institute, February 2017, https://www.clingendael.org/pub/2017/a_house_divided/.

21. Rend Al-Rahim, "Iraq Awaits the End of Its Political Deadlock," April 18, 2022, Arab Center Washington DC, https://arabcenterdc.org/resource/iraq-awaits-the-end-of-its-political-deadlock/.

22. Maya Mikdashi, *Sextarianism: Sovereignty, Secularism, and the State in Lebanon* (Stanford: Stanford University Press, 2022).

23. Haddad's work has rejected both primordial atavism and external intervention as adequate explanations for the sectarianization of Iraqi politics, emphasizing instead the interaction of domestic, foreign, top-down, and bottom-up

dynamics. See, for instance, Fanar Haddad, *Sectarianism in Iraq* (New York: Columbia University Press, 2011). Haddad's theoretical approach to sectarianism aligns with Ussama Makdisi's historical work on the emergence of sectarian politics in Lebanon. See Ussama Makdisi, *The Culture of Sectarianism* (University of California Press, 2000).

24. Faleh al-Jabar, *The Shi'ite Movement in Iraq* (Dar al-Saqi, 2003),

25. Toby Dodge, "Seeking to explain the rise of sectarianism in the Middle East: The case study of Iraq," Project on Middle East Political Science, March 9, 2014, https://pomeps.org/seeking-to-explain-the-rise-of-sectarianism-in-the-middle-east-the-case-study-of-iraq.

26. Faleh al-Jabar, "From Identity Politics to Issue Politics—the Iraqi Protest Movement. The End of Conformity, the Beginning of Accountability," Iraqi Economists Network, January 28, 2017, http://iraqieconomists.net/en/2017/01/28/from-identity-politics-to-issue-politics-the-iraqi-protest-movement-the-end-of-conformity-the-beginning-of-accountability-by-faleh-a-jabar/.

27. Toby Dodge and Renad Mansour, "Sectarianization and De-Sectarianization in the Struggle for Iraq's Political Field," *The Review of Faith and International Affairs* 18, no.1 (2020): 58–69.

28. Fanar Haddad, "The Waning Relevance of the Sunni-Shia Divide," The Century Foundation, April 10, 2019, https://tcf.org/content/report/waning-relevance-sunni-shia-divide/.

29. Lahib Higel, "A Way Out of the Iraqi Impasse," International Crisis Group, August 10, 2022, https://www.crisisgroup.org/middle-east-north-africa/gulf-and-arabian-peninsula/iraq/way-out-iraqi-impasse.